ACKNOWLEDGEMENT

My thanks are due to Nissan-Datsun (UK Concessionaires) Ltd for their unstinted co-operation and also for supplying data and illustrations.

I am also grateful to a considerable number of owners who have discussed their cars at length and many of whose suggestions have been included in this manual.

Kenneth Ball G I Mech E
Associate Member Guild of Motoring Writers

Ditchling Sussex England.

**This book is to be returned on or before
the last date stamped below.**

STORE

23. MAR 87		
29. AUG 87		

DATSUN 510 SERIES, 1300, 1400, 1600 1968-72

Workshop Manual for
Datsun 1300 1968-70
Datsun 1400 1970-72
Datsun 1600 1968-72
Datsun 1600 SSS 1968-72

by

Kenneth Ball G I Mech E

and the

Autopress team of Technical Writers

AUTOPRESS LTD   GOLDEN LANE   BRIGHTON   BN1 2QJ   ENGLAND

The AUTOBOOK series of Workshop Manuals is the largest in the world and covers the majority of British and Continental motor cars, as well as all major Japanese and Australian models. For a full list see the back of this manual.

CONTENTS

ISBN 0 85147 357 1

First Edition   1970
Reprinted   1971
Reprinted   1971
Second Edition, fully revised   1972
Third Edition, fully revised   1972

Printed and bound in Brighton England for Autopress Ltd by G Beard & Son Ltd

INTRODUCTION

This do-it-yourself Workshop Manual has been specially written for the owner who wishes to maintain his car in first class condition and to carry out his own servicing and repairs. Considerable savings on garage charges can be made, and one can drive in safety and confidence knowing the work has been done properly.

Comprehensive step-by-step instructions and illustrations are given on all dismantling, overhauling and assembling operations. Certain assemblies require the use of expensive special tools, the purchase of which would be unjustified. In these cases information is included but the reader is recommended to hand the unit to the agent for attention.

Throughout the Manual hints and tips are included which will be found invaluable, and there is an easy to follow fault diagnosis at the end of each chapter.

Whilst every care has been taken to ensure correctness of information it is obviously not possible to guarantee complete freedom from errors or to accept liability arising from such errors or omissions.

Instructions may refer to the righthand or lefthand sides of the vehicle or the components. These are the same as the righthand or lefthand of an observer standing behind the car and looking forward.

CHAPTER 1

THE ENGINE

1:1 Introduction

The range of cars covered by this manual may be equipped with any one of three different size engines, viz 1296cc, 1428cc or 1595cc. For convenience these are referred to as 1300, 1400 and 1600 respectively. The 1300 and 1400 are virtually identical cars, the engine simply being enlarged in 1970.

The 1300 (L13) has bore and stroke measurements of 83 x 59.9 mm and a compression ratio of 8.5:1. The 1400 (L14S) is of identical design with dimensions of 83 x 66 mm and a raised compression ratio of 9.0:1.

The 1600 may be fitted with either single (L16S) or twin (L16T) carburetters. Bore remains at 83 mm but the stroke has been increased again to 73.7 mm and the compression ratio is 8.5:1 or 9.5:1 respectively.

Earlier cars were fitted with a threespeed gearbox with a column mounted change, this was later altered to a fourspeed box with the gear change mechanism on the floor. A threespeed Borg-Warner automatic trans-mission and fluid torque converter is available on the larger models.

Two saloons are produced for each engine size as either standard or de luxe versions depending on internal trim, finish and additional accessories. Mechanically they are all similar and may be seen illustrated in **FIG 1:1**, while the estate car version is shown in **FIG 1:2**.

A general view of the smaller engine with the early threespeed gearbox is given in **FIG 1:3** and gives a good picture of the engine accessories and their locations. **FIG 1:4** shows the larger engine in twin carburetter form, although the carburetters themselves are hidden behind the air cleaner.

The L.13 engine develops a maximum output of 77 bhp at 6000 rev/min. The L.16 with standard carburetter develops 96 bhp at 5600 rev/min or, with twin SU pattern carburetters and the higher compression ratio, 109 bhp at 6000 rev/min. A sectional view of the engine along and across the crankshaft is given in **FIG 1:5**.

FIG 1:1   The 1300, 1400 or 1600cc Datsun family Saloon

The monoblock cast iron cylinder assembly incorporates the upper half of the crankcase with the journals for the five-bearing forged steel crankshaft. The aluminium alloy cylinder head supports the four-bearing camshaft, chain driven by double roller chain from the crankshaft sprocket, the aluminium bronze inlet and cast exhaust valve seats being shrink fits into the head. The lightweight cast aluminium slipper skirt pistons are of the concave bowl head pattern on the 1600cc single carburetter engine, other engine piston heads being flat, and are supported on the forged steel connecting rods by a hollow gudgeon pin, press-fitted into the small-end and a floating fit in the piston.

The inlet and exhaust manifolds are mounted side-by-side the inlet being of aluminium and the exhaust of cast iron. The inlet manifold is of monoblock construction for the standard downdraught carburetter but, where the twin SU pattern carburetters are fitted, two separate two-cylinder manifolds are utilized and the cylinder heads are of different pattern with larger valves.

Engine cooling is conventional with thermostatically controlled circulation but an unusual feature is the clutch

FIG 1:2   The 1600cc Datsun Estate car

FIG 1:3   The 1300cc engine with three-speed gearbox

FIG 1:4   The 1600cc engine with twin SU carburetters and four-speed gearbox

drive to the fan which comes into operation only when the cooling water circulating through the pump has reached a satisfactory temperature for efficient engine operation.

Pressure-feed lubrication is maintained by a double-rotor pattern oil pump circulating oil from the sump around the engine through the fullflow cartridge pattern filter. Ignition is conventional from battery and ignition coil through a distributor but on later models a special ignition coil and circuit, with ballast resistor, ensures a good spark at the plugs when the battery voltage is depressed by the heavy starting current.

The electrical system is standard 12 volt negative earth derived from a belt driven alternator with silicon rectifying diodes and lead/acid type battery.

1:2 Removing the engine

All normal servicing procedures applicable to a front mounted engine can be carried out with the engine in the

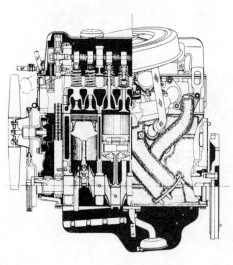
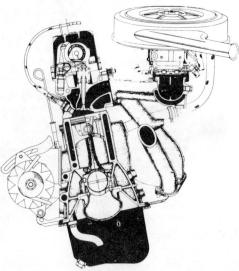

FIG 1:5   Sections through the ohc engine

FIG 1:6   The engine compartment

car, including decarbonizing, checking and setting tappet clearances, make-and-break points, cleaning and resetting sparking plug gaps, adjusting drive belts, changing air and oil filters, carburetter adjustments and oil and water changing, etc. For more extensive maintenance, it will be necessary to remove the engine from the car, keeping to the following procedure.

First, disconnect the battery terminals and remove the battery from the engine compartment. Scribe around the hinges on the bonnet, unbolt the bonnet from the hinges and remove to a safe place. Protect the surrounding paintwork by thick fabric or foam sheeting.

Remove the radiator filler cap, open the radiator drain cock and the plug at the bottom of the cylinder block and drain the cooling system. Check that the water is also drained from the car heating system.

Disconnect the extractor hose from the rocker cover, then loosen and remove the air filter. Unbolt and remove the radiator grille, disconnect the hoses to the radiator and engine, loosen the radiator fixing bolts and remove the radiator. **If the car has automatic transmission, disconnect the cooling pipes from the radiator to the gearbox.**

Slacken the drive belt and remove from the fan and alternator pulley, then remove the fan and pulley. Disconnect the fuel pipe from the fuel pump and plug to prevent drainage of fuel from the tank.

Remove the linkage connecting the accelerator and choke controls to the carburetter. Remove the heavy duty electrical cables from the starter motor and all other LT cables to the generator, starter solenoid, warning transducers and transmitters, etc., marking each one for ease of identification on reassembly.

Unbolt and remove the clutch operating cylinder with its return spring (see **FIG 1:7**). Disconnect the speedometer cable. Remove the HT lead from the ignition coil to the distributor. Check that all electrical connections to the engine are free and supported out of the way.

Raise the car and support on stands.

From beneath the car disconnect the linkage to the gearbox shift lever and remove the cross-shaft assembly. Disconnect the exhaust manifold from the exhaust tube and ease apart. If necessary, loosen the exhaust pipe supports so that the manifold can be extracted from the engine.

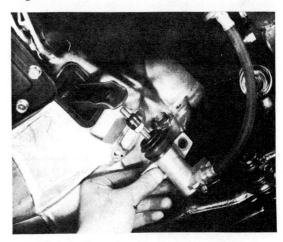

FIG 1:7   Removing the clutch slave cylinder

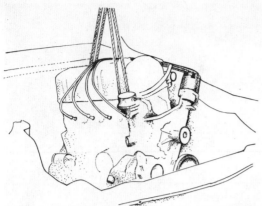

FIG 1:8 Lifting the engine from the front compartment

FIG 1:9 Removing the thermostat and housing from the cylinder head

From beneath the car, unbolt the universal joint connecting the propeller shaft to the gearbox drive shaft flange. Take the weight of the engine on a jack and then unbolt and remove the rear engine supporting crossmember. The handbrake cable clamp is secured by one of these bolts.

Support the engine from a crane by cables attached to the hooks secured to the front and rear of the cylinder head. Remove the bolts securing the front of the engine to the crossmember on its insulators, then slowly raise the engine clear of the compartment, tilting the gearbox downwards carefully to ease it through the rear opening and making sure that it does not foul any of the side installations in the compartment. Transfer to a bench or mounting stand (see **FIG 1:8**).

1:3 Dismantling the engine

With the engine at the bench or, preferably, secured to an engine stand, first remove the alternator, starter motor and distributor and cover the inlet to the carburetter with a waterproof plastic bag. Thoroughly clean the exterior free from road dirt and/or grease using, preferably, a proprietary compound such as Gunk or Teepol in accordance with the instructions provided, brushing into crevices,

and applying a strong jet of water to clear the loosened deposits. Allow to drain and dry.

Remove the drain plug from the sump and allow the oil to drain from the engine. Remove the distributor cap, HT leads to sparking plugs and extract the sparking plugs. Unbolt and remove the thermostat housing and thermostat (see **FIG 1:9**) and the unbolt and remove the carburetter. Unbolt and remove the gearbox and remove the clutch assembly and driven plate from the flywheel (see **Section 5**).

Unbolt and remove the distributor support casting from the seating in the crankcase front cover and extract the distributor assembly. Unbolt and remove the inlet and exhaust manifolds and gaskets (see **FIG 1:10**). Unbolt and remove the crankshaft pulley.

FIG 1:10 Removing the exhaust manifolds

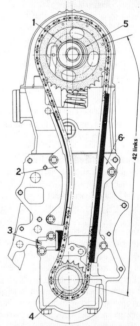

FIG 1:11 Details of the overhead camshaft drive showing chain guides, tensioner and timing marks

Remove the fan pulley from the water pump flange coupling. On vehicles with air-conditioning installed, this will also involve removal of the fan clutch. Unbolt and remove the water pump from the crankcase front cover and then extract the fuel pump from its seating. Remove any remaining hose connections.

Next, remove the rocker cover and gasket and follow up by removing the front cover to the cylinder head. This necessitates the removal of the return cooling water pipe from the inlet manifold to the circulating pump which is retained by a clip under one of the cover securing bolts. Remove the crankcase cover.

Remove the timing chain adjuster 3 (see **FIG 1 : 11**) and unbolt and remove the two chain guides, 2 and 6. Remove the nut securing the sprocket and fuel pump cam, 5 and 6, to the camshaft and extract both sprockets and cam. Loosen and remove the timing chain.

The cylinder head, complete with valves and overhead camshaft, can now be unbolted and removed as an assembly for further treatment later on. Also remove the cylinder head gasket.

When removing the cylinder head for a simple decarbonization procedure, it will not be necessary to remove the timing chain which can be supported by a special tool ST.49350000 (see FIG 1 :12) so preserving the linkage between crankshaft

FIG 1 :14   Removing front oil seal

FIG 1 :15   Removing baffle and net from cylinder block

sprocket and chain. On reassembly, the retiming of the camshaft is then simplified by setting the timing marks on the chain adjacent to those on the camshaft sprocket. There are 42 chain links between the two timing marks on the chain and the arrangement can be seen in FIG 1 :11. However, before dismantling, study the timing marks on both sprockets and chain so that there shall be no misunderstanding when reassembling.

Turn the engine over and remove the sump and oil strainer. Unbolt and remove the oil pump and drive gear and then extract the crankshaft worm and chain drive sprocket from the crankshaft.

Now unbolt the big-ends from the connecting rods and extract the piston and connecting rod assemblies through the top of the cylinder. **Note carefully the position in the cylinder block of each assembly and record for reinstallation later and also check that the bearing caps are replaced on the same connecting rods and the right way round. Look for any identifying marks to facilitate recognition.**

Unbolt the flywheel from the crankshaft, using a pawl engaged in the ringwheel to prevent turning, again checking the relationship between flywheel and crankshaft for identical reinstallation (see **FIG 1 :16**). **Failure to do this may result in an unbalance of the final assembly.**

Remove the rear main bearing cap, using the special tool ST.4463000D (see **FIG 1 :13**) and then the oil seal (see **FIG 1 :14**). Unbolt and remove the remaining

FIG 1 :12   Use of chain support tool to maintain chain on lower sprocket during decarbonization

FIG 1 :13   Removing front bearing cap with extraction tool

FIG 1:16 Removing flywheel from crankshaft. Note restraining pawl.

FIG 1:17 Removing crankshaft journal bearing caps

journal bearing caps (see **FIG 1:17**) and ease the crankshaft free of the cylinder block. Remove the baffle plate and net from the crankcase (see **FIG 1:15**). The engine is now completely dismantled.

As each part is dismantled, examine for identifying marks and record position, way up and presence of washers, shims and/or lockwashers, on paper. Do not rely on memory alone. The wrong part inserted, the wrong order of assembly is not only a waste of time in rectifying, but can result in some damage to stressed parts or unbalance of moving parts leading to less-than-perfect performance.

1:4 Servicing the cylinder head

Each rocker bar is pivoted at one end in a ball and socket joint, the ball being part of a screw support pillar to which it is secured by a saddle spring, with the other end resting on the end of the valve stem. The rocker bar is depressed by the overhead cam acting on its centre area and the valves are secured in position by a conventional arrangement of spring, spring cup and collet with oil seal. Valve opening adjustment is by means of the screw support pillar.

To dismantle, first remove the valve rocker saddle springs in turn, slacken the screw pillar locknut and reduce the height of the pillar. The rocker arms can then be removed by depressing the valves against their springs using a screwdriver with the camshaft **but not the cam face** as a fulcrum (see **FIG 1:18**).

Unbolt and remove the camshaft locating plate (see **FIG 1:19**) and ease the camshaft through the bushes to remove it from the head. **Take particular care not to allow the camshaft or cam faces to scratch the inside of the bushes during removal or replacement as these are integral with the cylinder head. Wear or damage beyond the limited amount necessitates complete replacement of the cylinder head.**

Next remove each valve using a valve lifter to depress the spring enabling the collet to be extracted and the valve stem released from the spring cup. Carefully identify each assembly with the cylinder from which it was removed and replace in the same position later.

Do not, in any circumstances, loosen or unbolt the camshaft bearing supports. These are bored in situ with a special boring bar to ensure perfect alignment with the camshaft journals. Any movement of the supports is almost certainly bound to upset the alignment and a precise machining

FIG 1:18 Removing valve rockers from cylinder head

FIG 1:19 Removing sprockets from camshaft to reveal camshaft locate plate behind

operation is necessary to restore it. Should the alignment be accidently disturbed and a replacement head and camshaft assembly is not available, grind with a mirror finish a length of steel bar, long enough to pass through all four bearings, to the exact outer diameter of the camshaft journals, loosen the two inner support studs and then insert the bar, lightly oiled, in position. Adjust and tighten the bolts so that the bar can be turned easily in the bearings and, subsequently, withdrawn without effort. The camshaft can then be inserted carefully and checked for smooth and effortless rotation.

Thoroughly examine the cylinder head casting for signs of cracking or corrosion and clean the surface where it is in contact with the cylinder block gasket. Check the surface for flatness against a straightedge endeavouring to insert a .003 inch feeler gauge between the head and the straightedge (see **FIG 1:20**). If the gauge can be inserted in more than three places, resurface on a surface grinder, taking the absolute minimum cut.

Check the valves for stem wear and the heads for deformation or, in the case of exhaust valves, burning. Clean each stem and head free from carbon deposits and polish. Check the state of the faces and reface if necessary.

FIG 1:22 Checking cylinders with bore gauge

FIG 1:23 Checking crankshaft for alignment with dial gauge

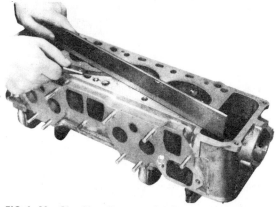

FIG 1:20 Checking flatness of cylinder head. Make a similar check on cylinder block head

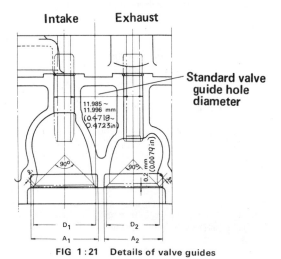

FIG 1:21 Details of valve guides

Remove any carbon deposits from the cylinder areas and valve pockets and blow the ports clear of carbon dust and particles. Inspect the valve seatings and the condition of the valve guides. Check for any sloppiness between the valve stems and guides and replace if the clearance is outside permitted limits, .0006 to .002 inch. Check the condition of the screw threads on the manifold securing studs. The valve guides are an interference fit in the head and must be extracted and inserted with a hydraulic press.

When inserting new guides, the interference fit in the guide hole must be between .001 and .002 inch. The head must be heated in an oven to around 200°C before insertion and the guides reamed to size afterwards. Note that the inlet valve guide has a tapered end and projects into the valve pocket whereas the end of the exhaust valve only just emerges from its seating (see **FIG 1:21**).

Check the condition of the valve springs. These should all be of the same free length, 1.89 inches, and must be free from cracks or distortion. The valve rockers, too, must be in good condition, particularly in the areas swept by the cam faces.

Reinsert the valves in position, grinding them in with coarse and fine carborundum paste in the conventional manner. When the seatings are satisfactory, clean thoroughly and replace the valves, with springs and

FIG 1:24 Determining bearing play with Plastigage strip and gauge

FIG 1:25 Checking piston ring clearance in gap before installing

collets in the positions they occupied before dismantling. With new valves or seatings, recutting may be necessary.

Lightly oil the camshaft and reinsert in the bearings, securing in place by the location plate. Refit the rocker bar assemblies and adjust the height of the support pillars to give a clearance of .008 inch between inlet cam and rocker and .010 inch between exhaust cam and rocker. Lock by means of the locknut. See **Technical Data** for hot clearances.

This completes the cylinder head overhaul.

1:5 Servicing the cylinder block

Examination of the cylinder block is confined, mainly, to inspecting for cracks and flaws or rust marks indicating a leak of some sort and a check of flatness across the block head. The latter is determined in the same manner as already described for the cylinder head and if the limits of out-of-true exceed .004 inch the surface must be reground.

Should the engine have been in service for an extended period, a check of bore dimensions is advisable. Wear can be in one of four aspects, scoring of the cylinder walls, excessive increase in bore while still perfectly cylindrical, wear in one diameter causing the section to become oval and excessive wear at the bottom of the cylinder causing the bore to taper.

A bore gauge is used to determine the degree and type of wear (see **FIG 1:22**) and the measurements are made in two diameters at right angles to each other at points 20, 60 and 100 mm from the top of the bore. The standard bore diameter is 83 mm with a maximum of 83.05 mm when new and a wear limit of 83.25 mm. The maximum difference between two diameters at any one level (ovality) must not exceed .015 mm and that between top and bottom (taper) also .015 mm.

If these figures are exceeded or the cylinder walls are so scored as not to be rectifiable by honing, reboring is necessary. This is a specialist task which must be entrusted to a garage with the necessary equipment and oversize pistons and rings will also have to be fitted.

1:6 Servicing the crankshaft and journals

Dealing, first, with the crankshaft, the first check is for straightness. Mount the crankshaft on V-blocks at the ends and rotate slowly while a dial gauge is applied to the three intermediate bearing surfaces. The variations in indication represent the degree of bending or out of truth but the difference between maximum and minimum indication is double the divergence from straight. There is, of course, an added possible error if the bearing surface is not perfectly round and, before actually deciding that the indicated error is due to bending, check the diameter of the bearing with a micrometer (see **FIG 1:23**). The crankshaft should not be more than .002 inch out of true.

Now check the big-end journals for roundness and inspect for scoring or cracking. Inspect the oilways and check that none are blocked. Examine the shell half-bearings for wear and replace if necessary. Make a trial assembly of the crankshaft in the cylinder block and check the clearance with Plastigage, cutting a strip the width of the bearing and inserting it parallel with the crankpin, clear of the oil hole between the journal and the shell bearing. Install the bearing caps and tighten to a torque of 30 lb ft. Remove the bearing cap and shell and measure the width of the now flattened strip of Plastigage thread against the scale to give the bearing clearance. This should be not less than .0008, nor more than .0024 inch (see **FIG 1:24**). **Do not turn the crank in the bearing during the operation.**

If the clearance is in excess of .0024 inch, replace the bearing shells by the next undersize and regrind the crankshaft journals to suit.

1:7 Servicing the piston assemblies

Carefully inspect each piston and connecting rod assembly for signs of damage or excessive wear and decarbonize and polish the piston heads. Check the condition of the piston rings and that they are free in the ring grooves around the piston. Check the connecting rod for side play in the piston as an indication of gudgeon pin or bearing wear. There should be no noticeable play but the connecting rod should swing on the gudgeon pin without friction.

If these are satisfactory, examine the state of the big-end bearing shells and check the clearance when mounted on to the crankshaft again using the Plastigage method. When tightening the big-end bearing cap nuts, set the torque spanner to 24 lb ft.

Replacing a broken piston ring is a fairly straight-forward operation. Determine the thickness of the broken ring and obtain a new one of the same thickness. Check the clearance of the new ring in the piston groove with a feeler gauge (see **FIG 1 : 25**) and, if it is between .0016 and .0030 inch for the top ring, .0012 and .0025 for the middle ring or .001 and .0025 for the lower or scraper ring, it is satisfactory for gapping. This latter operation comprises the measuring of the gap between the ring ends when fitted in the bottom of the cylinder bore. In **FIG 1 : 26** this operation is being shown at the upper end of the bore for viewing. The ring must be square within the bore and the gap must be between .009 and .015 inch for the top ring, or between .006 and .012 inch for the lower two. If the gap is too small, it can be opened by carefully filing the ends. If it is too large, select a larger ring.

If wear necessitates the replacement of gudgeon pin, piston or connecting rod, dismantle the assembly, first by removing the rings from the piston grooves and then extracting the pin in a suitable hand press. A special piston ring removal tool facilitates ring removal without breaking (see **FIG 1 : 27**). Should a new piston be necessary, check that the new one is the same size and weight as the old. Similarly, if damage or twisting necessitates the replacement of the connecting rod, this too, must be within .2 oz of the weight of the old one.

Check that the gudgeon pin is a finger press-fit into the piston holes at room temperature but is an interference fit in the little end bearing of the connecting rod. Insert in position with the connecting rod properly centred and press home in a press. **Do not attempt to hammer home.**

If the cylinder has been rebored, oversize pistons and rings will be necessary. These will be supplied by the garage undertaking the reboring but, unless they are also carrying out the engine reassembly, the fitting of the pistons to the connecting rods will be your responsibility. Again, do not interchange the pistons in the cylinders but preserve the order as fitted by the garage or agent.

An alternative method of fitting the gudgeon pin if a press is not available is to heat the connecting rod in an oven to 200°C while storing the gudgeon pin in a refrigerator. Then, supporting the hot connecting rod in a vice, quickly position the piston and insert the cold gudgeon pin which, for convenience, should be supported on a suitable mandrel. Allow to cool and remove the mandrel.

The next step is the preassembly of the pistons and crankshaft into the cylinder block.

1 : 8 Cylinder block preassembly

With the engine block on the stand, set the main bearing shells in position, after checking that all oil holes and channels are clear, ready to accept the crankshaft. Note the differences in the bearing shells and, in particular, the flanged shells for the centre bearing. Check that oil holes in the shells coincide with those in the seatings. Lightly oil the surface of the shells with engine oil and lay the crankshaft in position. Position the mating halves of the bearing shells on the crankshaft main bearings, oiling the surfaces at the same time, and install the bearing caps, tightening the bolts to a torque of 40 lb ft.

Check the end play with a feeler gauge inserted between the centre shell flange and the crankshaft web (see **FIG 1 : 28**). This should be between .002 and .006 inch when new but should not exceed .012 inch on an engine that

FIG 1 : 26   Checking gap in piston ring before fitting to piston

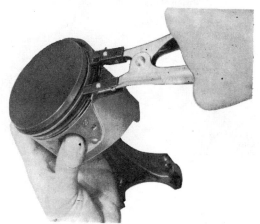

FIG 1 : 27   Use of tool for removing piston ring from groove

has seen service. Insert the rear oil seal in the cavity around the rear boss (see **FIG 1 : 14**) using the special tool ST.49370000 if available. A special shim may be inserted if excessive wear is apparent between the oil seal face and crankshaft bearing surface.

Bolt the rear end plate into position, turn the cylinder block with the flywheel end uppermost and install the flywheel and ring gear. Before fitting the flywheel, check that the ring gear is in good condition and that none of the teeth is chipped, and examine the clutch disc contact surface for damage or wear. The face can be resurfaced if excessively scored. The gear is shrink-fitted to the flywheel and, should the teeth be worn or damaged, it must be replaced.

Drill through the ring at two points diametrically opposite and at the root of a tooth space. A sharp blow with a hammer and chisel across the hole should then suffice to split the ring and free it from the flywheel. Thoroughly clean the exposed surface and check that the replacement ring is too tight to fit cold. Heat the ring to 200°C and, if possible, store the flywheel in a refrigerator for about 1 hour. Transfer the ring while hot to the flywheel and it will be found to fit closely. Clamp right home and

FIG 1:28 Checking crankshaft end play in main journals

FIG 1:29 Refitting flywheel. Note backplate in position

leave the clamps in position until the flywheel and ring are at the same temperature. Check for tightness.

When heating the ring, place it in an oven, thermostatically controlled. Do not, in any circumstances, use a blow torch or the hardened surfaces of the teeth will be impaired and wear will be rapid.

After fitting a new ring gear, rebalance the flywheel by mounting it on a close fitting arbor and swinging on two knife edges. Drill out in small amounts at persistent low points in the flywheel rim until perfect balance is restored. Alternatively, use a dynamic balancer if available.

When refitting the flywheel and ring gear on to the crankshaft, check that it is in the same relative position as before dismantling and secure by the six bolts tightened to 80 lb ft (see **FIG 1:29**).

Fit piston ring clamps to the pistons in turn and insert them into their respective cylinders from above. Lightly oil the cylinder bores before inserting the pistons which will shed the clamps as they enter. Check that the bearing shell halves are in place in the connecting rod big-end, oil the surfaces and locate on the crankshaft. Fit the bearing caps and half shells and secure, tightening the nuts to a torque of 25 lb ft. Check end play between the big-end bearings and the crankshaft webs (see **FIG 1:30**). This should lie between .008 and .012 inch. Finally, check that the flywheel can be turned with the crankshaft and piston assemblies in the cylinders and that there is no stiffness or binding at any point.

1:9 Servicing the camshaft and bearings

As already mentioned in **Section 1:4**, the camshaft bearings are not replaceable on account of the necessity for strict alignment. Should the bearing surfaces of the camshaft or the bearing surfaces of the bushes be worn or scored, the only remedy is to fit a new cylinder head assembly. All that can be done in the way of servicing the camshaft itself is to hone out any slight marks on the cam faces. The camshaft sprocket and drive cam are secured to the end of the camshaft by a single bolt but provision is made to fit the camshaft sprocket in one of three positions to ensure accurate valve timing regardless of chain wear within certain limits. This adjustment, and consequently, the fitting of the sprocket can take place only when installing the timing chain.

1:10 Oil pump and strainer

The oil pump is installed at the bottom of the front cover, being secured in position by four bolts, and is driven by the same multi-start skew gear on the crankshaft as that which drives the distributor (see **FIG 1:31**). This drive axle with central gear is an extension of the distributor shaft with a single dog coupling for the shaft of the oil pump. The pump is of the eccentric bi-rotor pattern an exploded view of which is given in **FIG 1:32**. It can be

FIG 1:30 Checking end play in big-end bearings

FIG 1:31 Installing oil pump. Note the drive shaft in end housing

removed while the engine is in the car, if necessary, by draining the sump, removing the front stabilizer, distributor and splash shield and then unbolting and withdrawing downwards.

To dismantle, remove the end plate and then check the clearances between the rotor and rotor ring and between the ring and the body with a feeler gauge. These clearances should not exceed .006 inch and, should the clearances be excessive, replace both rotor and ring by a new matched pair. Check the end float by means of a straight-edge placed across the face of the rotor when in the body and inserting a feeler gauge. Replace the rotors if the clearance exceeds .005 inch.

The end plate houses a spring-loaded relief valve opening at around 50 lb/sq in enabling the oil to bypass the lubricating system should the oil pressure exceed this value. It is not adjustable but the spring and valve can be extracted for a check on spring free length by unscrewing the cover nut. The free length should be 2.24 inches and, of course, the spring should not be deformed. When reassembling, check that the valve is a free sliding fit before finally securing the nut in place.

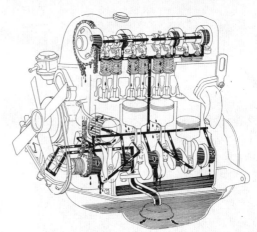

FIG 1:34 Diagrammatic view of lubrication system

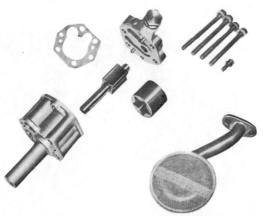

FIG 1:32 Exploded view of double rotor oil pump and strainer

FIG 1:33 Position of distributor spindle at No. 1 cylinder TDC, just after ignition. Make-and-break points just closing with rotor on No. 1 plug terminal

FIG 1:35 Replacing a new cartiridge oil filter element

Reassembly and reinstallation is a simple reversal of the dismantling procedure but a new gasket should be fitted and care taken not to damage it during the reassembly or reinstallation.

In operation, the oil pump draws oil from the sump through a foot strainer and circulates it, through a fullflow filter to a lateral duct in the cylinder block from whence it is distributed six ways. Three of these go direct to the end and centre crankshaft bearings, draining via oilways in the crankshaft, to the big-end and intermediate main journals and back to the sump. Two others, to the intermediate journals, distribute oil via the intermediate bearings to the crankshaft webs where they spray onto the cylinder walls. The last, a single channel rises to a lateral channel in the cylinder head, up through the camshaft bearings and along the camshaft to spray on to the rocker gear draining down to the sump. The camshaft timing chain is lubricated by spray from two auxiliary channels (see **FIG 1:34**).

1:11 Oil filter, fuel filter

The fullflow oil filter is of the replaceable cartridge type and is easily fitted in place on the special seating at the left of the engine to the rear of the alternator (see **FIG 1:35**). No special tools are needed, the whole operation

FIG 1 : 36 Fuel filter and clip in position in engine compartment

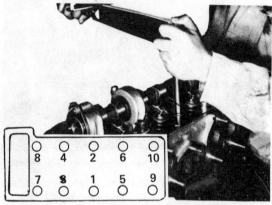

8	4	2	6	10
7	3	1	5	9

FIG 1 : 37 Tightening down the head nuts showing, (inset) the correct tightening order

of changing by hand taking a minute or so. The sealing ring is of a type which seals with the minimum of pressure; in fact, too tight a fitting may even cause leakage around the joint.

The filter element must be changed every 6000 miles or oil circulation will be reduced with consequent excessive wear at the lubrication surfaces.

The fuel filter is also of the cartridge type being inserted in the fuel hose line and secured by clips (see **FIG 1 : 36**). The straining element is a fibre mat supported within the transparent container in a nylon collar. Normally, the unit does not need replacement before the 24,000 mile service.

When replacing, unclip the filter from its support and slacken the two clips. Have the unit handily. Holding the inlet pipe in one hand, raise it to its greatest height above the level in the fuel tank, then quickly disconnect the outlet pipe, exchange the unit while still holding the assembly high. Fit the outlet pipe before lowering and then tighten

the clips. Reinsert in the supporting clip and check the unions for leaks.

1 :12 Reassembling the engine

With all components serviced, the engine can now be reassembled. The first step is to reinstall the cylinder head assembly. Fit a new head gasket. (The makers recommend the use of a sealing agent between the gasket and the two surfaces which is not in accordance with current British practice. It may be advisable to adopt their recommendation.) Carefully lower the head with valves and rockers assembled, checking that the oil feed to the camshaft support is not blocked, and insert the ten securing bolts. **Note that these are of different lengths and be sure to insert the right ones in each position.** Using the special tool, ST.4901 0000 tighten them in the order shown to a final torque figure of 43 lb ft (see **FIG 1 : 37**).

There are two very important precautions to be taken when fitting the cylinder head or damage to the pistons and/or valve heads may result. The first is to turn the crankshaft so that all pistons are level at mid point in the cylinders. The second is to avoid turning the crankshaft from this position until ready for timing.

FIG 1 : 38 Timing chain sprocket and distributor drive gear on crankshaft showing key position for No. 1 cylinder TDC. The extension takes the fan and alternator drive pulley

Notch for timing check

Camshaft locate hole

Timing mark

FIG 1 : 39 Timing marks and notches and the three holes for locating on the pin of the camshaft flange, to be found on the camshaft sprocket

At the front end, install the crankshaft sprocket and distributor drive gear and fit the oil throwers into position (see **FIG 1:38**). Fit the sprocket temporarily on to the camshaft with the pin in the centre of the three holes (see **FIG 1:19**). Rotate the camshaft until both valves are closed in No. 1 cylinder and the centre one of the three timing marks (see **FIG 1:39**) is at approximately 72 degrees as shown. Now rotate the crankshaft through 90 degrees, not more, in either direction to bring No. 1 piston to TDC. This is when the key on the crankshaft (see **FIG 1:38**) is at 12 o'clock. The timing mark on the crankshaft sprocket (4 in **FIG 1:11**) should then be about 18 degrees below the horizontal on the right.

Loop the timing chain around the two sprockets as shown and count to get 42 links between the two timing marks when tensioned on the left. (Some chains may have the 42 link marks scratched or engraved on them. If not, it may help to mark two links exactly 42 apart before fitting.) Temporarily fit the lefthand chain guide 2, to take up the slack and holding the righthand section taut, observe the position of the timing notch against the oval hole engraved in the locate plate (see **FIG 1:40**). If it is more or less central, the sprocket is in the right position. If it is to the left or right of the oval hole, change the position of the sprocket so that the pin is in one of the other two holes and recheck.

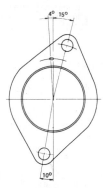

FIG 1:40 Camshaft locate plate showing position of the oval groove used with sprocket notch to check chain stretch

FIG 1:41 Adjusting the clearances between cam face and rocker. Note the measurement does not take place between rocker and valve stem

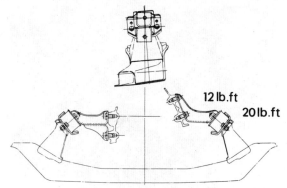

FIG 1:42 Detail of front engine mounting with the securing bolt torque values

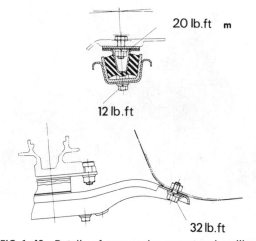

FIG 1:43 Details of rear engine mount and resilient bush

The purpose of this adjustment is to compensate for chain stretch and each position corresponds to an alteration in timing of 4 degrees at the crankshaft (two degrees at the camshaft). If it is not possible to set the timing notch within the area of the hole in the locate plate, the chain has stretched excessively and must be replaced. **It is, of course, important that the crankshaft be set at exactly top dead centre as the adjustment is only a matter of a degree or so.**

Fit the fuel pump cam in position and insert the bolt. Tighten to a torque of 40 lb ft. Fit and secure the remaining chain guide and tensioner and tighten all six bolts. Lightly oil the chain with engine oil and drip a little down the chain guides. Press a new oil seal into the front cylinder block cover, fit new gaskets, with sealing compound applied to both faces, and bolt into position. Refit the cylinder head coverplate.

Next, install the crankshaft pulley and the water pump, using new gaskets wherever necessary, and reinstall the oil pump and distributor driving spindle (see **Section 1:9**).

Bolt into position the fuel pump, water inlet elbow, thermostat housing front, engine sling hook, thermostat

FIG 1:44 Checking belt tension on alternator and fan drive

FIG 1:45 Installing the alternator. Note the timing pointer ringed at bottom right

and water outlet elbow. Turn the engine over and install the oil strainer, baffle plate and net, then fit a new sump gasket and secure the sump into position with a liberal coating of sealing compound on both faces of the gasket. Tighten the nuts diagonally in clockwise rotation to a torque of 5 lb ft. Insert the drain plug.

Turn the engine over. With No. 1 cylinder at TDC and the valves both closed, set the distributor rotor arm to No. 1 cylinder plug position and mount into position to link with the drive coupling as shown in FIG 1:33 and fit the fixing bolts.

Install the rear engine sling hook, exhaust manifold and intake manifold(s) with carburetter(s). Check the setting of the valve clearances .008 inch, inlet, and .010 inch, outlet (see FIG 1:41) then fit the cylinder head cover and gasket. Reinstall the heating pipe between the inlet manifold and water pump, securing in position by the clip under the cylinder head front cover bolt.

Refit the clutch and clutch driven plate to the flywheel (see Section 1:5) and bolt the gearbox into place on the engine. Install the sparking plugs, fit the distributor head and connect the HT leads between the plugs and distributor. Install the fuel line between the fuel pump and carburetter float chambers, circulating water hoses, alternator bracket, engine mountings, oil pressure transducers and oil level transmitter, water drain plug, etc.

Install the vacuum line between the distributor and inlet manifold.

Fill the engine sump with 7.25 pints of HD 10W.30 oil (Shell X.100) through the filler cap in the cylinder head cover. The engine and gearbox assembly can then be slung ready for reinstallation in the engine compartment.

1:13 Reinstalling the engine

Place a garage jack under the car to take the weight of the gearbox, then transfer the engine and gearbox on a moveable crane to above the engine compartment. Carefully lower into place, taking every precaution to see that the assembly does not catch, foul or damage any of the components already in the engine compartment, easing it backwards until it is possible to position the jack under the gearbox.

Raise the jack simultaneously with the lowering of the engine on the crane to bring engine and gearbox on to a level axis and right for dropping into the engine and gearbox supports. Secure the front to the engine mounting brackets on the forward crossmember (see FIG 1:42) and refit the rear engine crossmember and engine support brackets.

Recouple the propeller shaft to the gearbox drive shaft flange. Check that the engine is now seating properly for perfect alignment with the propeller shaft and finally tighten the mounting nuts to the torques shown in FIGS 1:42 and 1:43.

Reinstall the alternator and fan with pulleys, position the drive belt and adjust to give .5 inch play as shown in FIG 1:44. Fit the oil filter into place. Recouple the carburetter controls.

Beneath the car, reconnect the gearchange linkage and replace the clutch slave cylinder in position. Reconnect the exhaust manifolds to the exhaust pipes and secure the pipes and expansion chamber in place. Reinstall the starter motor.

Refit all hose connections and securely clamp in place. The only connections to be left at this stage are those to the radiator. Reconnect the fuel line from the filter to the fuel pump. Refit all electrical transducers and transmitters and reconnect all LT cables to their original positions, (alternator terminals, motor starter solenoid, distributor make-and-break, transducers, transmitters, etc.), and the heavy duty cables to the starter and engine earth terminal. Reconnect the central HT terminal on the distributor to the ignition coil. Refit the air filter.

Reinstall the radiator and make the last of the hose connections. Close the radiator drain cock and fill the cooling system with water, check for leaks and tighten clamps as necessary.

Make a final inspection of the engine to ensure that all the necessary reinstallation and reconnections have been made and the reconnect the battery cables.

Reinstall the radiator grille and refit the bonnet. The engine is now ready for the initial run. On pressing the starter switch, the crankshaft should turn but it will take a short while before the engine fires as the fuel pump must first charge the carburetter float chambers. If the engine does not start then, make a further check of HT connections and fuel flow before trying again.

Run the engine for a while to allow the cylinders to reach the proper operating temperature reset the valve clearances to the hot setting (see Technical Data) then

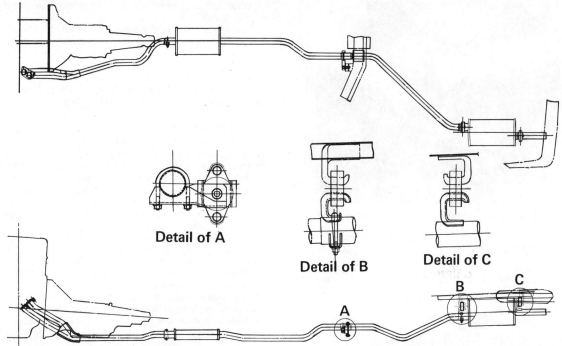

FIG 1:46 Details of exhaust pipe and mufflers with mountings

Detail of A

Detail of B

Detail of C

carry out the final tuning procedure. At the end of the test retorque the cylinder head bolts while the engine is still hot and make a further retorque after the first 100 miles running.

1:14 Tuning the engine

First run the engine until it has reached a steady temperature and adjust the throttle setscrew on the carburetter to give a steady turning speed of 600 to 700 rev/min. Adjust the idling screw until the engine speed increases, then reduce speed by the throttle screw again. Repeat on both adjustments until the crankshaft is rotating at around 550 rev/min and further adjustment of the idling screw will not increase, but may decrease, the speed.

For adjustments of the twin SU pattern carburetters, where fitted, see **Chapter 2, Section 2:13**.

The vacuum ignition control and centrifugal advance are not adjustable but are inherent in the construction of the distributor selected by the manufacturers for the individual engines. Coarse setting of the static advance is provided by the meshing of the distributor drive shaft gear with that on the crankshaft extension. Fine setting is by a slotted plate and setscrew immediately beneath the distributor housing (see **Section 1:3**).

To make the most of this setting, with the engine running at 500 rev/min, slightly lower than the normal idling speed, and with the vacuum advance line disconnected from the inlet manifold, in which circumstances both automatic controls are inoperative, the static setting can be checked and, if necessary, finely adjusted with the use of a stroboscopic light. A pointer secured to the front timing cover, clearly visible in **FIG 1:45**, is referenced against timing marks on the rim of the adjacent pulley. Each mark corresponds to a 5 degree advance from the TDC

in a clockwise direction, the lefthand, or zero advance, mark being TDC.

By adjusting the speed of the flashing light from the stroboscope to correspond with ignition on one of the cylinders, the timing marks can be made to appear stationary, regardless of engine speed. As the timing marks are set for TDC at No. 1 cylinder, the selection of this sparking plug as the datum enables the exact degree of advance to be viewed while fine adjustment is being made. This should be 10 deg. BTDC when the pointer should be opposite to the second timing mark (see **FIG 1:48**).

The only other factors which are likely to affect performance are wrong setting of the camshaft timing, wrong clearances between cams and rockers and wrong gapping

FIG 1:47 Exhaust pipe run beneath car showing the expansion chamber

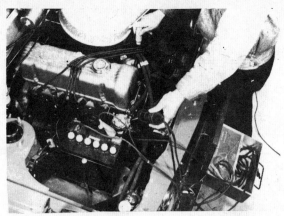

FIG 1:48 Use of stroboscopic light for precise timing

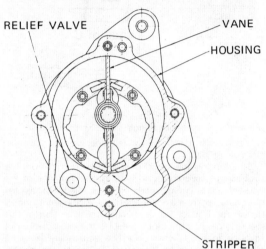

RELIEF VALVE

VANE

HOUSING

STRIPPER

FIG 1:49 Diagrammatic section through two-blade exhaust emission control compressor. The three-blade compressor is similar

of the distributor make-and-break. Providing that all of these have been set as laid down in the overhaul procedure, no troubles in this direction need be anticipated. Only if the engine performance is badly out of tune should a recheck be made.

After tuning, remember to reinstate the vacuum line and to tighten the distributor fine adjustment stud.

1:15 Exhaust system

The exhaust system comprises six parts, the front pipe, expansion chamber, two sections of exhaust pipe, silencer and tail pipe. The general layout of these is shown in **FIG 1:45**.

The front pipe is branched for connecting to the exhaust manifold and is secured to the forward end of the oval expansion chamber by a pipe clamp. The forward centre tube is secured to the expansion chamber and is clamped to the rear centre tube at bracket A where it is secured to the underframe. These three sections float between the bracket and the exhaust manifold and run down the

centre of the car immediately below the propeller tunnel (see **FIG 1:47**).

The opposite end of the rear section enters the silencer of circular cross section where it is supported from the underframe by an elastic hanger strap, the tail pipe being similarly supported at the opposite entry. In each case the strap bracket and pipe clamp are integral.

The whole assembly is readily accessible for replacement from under the car as and when necessary.

1:16 Exhaust emission control

The problem of air pollution is now such an international issue that certain authorities are insisting on the fitting of systems to cars which will control the emission of exhaust gases to contain only mineral content of unburnt hydrocarbons and carbon monoxide, the latter resulting from incomplete combustion or hydrocarbon/air mixtures and the former occurring on the use of the engine as a brake after bursts of high speed.

Provided that sufficient air is made available and the temperature is high enough for ignition, both the carbon monoxide and unburned fuel vapour can be reduced to relatively harmless carbon dioxide and water in transit from the engine exhaust ports to the tail pipe.

The Datsun emission control system, where fitted, tackles the problem in two ways, apart from the crankcase ventilation system described in **Chapter 2, Section 2:15**. The first is to substitute the standard carburetter by a modified one incorporating a solenoid valve operated by

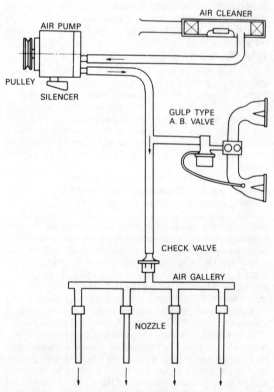

AIR CLEANER

AIR PUMP

PULLEY

SILENCER

GULP TYPE
A. B. VALVE

CHECK VALVE

AIR GALLERY

NOZZLE

FIG 1:50 Schematic view of air injection system for exhaust emission control

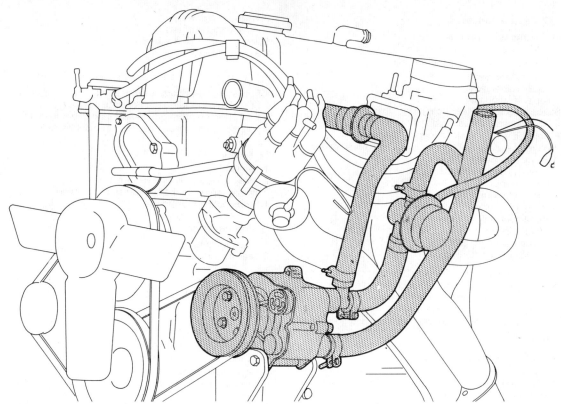

FIG 1:51 Left, the 1600cc engine with exhaust emission control installed and, right, a diagrammatic presentation of the air injection installation

a switch on the accelerator pedal. The second is to install a belt driven air pump to inject under pressure into the exhaust manifolds as close as possible to the ports where the gases are still in an incandescent state. The effect of these two is to produce a small fall-off in performance which is compensated for by altering the advance of the ignition timing through the unusual step of a second make-and-break (see **Chapter 3, Section 3:1**).

The modifications to the carburetters are dealt with in **Chapter 2**. The air pump comprises a rotor with two or three vanes within an aluminium housing (see **FIG 1:49**). The vanes are pivoted through bearings on a pin central with the housing but off-centre to the hollow rotor through which they protrude and extend to but do not quite touch the housing walls. The slot through which the vanes pass is sealed and an additional stripper seal between the inlet and exhaust ports bears on the periphery of the rotor, the vanes being withdrawn into the rotor as it passes this point.

Rotation in an anticlockwise direction has the effect of drawing air in from the righthand port, compressing it in the upper part of the housing and delivering it under pressure to the port on the left. From here it is ducted to the four-pronged injector assembly (see **FIG 1:50**) mounted on the engine with the injector nozzles protruding into the manifold adjacent to the exhaust ports. The ducting is through a large bore rubber hose and an exhaust check valve is incorporated to prevent possible back flow of gases from the exhaust system into the pump.

The pump is serviced as an assembly and is not suitable for dismantling. If trouble is experienced, fit a new pump and return the faulty one to the agents.

Since the air enriched exhaust gases depend on the high temperature at the exhaust port for ignition (that is, there is no separate ignition system), it may happen that a charge of unburned gas, followed on a sudden closure of the throttle at high speed, may find its way to the silencer to be exploded by a subsequent hot discharge, causing the familiar but unpleasant engine backfire. To minimise this risk, a backfire suppressor valve is incorporated which opens on sudden inlet manifold depression to admit pumped air from the compressor into the manifold. The resultant weakened mixture burns more readily in the cylinder but with little force and passes as normal exhaust to the silencer. It must be appreciated that overrich mixtures do not ignite as readily as those with correct fuel/air proportions.

A general view of the installation is shown diagrammatically in **FIG 1:51**, the air intake coming from the main air filter.

Generally speaking, the adjustment of an exhaust emission control system is a precise operation calling for various gauges, unions etc and its efficacy is insisted on in those places where Exhaust Emission Control is mandatory. Do not attempt the adjustments yourself but take the car to an agent with the proper equipment and experience.

1:17 Fault diagnosis

(a) Engine will not start

1 Flat battery
2 Loose or corroded battery terminals
3 Faulty starter switch
4 Faulty starter motor
5 Faulty ignition coil
6 Disconnected HT lead from coil to distributor
7 Disconnected LT lead to distributor
8 Break in wiring to distributor
9 Worn or excessively gapped make-and-break points
10 Faulty capacitor
11 Crossed-over HT leads to plugs
12 Faulty plugs
13 Choked fuel line of filter
14 Faulty fuel pump
15 Empty fuel tank
16 Air lock in fuel line
17 Condensation on plugs, in distributor or on HT leads
18 Choked carburetter jets

A little commonsense will tell which of the many possible causes is the most probable one. If the engine won't turn, suspect, battery, starter switch and starter in that order. If the engine turns but will not fire, suspect low fuel, damp distributor or plugs, faulty capacitor, choked carburetter jets, etc.

(b) Engine fires, then stalls

1 Idling jet out of adjustment
2 Choke not out
3 Throttle control set too fine
4 Faulty plugs

(c) Engines runs without power

1 Ignition timing slipped
2 Automatic or vacuum advance not working

3 Valve springs weak
4 Worn distributor cam
5 Wrong tappet clearances
6 Burnt valves or seats

(d) Engine runs but fades at speed with load

1 Fuel starvation through faulty pump
2 Fuel starvation through choked fuel filter
3 Fuel starvation through choked carburetter inlet jet
4 Fuel starvation through air lock or blocked fuel line

(e) Engine fires erratically

1 Faulty plug
2 Weak valve spring on one or more cylinders
3 Wrong tappet adjustment on some cylinders
4 Wrong idling adjustment

(f) Engine 'spits'

1 Water in carburetter
2 Leaking head gasket

(g) Engine 'pinks'

1 Wrong octane fuel
2 Ignition too far advanced

(h) Engine overheats

1 Shortage of water in radiator
2 Slipping fan and pump belt
3 Ignition too far retarded
4 Gasket blown in head

(j) Engine backfires

1 Weak valve spring
2 Sticking valve stem in guide
3 No clearance between rocker and cam
4 Transposed plug connections

CHAPTER 2

THE FUEL SYSTEM

2:1 Fuel pump and strainer

Fuel from the rear mounted tank, of approximately ten gallons capacity, is passed over the rubber pipeline and via the cartridge type fuel strainer to the fuel pump. The pump is of a fairly conventional diaphragm pattern mounted high on the cylinder head with the diaphragm rocker arm projecting into the rocker chamber, an extension to the arm resting on the pump driving cam mounted on the camshaft forward of the camshaft sprocket (see **FIG 2:1**).

The rocker arm is of the rigid pattern causing the pump to deliver a fixed quantity of fuel at each stroke regardless of the requirement of the carburetter. This quantity, in excess of the maximum required for top engine demand, is passed over a second rubber pipeline to a fuel return valve and through it to the carburetter. The function of this valve is twofold. First, it relieves any excess pressure caused by pumping against a closed needle valve in the float chamber and, second, it promotes circulation of fuel at periods of high ambient temperature so preventing vapour locks common to many fuel systems under tropical conditions. Fuel bypassed through the relief valve is returned to the tank via another rubber pipeline.

Sections through two types of relief valve, as applied to downdraught two-barrel and SU twin carburetter installations are shown in **FIG 2:2**. In each case, the fuel return valve is held closed by a cantilever leaf spring of bi-metal, the valve being opened either by pressure developed in the fuel pipeline from the pump when the float chamber needle valve is held closed or by deformation of the bi-metal leaf at high ambient temperature. In operation, the effect is that the pressure required to open the valve falls with a rise in temperature and only at a maximum ambient is it left on the point of opening at the slightest indication of back pressure from the float chamber. If, by maladjustment, the valve were to remain open with no back pressure, the division of flow between float chamber and fuel return pipe might be such that, at maximum engine demand on a hot day, the requirements of the engine could not be met by the fuel pump. **It is, therefore, imperative that the setting of the valve should not be tampered with and that any failure of the valve dealt with by immediate replacement.**

The cartridge strainer is of a new pattern and comprises a sealed transparent plastic case with an internal fibre mat filter interposed between inlet and outlet connections. It

FIG 2:1   End view of engine with covers removed to show position of fuel pump, rocker arm extension and cam

is secured to the car framework in the engine compartment by a spring clip and the fuel pipe connections are clamped to the filter inlet and outlet pipes (see **FIG 2:3**). A section through the filter is also shown.

The filter cannot be cleaned and must be replaced as and when necessary but in any case at intervals of not more than 24,000 miles. **As there are no cocks in the fuel line, it is important to hold the strainer high enough for the inlet pipe to be above the level of the rear tank when changing, otherwise spillage of fuel will result.**

2:2 Removal and dismantling the pump

To remove the pump, first disconnect the fuel lines to the carburetter and filter, taking precautions against fuel spillage. Normally the inlet to the pump is well above fuel level in the tank and providing that this level can be maintained, no other step need be taken. Alternatively,

cork the end of the fuel pipe or clamp the pipeline with a suitable screw clamp.

Remove the nuts securing the pump to the cylinder head and ease clear through the hole. Take off the gasket and throw away. At the bench, separate the upper and lower bodies by removing the six screws, then dismantle the upper half by removing the centre and four peripheral screws and extracting cover and gasket.

If necessary for valve replacement, remove the valve retainer clip (7 in **FIG 2:4**) and push out the valves from above. **Do not interfere with the valve assembly if it is working satisfactorily and, when replacing the valves, take care to see that they are inserted the right way round.**

Depress the diaphragm centre downwards and free the end of the pullrod 10 from the end of the rocker arm 24, by pushing it to one side with a screwdriver (see **FIG 2:5**). Extract diaphragm, spring, seal and washer from the lower body. Drive out the rocker arm pin 25 and remove rocker arm, spring and washers. Thoroughly clean all parts in carbon tetrachloride and dry.

2:3 Inspection and replacement

Inspect all parts for signs of wear or damage, paying particular attention to the state of the diaphragm, seal and diaphragm spring. Replace by new components as necessary. In particular, check that the rocker arm pin is a tight fit in the lower body since wear at this point can result in oil leakage from the camshaft area and cause a dirty engine.

If there is wear in the pin hole in the body, replace the whole pump.

Commence reassembly by installing the rocker arm and spring in the lower body. Lubricate the rocker arm bearing where the pin passes through and check that it is free on the pin: Insert the seal 13 and ring 12 (see **FIG 2:4**) in the lower body and position the spring 11. Place the diaphragm in position over the spring, checking that the tab on the external periphery is facing the flange side of the pump and that the holes coincide with those on the body, depress and rock to one side so that the end of the pullrod can be re-engaged with the slot of the rocker arm. Operate the rocker arm a few times and check that the diaphragm moves up and down and is parallel with the upper flange of the body.

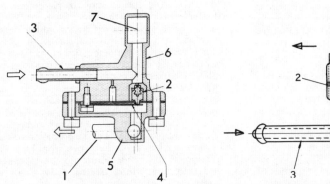

FIG 2:2   Sections through relief valves for downdraught (left) and SU (right) carburetters

Key to Fig 2:2   1 Pipe to fuel tank   2 Relief valve   3 Pipe from fuel pump   4 Bi-metal leaf spring   5 Cover   6 Body   7 To float chamber

Check that the valves are in position on the upper body and that the retainer clip 7 is secured by the screw 8. Place in position over the lower body, check that the holes coincide with those around the lower body flange and the diaphragm, then insert the six screws and clamp down. Check that no part of the diaphragm edge, apart from the tab, shows outside the flange joint. Fit the top cover with a new gasket 4, and secure in place first by the four outer screws and, finally by the centre screw and washer. **Do not overtighten this one or leakage from the outer edges may result.**

2:4 Testing and installation

It is advisable to give the pump a test before installation. Fit two short lengths of rubber tube to the inlet and outlet pipes and temporarily secure the pump upright with the jaws of a vice lightly gripping the lower body. Insert the inlet pipe into a container of paraffin a short distance from and slightly below the pump. Insert the free end of the outlet pipe into a glass measuring jar and, with strokes of the rocker arm, draw paraffin from the container through the pump and into the measuring jar.

Should the paraffin refuse to flow, it may be because the valves are not sealing properly. Remove the cap and insert a small quantity of paraffin into the valve chambers to wet the valve seatings, then reinstall the cap. When the liquid is flowing, stop pumping and return that in the measuring jar to the container and follow up by operating the cam lever about ten full strokes, catching the outflow in the measure. It should average not less than .5cc per stroke. Check that at no time are bubbles pumped through.

Finally, remove the inlet connection and cover the pipe with the pad of one finger. Operate the lever. A distinct suction should be felt and, on removing the finger, a slight inrush of air should be heard.

Fit new gaskets to the mounting flange, and reinstall the pump on the engine, tightening the nuts securely.

Remove the overhead camshaft cover and check that the rocker arm extension is in contact with the fuel pump

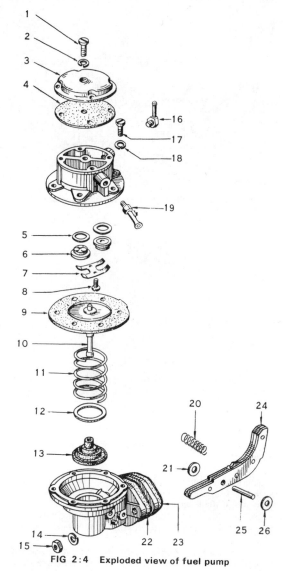

FIG 2:4   Exploded view of fuel pump

Key to Fig 2:4   1, 2, 17, 18 Cover screws and lockwashers
3 Cover   4 Gasket   5, 6 Valves and washers
7 Valve retainer clip and screw   9 Diaphragm   10 Pullrod
11 Diaphragm spring   12 Washer   13 Seal
14, 15 Mounting nut and washer   16, 19 Inlet and outlet pipes
20 Rocker return spring   21, 26 Washer   22, 23 Gaskets
24 Rocker arm

cam and that it oscillates freely when the engine crankshaft is turned. Replace the camshaft cover.

With the engine running, check for oil leaks around the mounting flange and fuel leaks at joints and gaskets.

2:5 Carburetters

Two types of carburetter are used, a downdraught pattern with two barrels modelled on the Stromberg Zenith design, and twin side draught variable venturi carburetters modelled on the SU design. The latter are used only on 1600 models.

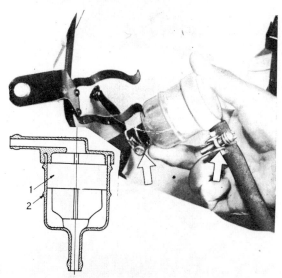

FIG 2:3   Cartridge type fuel filters showing internal construction and method of installation

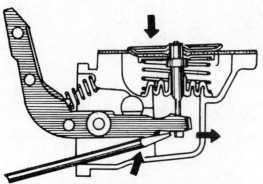

FIG 2:5 Section through fuel pump body showing method of disengaging pullrod from rocker arm

FIG 2:6 General view of type DCK.306 downdraught carburetter

The downdraught carburetters are similar in design for both the 1300, and 1600 cc engines, differing mainly in the venturi diameters and jet size numbers. These are designated type DCK.306 for the 1300 cc and DAF.328 for the 1600 cc engine. The twin SU type is designated HJL38W.

On the 1600 cc engine where exhaust emission control has been installed, a modified downdraught carburetter is fitted. This bears the type No. DAF.328.6 or DAF.328.8 according to whether the transmission is manual or automatic, and incorporates a solenoid valve opening an enrichment channel into the secondary barrel on overrun. Evaporative emission control may also be found in association with exhaust emission control. This is a sealed fuel tank system exhausting into the carburetter induction but using the crankcase as a reservoir for fuel vapour when the engine is at rest. A non-return valve in the vapour vent line and a vapour/liquid separator effectively prevents any chance of explosive blow-back into the tank area.

2:6 DCK and DAF, description of operation

Dealing first with the downdraught carburetters, a general view, removed from the engine, is given in FIG

2:6. The DAF.328 as fitted with automatic transmission on the 1600 cc engine incorporates an additional dashpot (see **FIG 2:7**).

In each case, the carburetter comprises a primary and a secondary system, each with its own venturi and jets, discharging side by side into the inlet manifold. Both systems share a common float chamber and float mechanism, the primary throttle valve, regulating over the normal running range, being manually operated from the accelerator pedal, the secondary throttle valve opening for full load running under the control of the vacuum capsule sensing the depression in the throats at the venturi outlets. (In the DAF.328, the primary system is modelled on Solex design with the secondary on Stromberg Zenith. In DCK.306 both are based on Stromberg Zenith.)

Taking, first, a section through the DCK.306 (see **FIG 2:8**), air drawn down the primary duct passes through and around the small venturi 14, inducing a flow of vaporized fuel through the main nozzle 15 from the emulsion tube 21, where air from the jet 16, and fuel from the main jet 22 are mixed. When the throttle valve is closed, air from 17 and fuel from 18, the idling combination, bypass the throttle valve entering the induction manifold via hole 23. This flow ceases when the valve uncovers hole 24 destroying the depression in the idling system.

FIG 2:7 General view of type DAF.328 carburetter with, below, the same type fitted with dashpot for automatic transmission installations

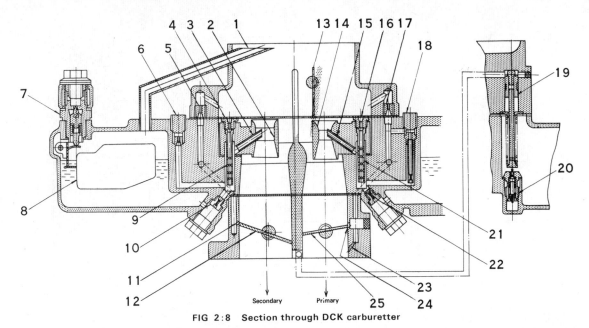

FIG 2:8 Section through DCK carburetter

Key to Fig 2:8   1 Float chamber air vent   2 Secondary venturi   3 Secondary main nozzle   4 Main air jet   5 Idling air jet
6 Idling jet   7 Needle valve   8 Float   9 Emulsion tube   10 Secondary main jet   11 Bypass   12 Secondary butterfly valve
13 Choke   14 Primary venturi   15 Primary main nozzle   16 Main air jet   17 Idling air jet   18 Idling jet
19 Power valve piston   20 Power valve   21 Emulsion tube   22 Main jet   23 Bypass   24 Progression hole   25 Primary
butterfly valve

When the choke valve 13 is held closed for starting, the entry of air to jets 16 and 17 is restricted and the depression in the inlet manifold draws almost pure fuel into the venturi to give an excessive rich starting mixture. As, however, the valve is eccentrically mounted, and the control is through a spring coupling, as soon as the engine fires, the inflow of air opens the choke valve against the spring to reduce the richness of the fuel vapour.

Under heavy load conditions, the depression in the venturi throats is communicated to the vacuum capsule which progressively opens the secondary throttle valve 12, drawing vapour through the secondary venturi 2, with additional vapour from the emulsion tube 9, where air from 4 and fuel from 10 are mixed. Mechanical linkage between the two throttle valves, external to the chambers, prevents opening of the secondary valve until the primary valve opening has reached 56 deg.

The power, or vacuum actuated boost valve 20, is normally held closed by the spring encircling the plunger 19, but when the depression in the manifold is high under light load with small throttle valve opening, this depression is communicated to the upper end of the plunger raising it to uncover the opening to the valve enabling extra fuel from the chamber to enter the passage to the emulsion tube ahead of the main jet. The effect is the same as though the main jet 22, were a variable opening one adjusting the flow not only in proportion to the depression in the venturi above the throttle but also in proportion to the suction below the throttle.

Opening the throttle suddenly has the effect of lowering the suction in the region of the venturi momentarily so that the intake of fuel from the main jet is reduced with the risk of fuel starvation and stalling of the engine. This is

overcome by the accelerating pump mechanism which, mechanically linked to the throttle, injects almost pure fuel into the area surrounding the venturi, at a rate proportional to the opening of the throttle valve by the accelerator pedal. The balance of fuel to air is therefore restored until the increase of depression with the acceleration of the engine re-establishes the flow through the main jet and stalling is avoided. When the throttle is closed, the pump plunger is raised, drawing a fresh charge of fuel into the cylinder ready for the next demand upon it (see FIG 2:9).

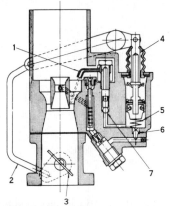

FIG 2:9 Section through accelerator pump

Key to Fig 2:9   1 Injector   2 Operating rod
3 Butterfly valve   4 Piston   5 Piston return spring
6 Valve   7 Ball valve

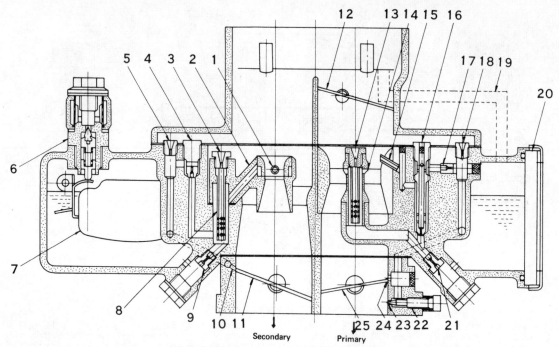

FIG 2:10 Section through DAF.328 carburetter

Key to Fig 2:10   1 Secondary venturi   2 Secondary main nozzle   3 Main air jet   5 Idling air jet   6 Needle valve
7 Float   8 Emulsion tube   9 Secondary main jet   10 Bypass   11 Secondary butterfly valve   12 Choke
13 Primary main air jet   14 Multi-orifice main nozzle   15 Bleed hole   16 Main air jet   17 Economizer bypass
18 Idling air jet   19 Float chamber air vent   20 Float chamber cover   21 Primary main jet   22 Slow-running adjustment
23 Slow-running jet   24 Progression hole   25 Primary butterfly valve

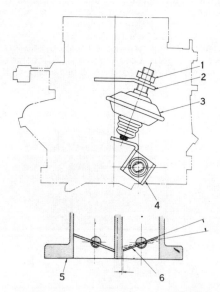

FIG 2:11   Action of dashpot on primary butterfly valve with automatic transmission

Key to Fig 2:11   1 Adjusting nut   2 Bracket
3 Dashpot capsule   4 Valve control arm
6 Primary butterfly valve   7 Carburetter body

The main differences in the standard DAF.328 are the omission of the power valve, the introduction of an adjustable throttle bypass 22 and 23 (see **FIG 2:10**), and the replacement of the small venturi in the primary throat by a multi-orifice main nozzle with the main air jet directly in the intake air-flow. The discharge of fuel vapour is then from a circumferential series of holes directed downward 14, in to the primary throat.

The mechanical linkage is set to open the secondary throttle valve only after the primary valve opening has reached 59 deg. The special dashpot attached to the DAF.328 for use with the Borg-Warner automatic transmission is securely fixed at one end to a bracket on the carburetter and the other end is in contact with a lever mounted on the main throttle spindle (see **FIG 2:11**). Removal of the foot from the accelerator pedal and to the brake for quick application could stall the engine but the action of the dashpot is to slow down the rate of closure of the throttle enabling the engine speed to decrease steadily, rather than stall, the slip being taken up in the hydrokinetic converter.

2:7 Dismantling and inspection

Remove the air cleaner and disconnect the vacuum line and choke and throttle linkages from the carburetter. Disconnect the fuel line to the carburetter. Unbolt and remove the carburetter from the inlet manifold and transfer to a bench for dismantling.

Thoroughly clean the exterior and drain the fuel from the float chamber.

Extract all main jets, idling jets, throttle stop screws accessible from the outside, noting the position of each one for replacement. Remove the splitpins and disconnect the accelerator pump linkage. Remove the return springs and dismantle the primary/secondary throttle interlinkage. Remove, but do not dismantle, the diaphragm capsule. Unscrew the four setscrews retaining the choke chamber in position and remove the choke chamber and gasket. Remove the top cover to the accelerator pump chamber and extract the piston and spring. **Be particularly careful not to lose the piston return spring and inlet valve at the bottom of the cylinder.**

The throttle chamber, below the main body, can also be detached by removing the four setscrews but, as this only contains the mechanical parts of the butterfly valves and spindles and removal breaks the joint through which the bypass holes traverse, there is little point in doing so.

Removal of the choke chamber gives access to the remainder of the jets and emulsion tubes and these can be extracted for cleaning and examination, again being careful to note the positions for reinstallation.

Access to the float chamber is by removal of the end cover and gaskets (see **FIG 2:12**). The float slides off from the internal spindle and the needle valve and union is removable from above the body.

Inspect all parts carefully for signs of damage and check that all jets are clear. **Do not endeavour to insert wire through the jets to clear them if they appear choked. This can alter the bore which is critical for carburetter performance. If they appear to be damaged or choked beyond clearing by blowing through them, replace the jets by new ones of the same number.**

Clean out the float chamber and obtain a new set of gaskets. When all parts have been inspected and worn or damaged parts replaced, reassembly can commence.

2:8 Reassembly and installation

Reassembly is a simple reversal of the dismantling procedure followed by adjustments to ensure maximum performance when installed.

During assembly, pay particular attention to the following points. First, check that all throttle and choke butterfly valves are free to turn on their shafts without fouling the sides of the throats in which they are located. Check that there is no excessive play in the bearing holes and lubricate with engine oil to provide both easy tuning and a perfect seal against the ingress of air to the chamber. If the play is excessive and the spindle holes are worn, replace the carburetter by a new one, returning the original one to the agent for reconstruction.

After inserting the float chamber needle valve and float, check that the float, on its spindle, moves between the stop 3 (see **FIG 2:13**) and the needle valve when fully closed to give a total movement of .06 inch (DAF.328) or .04 inch (DCK.306) at the valve end. **Unless the fuel level was wrong before dismantling, careful handling will enable float tab adjustment to be avoided on reassembly.**

Though it is possible to vary the jet sizes to give a change in engine performance, providing that the engine was

FIG 2:12 Exploded view of float chamber with float removed

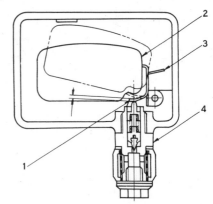

FIG 2:13 Float chamber showing points of adjustment of fuel level

Key to Fig 2:12 1 Valve seat arm 2 Float 3 Float stop 4 Valve body

FIG 2:14 View of twin SU type carburetter installed on 1600cc Saloon with air intake elbows removed

running to your satisfaction before servicing, it is advisable to retain the jet selection chosen by the manufacturers. To improve economy at the sacrifice of performance, reduce the size of the main **or** idling jets, alternatively, increase the size of the main **or** idling air bleeds. Conversely, to improve performance at the sacrifice of economy, larger jets **or** smaller bleeds may be installed.

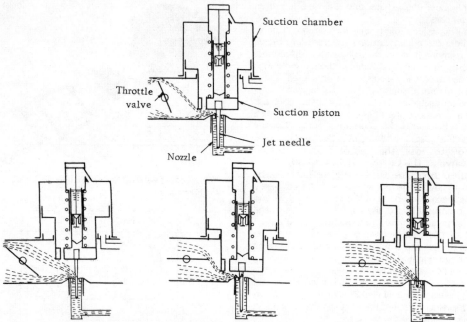

FIG 2:15 Operation of SU type carburetter showing position of piston and fuel vapour flow for typical engine conditions. (Above) idling, (Below left) low-speed, (Below centre) full throttle under load, (Below right) full throttle, top speed

Whenever servicing a carburetter, always use new joint gaskets and washers. Sets of gaskets, washers, splitpins etc., are available from the agents.

Installation is straightforward and care must be taken to ensure that the joint with the manifold is absolutley airtight. **This is most important.** When reassembling the mechanical linkages, be careful not to bend or alter their setting which is jig set in the first instance. This is particularly relevant of the primary and secondary throttle linkages.

As with all downdraught carburetters, be particularly careful not to drop any small screws or metal parts into the intake during assembly. These may be drawn into the valve ports at high engine speeds and do considerable damage.

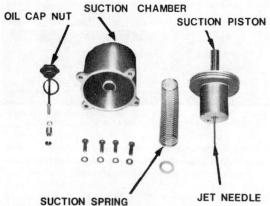

OIL CAP NUT **SUCTION CHAMBER** **SUCTION PISTON**

SUCTION SPRING **JET NEEDLE**
FIG 2:16 Component parts of dismantled SU control piston

2:9 Tuning for slow-running

Provided that no alterations to the jet selection have been made, tuning comprises the simple adjustment of two screws, the throttle stop and the idling adjustment screw. To commence with, carefully screw the idling adjust screw home until it bottoms in the jet, then unscrew three complete turns. Set the throttle stop so that it just rests on the throttle plate and then screw in two complete turns. Start the engine and adjust the throttle stop to give a speed of 500 to 600 rev/min. Allow to run until warm. Then adjust the two screws in turn until the engine speed is steady at 550 rev/min and any change in the setting of the idling screw only serves to slow the engine down.

Check operation of the accelerator pump by slamming the throttle wide open from idling. The engine should pick up without hesitation.

2:10 Twin SU type, description and operation

The two SU carburetters, identical in principle and operation, are structurally different only in the position of the float chamber in relation to the body. Each carburetter serves two cylinders through a two-branch manifold the forward carburetter, supplying cylinders 1 and 2, having the float chamber to the left, and the rear carburetter, serving cylinders 3 and 4, having it to the right (see **FIG 2:14**).

Fuel from the float chamber enters the carburetter throat through a vertical jet partially closed by a tapered concentric needle. This needle is supported on a piston in a vertical air chamber which is both spring-loaded and weighted to keep the needle in the position of greatest choke. At the same time, the piston end virtually closes the entrance to the carburetter throat. A small vent situated at the lower face of the piston communicates with the cylinder above and the depression caused by the induction of fuel/air into the inlet manifold is communicated to the cylinder above the piston. Since the lower face of that part of the piston in the cylinder proper is open to atmosphere, engine induction causes the piston to rise.

This has two effects. The first is that the withdrawal of the tapered needle from the fuel orifice increases its effective area and the amount of fuel inducted. The second is that, by increasing the effective area of the throat at this point, the air velocity for a given intake is reduced and a position of equilibrium is reached at which the opposing suction and spring forces in the cylinder balance to hold the piston stationary at its new position.

The air velocity is dependent on both engine speed and throttle valve opening and the position of the piston will therefore be changing to suit every alteration in engine speed as determined by load and accelerator pedal application.

The arrangement is very sensitive and, to avoid the occurence of hunting (instability as the result of interplay between the changing conditions and resultant piston positions), a dashpot is installed at the upper end to damp out random oscillations and to introduce a slight delay in the effect of a change. As a result, a sudden opening of the throttle causing a heavy induction across the face of the piston and jet is prevented from instantaneous change of jet effective size and the fuel vapour indicated, while adequate in quantity for the immediate engine requirement, is not rendered richer in fuel content until the engine speed has responded to the reduced throttle choke.

Two adjustments are provided for tuning. The first is the normal throttle stop screw acting on the throttle butterfly valve and the second is idling mixture control which is effected by raising or lowering the fuel jet carrier in relation to the tapered needle by means of the screw adjustment below the carburetter.

The operation can be understood from the four diagrams showing typical positions for throttle/speed conditions in **FIG 2:15**.

2:11 Dismantling and inspection

Disconnect the fuel line to the float chamber and uncouple the throttle linkage. Unbolt and remove the fuel overflow pipe from the float chamber. Unbolt and remove each carburetter from its manifold and thoroughly clean the exterior. Transfer to the bench.

Drain out the fuel from the float chamber, remove the top cover to the float chamber and extract the float. The valve and float lever are mounted on the cover with the float itself a free body in the chamber. Put both in a clean, safe place. Now remove the domed section chamber by extracting the four screws and lifting, complete with piston assembly, from the carburetter body. **Be careful not to bend the needle when withdrawing.**

Carefully dismantle the piston, spring and dahspot assembly (see **FIG 2:16**) but **do not remove the needle unless absolutely necessary.**

From below the carburetter, disconnect the fuel pipe from the float chamber and unscrew the nozzle adjusting nut. Extract the nozzle from the nozzle sleeve and remove

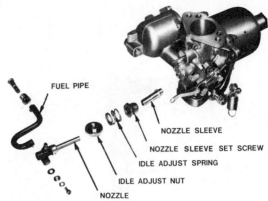

FIG 2:17 Component parts of fuel nozzle and sleeve

FUEL PIPE
NOZZLE SLEEVE
NOZZLE SLEEVE SET SCREW
IDLE ADJUST SPRING
IDLE ADJUST NUT
NOZZLE

FIG 2:18 Position of piston lifting pin

FIG 2:19 Adjusting the nozzle nut to regulate slow-running

both nut and spring. Next unscrew the sleeve setscrew and extract both screw and sleeve (see **FIG 2:17**).

Thoroughly wash all parts in clean petrol and blow through nozzles and passageways with a clean air jet. Examine for signs of damage and replace as necessary. Check operation of the throttle valve.

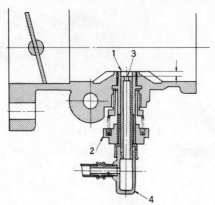

FIG 2:20 Setting the nozzle level showing, 1, the table, 3, the nozzle set 2.5 mm below the table by, 2, the nozzle nut and 4, the fuel inlet area of the nozzle

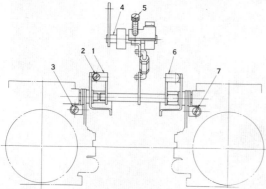

FIG 2:21 Control linkage between the two SU type carburetters

Key to Fig 2:21

3, 7 Carburetter throttle stops	1 Throttle coupling rod
4 Auxiliary shaft	2 Synchronizing screw
6 Non-adjustable stop	5 Combined throttle stop

2:12 Reassembly and installation

First, reassemble the piston assembly in the reverse order to dismantling leaving the dashpot assembly out for the time being. Check that the piston moves smoothly in the cylinder, that the needle projects into the nozzle socket and that, when held vertically, the spring-loaded lifting pin, situated between the body and the float chamber, rises and lowers the piston without friction or effort (see **FIG 2:18**).

Next, reposition and fit the nozzle sleeve and setscrew but do not tighten the setscrew yet. Insert the nozzle after fitting the adjust spring and nut in position and tightening well up, carefully easing it on to the needle and then pushing the nozzle up until it commences to lift the piston. Holding it in this position, raise the piston by means of the lifting pin, allowing it to fall. If it does not fall freely, the needle is not central in the jet. Ease the setscrew to enable the nozzle sleeve to centre itself with the nozzle around the needle and then tighten setscrew.

Raise the piston and adjust the nozzle nut until the tip of the nozzle is flush with the table in the carburetter

throat (see **FIG 2:20**) This can be seen from the inlet port. Turn the adjust nut back 2½ turns. This will lower the nozzle tip 2.5 mm approximately below the table level since one turn of the nut corresponds to 1 mm. Replace the dashpot assembly and again check that the piston is free by lifting with the lifting pin and releasing.

Reassemble the float chamber and reconnect the fuel pipe. Unless it has been necessary to fit a new needle valve, adjustment of the float arm will not be necessary. Remount in position on the engine and recouple the linkage. Reconnect the fuel pipes and install the overflow pipes. Take out the plungers from the dashpots and fill the cylinders with light oil up to the marks engraved on the plunger rod. Refit the plungers and screw the cap nuts home. **No lubricant is applied to the inside of the main cylinder or to the piston. These operate in a perfectly dry state.**

2:13 Tuning

Slacken back both throttle screws, pull out the choke lever and start the engine. Allow to run until the engine has warmed up. Ease back the coupling shaft adjusting screw (2 in **FIG 2:21**) and then adjust both throttle stop screws independently until the engine is turning over at 600 to 650 rev/min and the intake hiss, as heard through a short length of rubber tube applied to each intake in the manner of a stethoscope, is equal in volume at each opening (see **FIG 2:14**).

Push in the choke lever. It will have been observed that the choke operates to raise or lower the nozzle in the sleeve which, for a given needle position, varies the effective size of the jet, the setscrew determining the minimum size of jet opening. Adjust the coupling screw 2 until it just touches the tab on the throttle arm and slacken back the throttle screw on that arm to just clear the plate. If this unbalances the intake hiss, make the correction on the coupling screw 2.

Now adjust the common throttle stop 5, and back off the second throttle stop 7 half a turn. Again check the

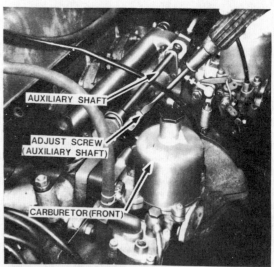

FIG 2:22 View of carburetter installation showing position of combined throttle stop adjustment screw on the auxiliary shaft

intake hiss balance. All subsequent setting is done on the common throttle stop which is now adjusted to give an engine speed of 650 rev/min and checked by opening the throttle and allowing it to fall back on the stop. The engine speed should return to the same rev/min each time (see **FIG 2 : 22**).

The final step is to check the setting of the nozzle set-screw. The easiest method is to slam the throttle wide open and note the response. If it is virtually instantaneous, the setting is correct. If there is a noticeable delay with apparent fall-off in speed, unscrew the idling adjust nut a fraction and try again (see **FIG 2 : 19**). Repeat until the best setting is obtained. It should be possible to get this response with not more than half a turn either way from the original setting of $2\frac{1}{2}$ turns (see **Section 2 : 12**).

When this setting has been achieved, recheck engine idling speed and readjust the common throttle screw, if necessary, to give 600 rev/min and make a final check on balanced hiss. Reinstall the air filter.

2 : 14 Air filters

The air filter for the single carburetter installations is of the circular pan pattern with a dry, replaceable, corrugated paper filter element. It is not intended that the filter shall be cleaned at any time and, under normal conditions, it should not need replacement until after some 24,000 miles. This figure should, however, be reduced for particularly dusty or sandy environments.

Filter replacement is quite simple consisting of, unscrewing the wingnut at the top and removing the cover and

FIG 2 : 23 Circular pattern air filter with expendable filter elemenet being removed

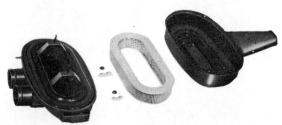

FIG 2 : 24 Oval pattern air filter as fitted to twin SU type installations

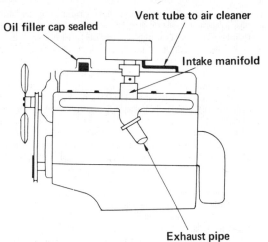

FIG 2 : 25 Crankcase ventilation through air filter to carburetter intake

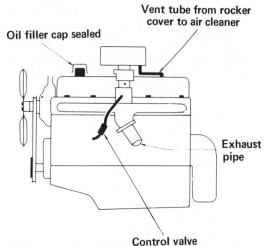

FIG 2 : 26 Combined system of crankcase venting and cooling

intake (see **FIG 2 : 23**). **Always brush out the interior surfaces of the cover and base plate before refitting a new filter and, if there are any sticky or oily deposits, wipe clean with a rag dipped in paraffin or petrol.**

The air filter for the twin SU installation is similar in construction but the shape of the pan and filter is oval instead of round (see **FIG 2 : 24**). The cover is secured by two wingnuts and there are, of course, two outlets, one to each carburetter intake. Flanged metal elbows on each carburetter, both turning inwards to face each other, are coupled to the filter outlets by substantial rubber hoses and clamps. These are clearly visible in **FIG 1 : 4**.

2 : 15 Crankcase ventilation system

Although strictly not a part of the fuel system, the controlled crankcase emission system which is a mandatory requirement in certain areas and which is now standard on Datsun cars, is linked with the fuel system in that the vapours from the crankcase are vented into the inlet manifold either directly or through the clean air side of the air filter. The old practice of venting both crankcase and rocker box direct to atmosphere via a vent type oil cap and vent pipe respectively no longer applies.

On the 1300cc engine no crankcase vent is fitted and the oil filler cap is of the sealed pattern. A short pipe from the crankcase cover terminates on the inside area of the air filter (see **FIG 2 : 25**) and oily vapours from the crankcase are drawn up into the rocker box and into the carburetter intake together with fresh air from the filter. The oil vapour then serves as an upper cylinder lubricant and is discharged, when carbonized by high cylinder gas temperatures, through the car exhaust system.

On the 1600cc engine the same applies but an additional pipe, with a special control valve inserted, is interposed between the crankcase and inlet manifold, bypassing the carburetter (see **FIG 2 : 26**). When the manifold depression is high, on part open throttle, the crankcase vapours are drawn through the control valve and into the manifold where they pass, with the fuel vapour, to the cylinders. The flow of filtered air from the filter then passes into the rocker box and down into the crankcase to replace the extracted vapours, helping to cool the crankcase as well as reducing vaporization. At high engine speeds and full throttle, the valve cannot handle the crankcase vapours since the manifold depression is not sufficient to extract them. The build-up of vapour pressure is then vented to the air cleaner in reverse entering the cylinders through the carburetter.

The pipes or hoses are of a special composition which is resistant to hot oil vapours but the resistance is not long term. It follows that the pipes must be inspected at frequent intervals and must be replaced at the first signs or deterioration.

At every 10,000 miles, the pipes should be disconnected and blown through with compressed air, the ventilation control valve checked for operation and the crankcase and manifold connectors examined. Parts which show any signs of blockage or deterioration must be replaced.

Apart from its purpose for reducing atmospheric contamination, it will be appreciated that the inlet to the manifold represents an air leak which must be controlled. The restriction of the control valve ensures that this leak is not sufficient to affect carburation but a broken or detached pipe to the manifold on the 1600cc engine introduces an uncontrolled leak which will affect engine performance to a marked degree. Good maintenance is, therefore, absolutely essential.

2:17 Fault diagnosis

The fuel system is dependent on the ignition and valve timing and settings and these should first be checked when trouble arises before assuming that it is the carburetter that is at fault.

(a) Engine will not start

1 Low fuel in tank
2 Faulty fuel pump
3 Choked filter gauzes
4 Sticking float or needle valve
5 Air leaks in induction system
6 Overrich mixture through excessive choke
7 Blocked main or idling jets
8 Vapour lock in fuel line.

(b) Engine starts but stalls

1 Idling setting too low
2 Idling jet choked
3 Throttle stop set too fine
4 Not enough choke

(c) Poor acceleration

1 Weak accelerator pump spring
2 Sticking pump valve
3 Choked pump jet
4 Low oil level in dashpot (twin SU)
5 Control piston sticking (twin SU)

(d) Fuel overflowing from carburetter

1 Punctured float
2 Sticking needle valve
3 Faulty float arm adjustment

(e) Excessive fuel consumption

1 Main jets too large
2 Air jets too small
3 Air jets clogged
4 Primary/secondary throttle coupling faulty
5 Worn jet needle (twin SU)
6 Worn nozzle (twin SU)
7 Slow-running adjustment faulty (twin SU)

(f) Engine 'hunts'

1 Low oil in dashpot (twin SU)
2 Jet needle wrongly fitted or loose (twin SU)

(g) Engine fades at speed

1 Faulty fuel pump
2 Faulty bypass valve

CHAPTER 3

THE IGNITION SYSTEM

3:1 The ignition system

The ignition system is a fairly conventional arrangement of ignition coil and distributor with make-and-break for the coil primary. A special coil is fitted on later models in which a ballast resistor of 1.6 ohms is connected in series with the primary across the 12-volt supply. This resistor is cut out of circuit by the motor starter switch during starting to compensate for the drop in volts across the battery terminals while the heavy starting current is flowing. A good spark is, therefore, ensured.

The distributor is of normal pattern with centrifugal and vacuum advance. A top-entry distributor cap is fitted and the drive is by skew gear from the crankshaft, an extension to the distributor shaft providing the fuel pump drive via a simple dog coupling (see **FIG 3:1**).

Where exhaust emission control installations have been fitted, the burning of rich hydrocarbon vapours on overrun with the throttle closed is facilitated by retarding the ignition. In some systems this is effected by a second overriding vacuum capsule on the distributor, moving the cam plate in the opposite direction to the vacuum advance capsule, connected to the inlet manifold when the depression is exceptionally low. In the Datsun system, the same effect is obtained by the use of a modified distributor with two contact breakers set to operate on opposite faces of

the cam and some 5 deg. apart. The retarded breaker is brought into service by a relay, coupling the two moving contacts electrically, when the accelerator pedal is released suddenly and the engine speed is high. The special distributor is the Hitachi Model D412.59 and replaces the D410.58.

3:2 Automatic ignition timing and controls

The automatic ignition timing is set by the manufacturers and cannot be changed except by changing the vacuum unit or the combination of weights and springs. The static advance is set approximately by the meshing of the skew gears and finely adjusted by the clamping plate at the foot of the distributor housing.

Setting the static advance can be done with the aid of a battery and lamp circuit across the make-and-break to give instantaneous indication of the opening and closing of the contacts. These are used with the ignition timing marks against the pointer on the crankcase (see **FIG 1:45**). Each mark represents a 5 degree variation before top dead centre on No. 1 cylinder and the contacts should be set to open at 10 deg. BTDC on the 1300 and 1600 cc engines using 85 octane fuel and 14 deg. BTDC on the twin SU engine using 95 octane fuel. On the 1400 the timing is 8 deg. BTDC.

FIG 3:1 Hitachi distributor and drive as fitted to the 1300 and 1600 cc engines

FIG 3:2 Vacuum capsule detached from the distributor

FIG 3:3 Removing the make-and-break from the breaker plate

FIG 3:4 Removing the breaker plate from the distributor housing

The vacuum advance will then give a maximum 9 deg. advance over the static advance, a total of 19 deg. while the centrifugal advance operates over a range of 10 deg. also in addition to the static advance and, at high speed, light load, the maximum vacuum advance.

This enables the optimum engine performance to be obtained under all conditions of engine speed and load which is dependent on several factors. These include cylinder head temperature, grade and temperature of the fuel vapour, compression ratio of the engine and the interval before TDC at which ignition commences in each cylinder. Some are a function of engine design based on predicted engine and ambient vapour temperatures and the cooling system is devised to achieve the conditions when running normally. The variables of engine speed and load are then dealt with by the automatic ignition features.

3:3 Removal and dismantling

To remove the distributor, first disconnect the HT and LT leads and unclip and remove the distributor cap. Unscrew the bolt securing the clamping plate to the distributor support casting and withdraw.

At the bench, commence dismantling on a clean surface and, as the work proceeds, lay the parts out on a clean sheet of paper in a recognisable order.

Unscrew and remove the clamping plate from below the body casting. Remove the screws securing the vacuum capsule assembly to the distributor housing and extract, lifting the operating arm clear of the pin on the breaker plate (see FIG 3:2). Disconnect the capacitor lead from the breaker plate assembly and unbolt and remove the capacitor.

Remove the cheese-head screw and slacken the two setscrews on the breaker plate holding the make-and-break assembly in position. Slide the latter clear, extract the terminal block from the distributor housing and remove the complete assembly from the distributor (see FIG 3:3).

Do not attempt to dismantle the breaker plate further as it comprises an upper and lower member running on steel balls interposed between each member and the breaker plate, but check that the balls are in position and secure by tightening the two setscrews until reassembly.

The breaker plate is removed from the distributor housing by extracting the two side screws which also hold the cap fixing clips and the earth lead (see FIG 3:4).

Next, extract the two pins securing the dog collar and skew gear to the shaft (see FIG 3:5). Remove together with packing washers, noting the number for eventual replacement.

The shaft and centrifugal plate can then be extracted as an assembly. Unless the springs are broken, it should not be necessary to dismantle the centrifugal gear further but, if spring replacement is essential, the cam and cam plate can be removed by extracting the screw in the centre of the cam (see FIG 3:6).

Thoroughly wash all parts in paraffin or carbon tetrachloride and dry off. Examine for signs of wear and, if any are present, replace the complete distributor and return the old one to the agents. The only part which is justifiably replaceable is the make-and-break assembly if the contacts are badly burned or worn down. Check that the bushings in the housing are in good condition and that there is no 'slop' in the shaft when fitted.

3:4 Reassembly and installation

Reassemble in the reverse order, packing grease in the circumferential space between the two bushings (see **FIG 3:7**) and petroleum jelly (vaseline) to the pivots of the governor weights and the ball tracks of the breaker plate. Remake all electrical connections and refit and connect the capacitor. With the make-and-break assembly in position, slacken the screws a trifle, rotate the shaft until the rocker arm pad is on a peak of the cam face (break fully open) and adjust the position of the make-and-break assembly on the breaker plate until the gap is .018 to .020 inch (see **FIG 3:8**). Tighten all three screws and recheck.

Refit the skew gear and dog on the shaft and drive home the pins. If end play on the shaft is excessive, adjust the thickness of the washer. If a spring retaining collar was present originally on the dog to secure the pin, refit it.

Refit the clamping plate. Replace the rotor and check position on casing corresponding to No. 1 cylinder. Turn crankshaft until piston is approaching TDC on No. 1 piston with both valves closed (compression stroke). Set it at 10 deg. BTDC by the pointer and timing marks. **Slacken the oil pump bolts and withdraw about ¼ inch to keep clear of the distributor shaft dog while timing.** Insert the distributor shaft into the support casting and, turning the shaft anticlockwise by about 30 deg. before the breaker points open with the rotor towards No. 1 cylinder, push home to engage with the crankshaft skew gear.

Without changing the position of the crankshaft, still 10 deg. BTDC, check the position of the make-and-break which should be on the point of opening since the meshing of the skew gears will have advanced the shaft about 30 deg. Insert the adjusting plate screw and rotate the distributor to obtain a precise point of opening at this setting and secure by tightening the screw. If the adjustment is not possible, withdraw the shaft and try again at the next thread in the skew gears. Precise adjustment can be effected by the use of the battery and lamp as described earlier.

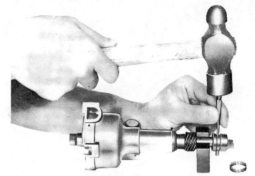

FIG 3:5 Extracting the securing pin from the oil pump drive dog

FIG 3:6 Removing the camshaft and plate from the drive shaft

With the distributor in position, remesh with the oil pump dog, turning the crankshaft to bring the two ends in line, and resecure the oil pump. Refit the distributor cap and remake the HT leads to ignition coil and sparking plugs and the LT lead to the distributor terminal.

3:5 The ignition coil

The ignition coil is of the solid insulation type, Hitachi Model C14.51. This is of the auto-transformer pattern with the common point between the primary and secondary windings going to the distributor make-and-break terminal (see **FIG 3:9**).

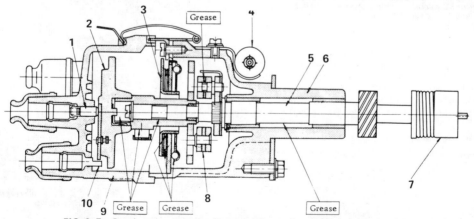

FIG 3:7 Section through distributor and cap showing lubricating points

Key to Fig 3:7   1 HT pencil   2 Rotor   3 Breaker plate assembly   4 Capacitor   5 Drive shaft   6 Body housing
7 Oil pump driving dog   8 Centrifugal weights   9 Distributor cap   10 HT terminals

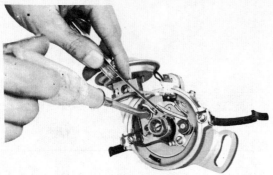

FIG 3:8 Setting the make-and-break gap with feeler gauge

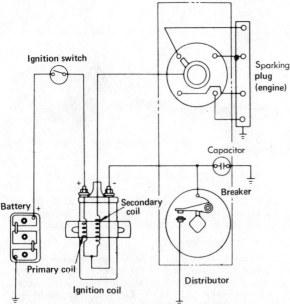

FIG 3:9 Ignition circuit for 1300 and 1600cc Saloons. On the twin SU carburetter installation a ballast resistor which is cut out while starting is inserted between the coil positive and the ignition switch

A section through the coil is shown in **FIG 3:10** and the primary winding resistance is between 3.2 and 4.1 ohms. The ignition coil for the twin SU carburetter 1600cc engine is of similar design but the primary winding is of lower resistance, 2.1 to 2.7 ohms for use with an external 1.6 ohm resistor. The Hatachi Model No. C6R.50.

3:6 Sparking plugs

The recommended types of sparking plugs for these engines are as follows:

Engine	Plug type
L13	N.G.K. BP.6E
L14	N.G.K. BP.5ES
L16 (early)	N.G.K. BP.6E
L16 (twin carburetter)	N.G.K. BP.6ES

There are, of course, several other equivalent types which are suitable if these are not available.

These are all 14 mm thread diameter with a reach of 19 mm, and the specified gap is .8 to .9 mm (.031 to .035 inch). **FIG 3:11** shows a section through one of these plugs.

Misfiring or uneven firing at low speeds may be due to faulty plugs. Check that the plug points are clean and that the gap is properly set. **When adjusting, always bend the outer electrode and never the central one. Use a proper sparking plug wrench for removal or insertion of plugs. Box spanners, unless skilfully applied, can break the plug porcelain.**

The usual deposit from a good engine plug is hard and white. Heavy black carbon deposits can indicate an over-rich mixture or over-cool running while a wet or oily deposit can indicate faulty piston rings. While any garage can recondition dirty plugs, the cost of a new set is so small as to make reconditioning uneconomical. So fit a new set every 10,000 miles or at each major servicing.

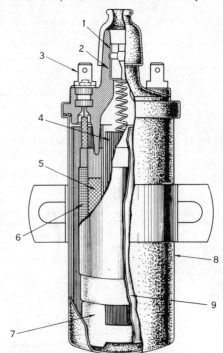

FIG 3:10 Part section through ignition coil

Key to Fig 3:10   1 HT terminals   2 Cap
3 LT terminals   4 Core   5 Primary winding
6 Secondary winding   7 Insulator   8 Casing
9 External iron core

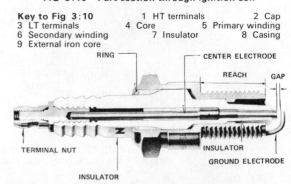

FIG 3:11 Part section through 14 x 29 mm sparking plug

3:7 Fault diagnosis

(a) Engine will not fire

1 Low battery volts
2 Dirty make-and-break contacts
3 Faulty capacitor
4 Broken or disconnected HT lead
5 Broken or disconnected LT lead
6 Faulty ignition switch
7 Condensation in or on distributor cap
8 Broken carbon pencil distributor cap

Low battery volts may not show across the battery terminals on open circuit but, if a cell is in a poor state, the voltage when the starting current (of the order of 150 to 180 amps) is flowing may drop to below 9-volt across the ignition coil, the minimum for creating a healthy spark unless the coil is fitted with a ballast resistor cut-out of circuit by the starting switch.

(b) Engine misfires

1 Faulty plug or plugs
2 Carbon track in distributor cap
3 Moisture on sparking plugs
4 Faulty HT lead
5 Shortcircuit on HT lead to earth
6 Too large a gap in one plug
7 Plug loose in engine

(c) Engine backfires

1 Ignition too far advanced
2 Weak or broken spring on centrifugal device
Both of these faults can also be indicated by 'pinking' with the recommended grade of fuel.

(d) Poor acceleration

1 Ignition too far retarded
2 Vacuum hose disconnected
3 Vacuum capsule faulty
4 Centrifugal weights seized on pivots
5 Cables fouling the advance mechanism.

CHAPTER 4

THE COOLING SYSTEM

4:1 Principles of operation

The water cooling system for the Datsun engine is conventional in that it comprises a radiator, water pump and fan, the radiator also being the heating source of the air-conditioning system.

The radiator, forward mounted behind the engine grille at the front of the body, is a vertical tube pattern with rows of vertical tubes being air cooled by horizontal rows gills. Water is circulated between the cylinder jacket and the radiator by a belt-driven pump of the centrifugal vane type mounted centrally immediately above the crankshaft. An extension of the shaft forward carries the hub to which is bolted the driving pulley and fan. Where air-condition equipment is installed, the hub incorporates a clutch mechanism operated by a thermostatic element sensing ambient temperature which prevents the fan from circulating air through the radiator until it has reached a predetermined level.

A thermostat mounted in the top radiator connection to the cylinder head also restricts the flow of coolant until it has reached a set temperature at which the engine can function efficiently. The coolant from the engine jacket passes through several outlets, each performing a particular function before returning to the pump for recirculation through the engine jacket. These include, (a) the flow through the radiator when the thermostat valve is open, (b) the flow through the air-conditioning heater when the water valve is open and (c) the flow through the inlet manifold jacket to provide a degree of preheat to the fuel vapour from the carburetter. All three returns meet at the inlet to the circulating pump (see **FIG 4:1**).

On cars with an automatic transmission, the fluid from the hydrokinetic converter is also cooled by the system via a heat exchanger inserted in the lower compartment of a special radiator. The capacity of the system, including the heater, is 12 pints and the system is pressurized by a spring-loaded radiator cap to achieve a boiling point of

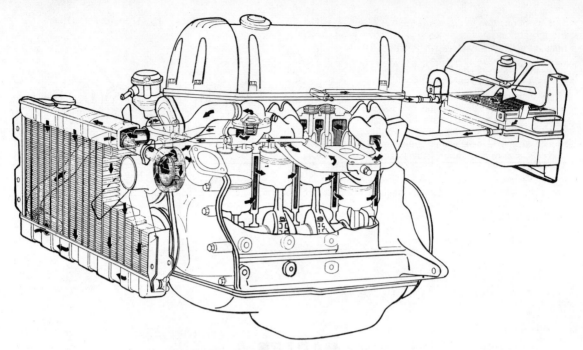

FIG 4:1   Diagrammatic view of the cooling system

around 120°C. Expansion of the contents is taken care of by an overflow pipe from the filler cap housing.

A temperature transmitter mounted in the cylinder head and supplied from a constant voltage source, a voltage stabilizer located at the rear of the instrument panel, provides an indication of coolant temperature on a gauge in the instrument cluster.

4:2 Maintenance and servicing

Maintenance of the cooling system is continued to periodical flushing of the radiator, refilling with antifreeze solutions for cold weather, checking that the fan is securely attached to the pump shaft and that the belt tension is properly adjusted. At frequent intervals, the

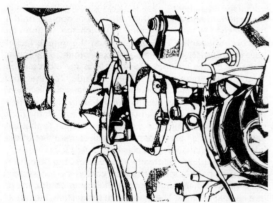

FIG 4:2   Removing the cooling pump rotor assembly from the casing

hoses and connections should be examined for leaks, particularly in view of the pressure that builds up in the system during normal running.

Draining of the radiator is effected by opening the cock at the bottom of the radiator and removing the filler cap. Failure to do the latter causes an air lock and slows down the draining. A plug in the cylinder block enables the water jacket to be drained as well. To drain the air-conditioning heater, leave the cock open while draining the radiator.

Before changing to antifreeze, ensure that all rust has been removed and that the system has been flushed with clean water until the drainings run clear. Any good anti-freeze solution incorporating a corrosion inhibitor may be used providing that it is mixed in accordance with the instructions given on the container.

Regular maintenance and frequent visual inspections of the cooling system can often disclose faults and conditions leading to faults before they have assumed serious proportions.

4:3 Water pump removal and inspection

To remove the water pump, first drain the system and disconnect the hose connections from the radiator. Unbolt and remove the radiator grille, loosen and remove the radiator. Slacken the drive belt and remove, then remove the fan and pulley. Loosen and remove the six screws retaining the pump in position and ease the pump from its housing (see FIG 4:2).

Clean out the interior of the pump housing and remove the gasket. Transfer the pump to the bench, clean thoroughly and examine for signs of wear or damage. A special cleaning agent, Nissan CSC, has been prepared for this purpose and can be used if available.

It is not possible to dismantle the pump further and, if the vanes show excessive corrosion or if there is too much play in the bearing, replace the pump as a unit.

4:4 Water pump replacement

Before reinstalling the pump, fit a new gasket and apply a good coating of sealing compound to both sides before putting into position. Relocate the pump in the housing and insert the six retaining screws, tightening evenly all round. Wipe off excess compound exuded from the joint.

Check that the pump rotor turns easily in the housing and does not foul, bind or squeak in operation. The bearing is prelubricated for life and does not need recharging. When the bearing starts to squeak, change the pump.

Refit the fan and pulley, reinstall and tighten the belt and reposition the radiator and grille. Connect up the hoses and tighten the clamps, refill the radiator and run the engine until the thermostat opens and the coolant is circulating freely. Check all points for signs of leakage and remedy.

4:5 Fan clutch

On saloons fitted with air-conditioning, the fan is driven from the pump drive pulley through a thermostatically operated clutch mechanism. On other models, the fan blades are bolted direct on to the pulley.

The exploded view of the clutch mechanism is shown in **FIG 4:3**. The drum and pulley are secured to the pump drive flange by four bolts. The spider assembly, comprising the outer spider, bearing and inner race are secured to the pump shaft extension by a circlip. The dust cover, lining and operation plate are attached to the spider and the whole is covered by the fan housing, all by the same four through-bolts.

The bi-metal strip on the housing expands with rising temperature to bring the lining into contact with the inner surface of the drum, so creating the drive from the pump/fan pulley to the fan itself. The temperature sensed is the ambient temperature within the engine compartment and the strip is designed to bring the fan into operation at around 65°C and to disconnect the fan drive at 54°C.

To dismantle, remove the four bolts securing the outer assembly to the spider and extract operation plate, dust cover, fan and lining (see **FIG 4:4**). Remove the circlip and ease the spider from the shaft extension. Examine the interior of the drum for wear or scoring and remove any accumulations of dust or dirt. Reassemble in the reverse operation.

4:6 Thermostat

The thermostat is of the wax pellet pattern and is designed to open at 83°C being fully open at 95°C. It is located in the housing on the right of the engine, viewed from the front, and is secured in position by the housing flange when bolted down (see **FIG 4:5**).

To remove for replacement, drain the radiator and remove the hose between the radiator and the thermostat housing. Unbolt and lift away the housing and gasket. The thermostat can then be extracted from its seating. When replacing, use a new gasket and apply a sealing compound to both sides before tightening the flange nuts.

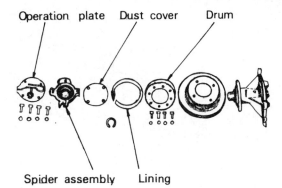

FIG 4:3 Exploded view of the fan clutch

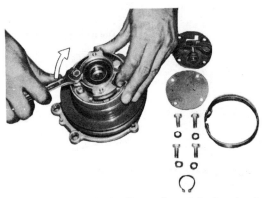

FIG 4:4 A stage in the dismantling of the fan clutch

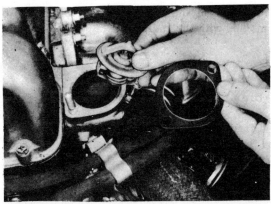

FIG 4:5 Removing the thermostat from its seating in the housing

As failure of the thermostat to open effectively seals off flow of the coolant through the radiator, the device is not of the fail-safe pattern. Should it be found that the thermostat is not opening and a replacement thermostat is not immediately available, remove the faulty unit and replace the housing leaving the flow through the radiator unimpeded until such time as the new unit is obtainable.

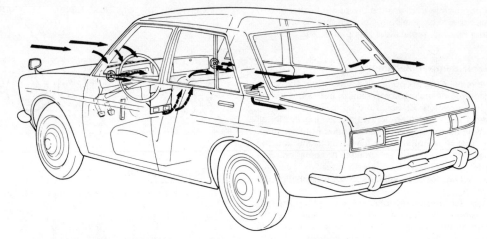

FIG 4:6   Diagrammatic view of the ventilation system in the Datsun saloon

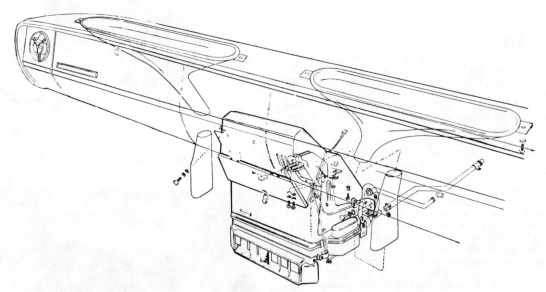

FIG 4:7   Diagrammatic view of the air-conditioning unit as installed in the Datsun saloon

4:7 Car heating unit

The car heating system is of a fairly conventional pattern, being mounted immediately beneath the front dashboard in the centre of the car and comprising a heat exchanger deriving its hot water from the cylinder jacket, an accelerating air flow fan and the usual controls for mixing and directing the air flow. Air circulation is by ram air while the car is in motion, the air entering through a horizontal grille immediately below the centre of the windscreen. Part of this air is ducted direct to two face-level outlets at the sides of the dashboard, these being fitted with directional louvres. The remainder is passed through the central air heater where part is circulated around the heat exchanger and part is bypassed, the two flows meeting to exhaust through the central louvred exit.

Flap controls apportion the flows between the two routes enabling the temperature of the emitted air to be regulated at will. A second flap control diverts all or part of the warmed flow through the windscreen demisters, slots on the upper surface of the windscreen frame immediately to the front of the instrument panel before both passenger and driver.

Air extractors at the rear of the saloon withdraw stale air from the interior exhausting to the sides (see FIG 4:6). On the estate car, these exhaust extractors are mounted centrally in the tailgate.

Should it be necessary to service the heat exchanger, first drain the radiator system and disconnect the hose to the rear of the air-conditioning unit. Disconnect the electrical connections to the fan motor and also the control cables at the unit end. Remove the oval duct

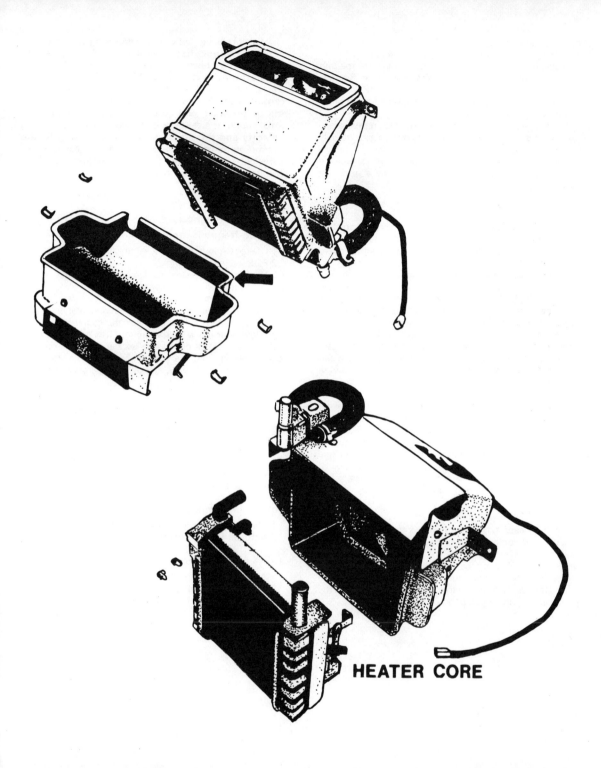

HEATER CORE

FIG 4:8 Stages in the dismantling of the air-conditioning unit with, above, lower cover removed and, below, the heat exchanger extracted

connectors at each side linking the unit outlets for demisting to the demister slots (see **FIG 4 : 7**).

Slacken and remove the fixing bolts and ease the unit clear of the body. Transfer as a unit to the bench. Remove the four spring clips securing the lower cover (see **FIG 4 : 8**) to gain access to the heat exchanger and fixing bolts. Remove the heat exchanger.

When reassembling, check that any packing extracted during the dismantling is replaced in position and securely fastened in place.

Generally speaking, it is not practicable to repair a leaking heat exchanger. Always replace by a new unit from the agents.

4 : 8 Radiator

The conventional pattern radiator is secured in position by four fixing bolts through mounting flanges on either side of the assembly. Removal is a straightforward procedure needing no special instruction.

Regular flushing through with clean water and the use of antifreeze solutions with corrosion inhibitors should maintain the heat exchanging efficiency at a high level over many years of service. If appreciable scale should appear to be present when draining the radiator, or should the drain cock appear to be choked, scale removal is advisable. Remove the drain cock completely by unscrewing and flush through until the water runs clear. Drain and insert a plug into the drain cock seating, then filling with a hot solution of sodium bicarbonate, one ounce to each pint of water, at a temperature of around 180°C and allow to stand until cool. Drain and flush with fresh water then replace the drain cock.

Refill and pressure test to 14 lb/sq in for signs of leakage. Pinhole leaks in tubes should not be repaired but the radiator replaced by a new one. The existence of only one pinhole is usually clear indication of a general state of deterioration and complete replacement is the only real safeguard on a pressurized cooling system.

4 : 9 Filler cap

The filler cap seals and pressurizes the contents of the radiator and cooling system. Should the cooling water boil, the pressure overcomes the seal maintained by the upper spring releasing the contents to the overflow pipe. On cooling, the contents contract and the fall in pressure within the system to below that of atmospheric, forces the lower spring valve open to admit air.

Always take great care in removing the filler cap after the engine has been running for any length of time. The pressurized system enables the water temperature to rise above 100°C the boiling point at normal ambient pressure. If the filler cap is removed at this or higher temperatures, lowering of pressure will enable the contents to flash into scalding steam which will emerge at high velocity and possibly disastrous resultants to the person concerned. A safe rule is not to remove the filler cap when the temperature gauge needle is in the upper half of the gauge scale

4 : 10 Fault diagnosis

(a) Too frequent topping-up of radiator

1 Leakage from joints or hose couplings
2 Faulty filler cap seal
3 Leak in heater system to air-conditioning unit
4 Leaking drain cocks or valves
5 Leaking cylinder head gasket

The last is a serious condition occuring after an engine overhaul through failure to check the cylinder head nut tightness after a few hours running. It is usually accompanied by a loss of power and occasionally by excessive condensation from the exhaust. Immediate strip down and the fitting of a new gasket is imperative if further damage is to be avoided.

(b) Excessive rise of coolant temperature

1 Broken or loose fan belt
2 Low water level in radiator
3 Obstruction in radiator passages
4 Faulty thermostat
5 Fault on temperature transmitter or circuit
6 Engine ignition too far retarded

(c) Coolant temperature will not rise

1 Thermostat jammed in open position
2 Ambient temperature too low

(d) Air heating inoperative

1 Air lock in radiator system
2 Broken or disconnected shutter cable
3 Broken or disconnected hot water valve cable.

CHAPTER 5

THE CLUTCH AND PROPELLER SHAFT

5:1 Introduction

Datsun cars with the 1300cc engine installed incorporate a dry, single disc coil spring clutch as the intermediary between the engine and gearbox. Cars with the 1400 and 1600cc engine utilize a diaphragm spring pattern clutch. In both cases the withdrawal mechanism is hydraulic.

5:2 Diaphragm clutch

The diaphragm clutch is a single plate pattern in which the driven plate and spring cushioned hub are clamped between the flywheel face and the clutch plate by a diaphragm pressure spring. This special diaphragm pressure spring maintains a constant load on the pressure plate irrespective of the degree of wear on the friction facings.

The drive from the engine is communicated to the gearbox drive shaft by clamping the facing ring of the driven plate between the pressure plate, part of the clutch withdrawal mechanism, and a machined facing on the flywheel. This pressure is applied by the diaphragm, secured at nine points to the clutch cover, against rings which act as a fulcrum around which the diaphragm bells when the centre section, divided into a group of eighteen radial segments, is deflected by the central release plate. The

torque between the pressure plate and clutch cover is taken by three straps and contact between the periphery of the diaphragm and the pressure plate is maintained by rivets at the diaphragm end of the straps, so preventing noise arising from any loose association between the two members.

The belling of the diaphragm has the effect of releasing the circumferential pressure on the driven plate, the straps slightly withdrawing the pressure plate. The clutch housing can then rotate with the engine crankshaft without transmitting the torque to the gearbox drive shaft.

FIG 5:1 shows a view of the clutch members as dismantled and **FIG 5:2** a diagrammatic section through the clutch cover assembly.

5:3 Removal and dismantling

Raise the car on stands and, working from beneath the car, disconnect and remove the clutch operating cylinder (see **FIG 1:7**). Disconnect the handbrake cable at the equalizer pivot and unscrew and remove the speedometer cable. From within the car, remove the gearlever. Loosen the two centre exhaust pipe clamps and ease the pipe and expansion chamber clear of the propeller shaft. Unbolt and remove the propeller shaft (see **Section 5:9**).

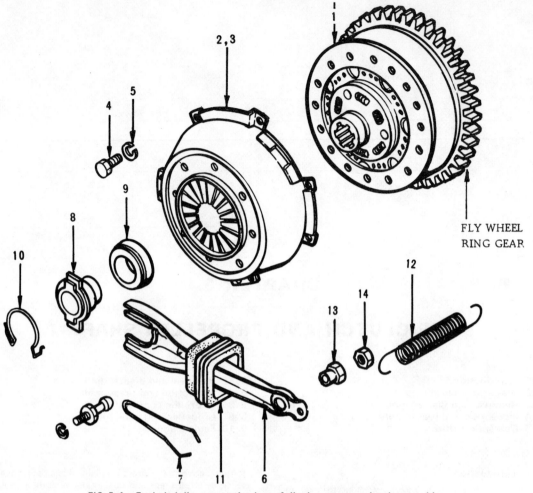

FLY WHEEL
RING GEAR

FIG 5:1   Exploded diagrammatic view of diaphragm type clutch assembly

Key to Fig 5:1   1 Driven plate   2, 3 Clutch cover and diaphragm   4, 5 Cover fixing bolt   6 Withdrawal lever
7 Spring   8 Sleeve   9 Bearing   10 Circlip   11 Boot   12 Spring   13, 14 Nut and locknut

Place a jack under the transmission housing and take the weight while the rear crossmember is unbolted and removed. **Do not position the jack under the sump drain plug but insert a wooden block between the sump and jack to prevent any distortion to the sump when the full weight of the transmission is on the jack.**

Disconnect the battery positive lead, then disconnect the cables to the starter motor and unbolt and remove the starter. Finally, unbolt the bellhousing from the crankcase and ease the transmission back and down to give access to the clutch assembly. The withdrawal lever and thrust bearing will come away with the transmission and bellhousing (see **FIG 5:3**).

Fuller instructions for the removal of the transmission are given in **Section 5:6**.

Insert the special support bar, ST49090000, into the centre of the clutch assembly to take the weight of the driven plate when the clutch assembly is removed, then unbolt the six studs around the clutch cover assembly to the flywheel a turn at a time in order across and around the periphery (1, 4, 2, 5, 3, 6, 1, etc., sequence) until the tension of the diaphragm spring has been released and the clutch cover can be removed over the end of the support bar. Extract the support bar with the driven plate.

From the bellhousing, remove the clutch withdrawl lever, bearing sleeve and bearing.

5:4 Inspection and reassembly

Thoroughly clean the surface of the clutch cover assembly, driven plate and flywheel and check that all parts are dry and free from oil or grease. If any oil or grease is present, examine the oil seals in the transmission and crankshaft bearings.

The friction surfaces on both flywheel and clutch cover assembly should be smooth and free from ridges. The surface of the flywheel, if slightly scored, may be honed

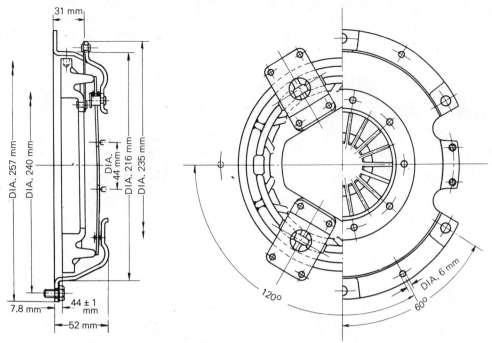

DIA. 257 mm
DIA. 240 mm
DIA. 44 mm
DIA. 216 mm
DIA. 235 mm
31 mm
7.8 mm
44 ± 1 mm
52 mm
120°
60°
DIA. 6 mm

FIG 5:2   Section through and part plan section of diaphragm clutch

smooth but, if the ridging is excessive, the flywheel will have to be removed and refaced on a lathe. For removal of the flywheel see **Section 5:1**.

The clutch cover assembly with the diaphragm spring and pressure plate is a riveted assembly and cannot be dismantled. Examine the diaphragm for cracks around the periphery and the driven plate for distortion or ridging. If excessive wear or damage is evident, scrap the assembly and fit a new one.

Check the friction surfaces of the driven plate and, if worn or scored, exchange for a new plate. It is possible to reface an existing plate with suitable friction material but the problem is to obtain the proper grade as specified by the makers and to ensure that, after fitting, the plate will run true.

Clean and examine the bearing sleeve and bearing and, if the bearing is satisfactory, repack with grease before reassembly. Should any signs of wear be apparent, replace oithor or both.

To reassemble, reinstall the driven plate in position on the special tool and relocate the clutch cover. Insert the six support studs and tighten progressively, across and around, until all are right down. Tighten finally with a torque spanner set to 19 lb ft. The driven plate should then be gripped between the pressure plate and flywheel face enabling the tool to be withdrawn ready for entry of the gearbox drive shaft.

In the bellhousing, reinstall the withdrawal lever, bearing sleeve and bearing, raise the complete transmission on the jack and ease into position with the gearbox drive shaft splines correctly meshed with those in the clutch driven plate. Check that the bellhousing to crankcase gasket is in place and insert the fixing bolts, tightening to a torque of 22 lb ft.

Reinstall the rear crossmember, remove the jack and reconnect the propeller shaft, starter motor and electrical connections, reposition and secure the exhaust system and, finally, reinstall the clutch slave cylinder and hand-brake cable. Inside the car, replace the gearlever.

5:5 Coil spring clutch

The coil spring clutch comprises a similar assembly of driven plate and clutch housing bolted to the flywheel but the pressure is applied by nine helical coil springs in housings distributed around the periphery of the pressure

FIG 5:3   Bellhousing with withdrawal lever, boot and bearing

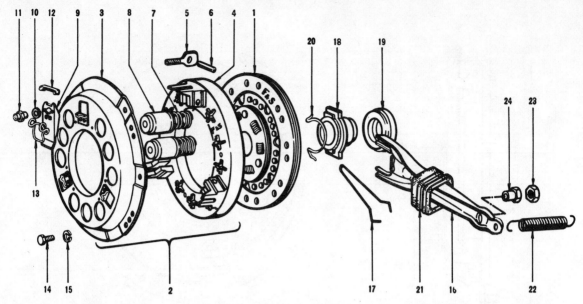

FIG 5:4　Exploded diagrammatic view of coil spring type clutch assembly

Key to Fig 5:4　1 Driven plate　2 Clutch assembly　3 Clutch cover　4 Pressure plate　5 Eyebolt　6 Pin　7 Coil spring
8 Spring cover　9 Lever　10, 11 Washer and eyebolt nut　12 Bridge　13 Mousetrap spring　14, 15 Bolt and washer
16 Withdrawal lever　17 Retainer spring　18, 19 Bearing sleeve and bearing　20 Circlip　21 Boot　22 Return spring
23, 24 Nut and locknut

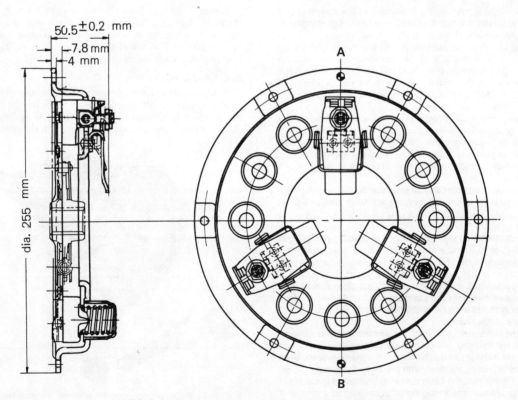

FIG 5:5　Section through and plan of coil spring clutch

plate (see **FIG 5:4**). A section through the assembly is shown in **FIG 5:5**.

The driven plate is of the spring cushioned pattern, the hub and hub plate being coupled, through six helical springs, to the cushion disc which, in turn, is riveted to the concentric ring supporting, on both faces, the bonded asbestos friction material. This ensures smooth engagement between the engine and gearbox drive shaft by damping out cyclical acceleration and retardation torques.

The drive from the engine is communicated to the gearbox by clamping the facing ring between the pressure plate in the housing and the machined facing on the flywheel. This pressure is applied by the nine helical springs, mounted in cups on the clutch cover, and three levers on the cover serve to withdraw the pressure plate against the spring pressure to release the clutch.

The innermost ends of the levers are depressed by the clutch withdrawal bearing to lift the pressure plate, bolted to the outer ends, against the fulcrum in the form of a bracket riveted to the clutch cover. A mousetrap spring, embracing the inner end of each lever, takes up loose play and prevents the levers from vibrating against the withdrawl bearing when the clutch is engaged.

Contact pressure on the driven plate by the pressure plate is regulated by the three eyebolt nuts on the levers, at the same time setting the amount of depression to release the clutch. The adjustment of these three nuts is, therefore, of paramount importance to efficient operation. If they are too slack, permitting the maximum pressure on the plate, the clutch pedal depression may be excessive or even ineffective to release the driven plate. If they are too tight, clutch slip and burnout of the facings can easily result.

5:6 Removal and dismantling

To gain access to the clutch for removal, the procedure is much the same as that for the diaphragm clutch but, since the coil spring clutch is fitted exclusively with the three-speed manual gearbox with column change, there is no removal of the gearlever to contend with. The

FIG 5:6 Clutch cover assemblies and driven plate of diaphragm (left) and coil spring (right) type clutches

FIG 5:7 Adjusting lever height for coil spring clutch

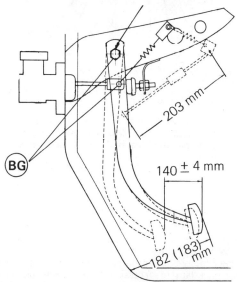

FIG 5:8 Details of pedal mounting and coupling to master cylinder

linkage to the gearchange levers beneath the transmission has to be disconnected. See also **Chapter 6**.

Removal of the clutch cover from the flywheel is also similar, including the use of the special tool to support the driven plate, but, unlike the diaphragm pattern, the clutch cover and pressure plate assembly can be dismantled on the bench and serviced. For this, however, a flat plate drilled to simulate the flywheel, is necessary. A special assembly tool, ST47990000 is available but if this cannot be obtained readily, and flat mild steel plate with six tapped holes drilled equidistant around a circumference of 9.56 inches and short studs, to pass through the clutch cover holes, to match will serve.

The clutch cover assembly, on removal from the flywheel, is clamped into position on the plate and the three eyebolt nuts are then removed from the levers. Each lever must be marked so that it goes back into the same position on reassembly and they are then extracted together with the mousetrap springs.

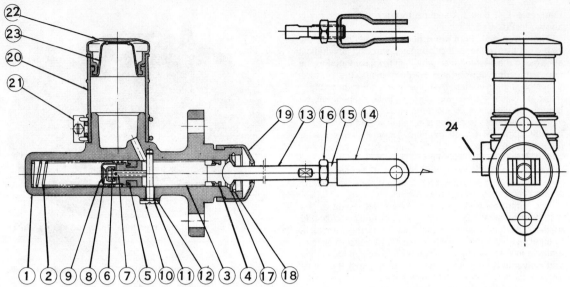

FIG 5:9 Section through master cylinder

Key to Fig 5:9   1 Master cylinder   2 Piston return spring   3 Piston   4 Secondary cup   5 Piston seal
6 Valve seat   7 Valve stem   8 Valve spring   9 Spring seat   10 Stop screw   11 Gasket   12 Ring   13 Pushrod
14 Clevis   15, 16 Headnut and locknut   17 Dished washer   18 Circlip   19 Boot   20 Reservoir   21 Band   22 Cap
23 Seal   24 Outlet

The six holding-down bolts are next released in the
now-familiar sequence and when all have been removed,
the cover can be lifted clear of the pressure plate, springs
and spring covers.

Clean and examine all parts for signs of wear or damage
and in particular check that there is no oil or grease
present in any part of the assembly.

5:7 Inspection and reassembly

Inspect the driven plate for worn facings, damaged
splines or defective cushion springs. If they are present,
replace the complete assembly.

Check the pressure plate for scoring or grooving and
reface on a lathe if necessary, taking the minimum of
material from the face, Check that all springs are of the
same length, are free from deformation and, if possible, are
equal in deflection under the same compressive load. If
all are satisfactory, check for freedom in the covers. **If any**

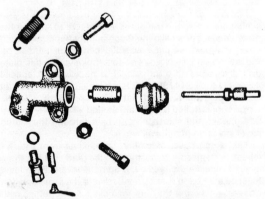

FIG 5:10 Slave cylinder in its component parts

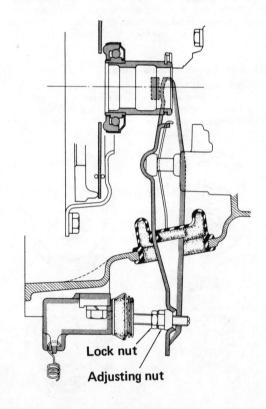

Lock nut

Adjusting nut

FIG 5:11 Slave cylinder and clutch withdrawal
assembly

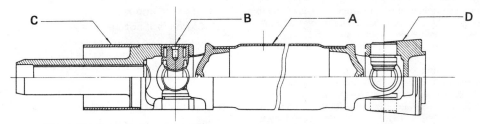

FIG 5:12 Propeller shaft showing shaft (A), coupling (B), sleeve (C) and flange (D)

one is unsatisfactory, replace the complete set for a new, balanced set from the agents.

Examine the clutch cover for deformation or cracks and the levers for signs of wear or distortion, particularly in the areas of the withdrawal bearing contact. Replace as necessary.

Remount the assembly on the plate with the springs in position and clamp down by means of the peripheral studs. Replace the withdrawal levers and mousetrap springs in their original positions and fit the eyebolt nuts.

Using a suitable surface gauge in the centre of the assembly, adjust the height of each lever tip to 1.99 inches (see FIG 5:7). Operate the levers once or twice simultaneously and bed them down on the fulcrum brackets and recheck the setting height.

With all parts inspected, passed or replaced, reassembly can commence. This follows closely the routine already set down for installing the diaphragm pattern.

5:8 Hydraulic controls

The clutch withdrawal mechanism comprises pedal, master cylinder and slave operating cylinder the piston of which bears directly on the clutch withdrawal lever.

The pedal is of the pendant type and is directly connected to the master cylinder by rod and clevis (see FIG 5:8). The master cylinder, a sectional view of which is shown in FIG 5:9, incorporates its own fluid reservoir and communicates directly with the slave cylinder by a short pipeline.

To dismantle the master cylinder, remove the pedal clevis pin, uncouple the fluid line to the slave cylinder and unbolt the master cylinder from the bulkhead. At the bench, drain the reservoir, extract the valve stem stop pin 10, withdraw the rubber boot 19 and extract the circlip 18. The pushrod can then be extracted and the piston assembly removed from the cylinder by applying air pressure to the fluid outlet.

Wash and examine all parts, using brake fluid only, and check that the cylinder is not scored. Replace all seals and piston cups and reassemble in the reverse order. Reinstall and reconnect the hydraulic pipeline and clevis coupling to the clutch pedal.

The slave cylinder at the far end of the hydraulic line is similarly dealt with (see FIG 5:10) and, after both cylinders have been serviced, fill the reservoir with brake fluid and bleed the system from the bleed valve in the slave cylinder.

Finally, adjust the nut on the slave cylinder rod so that with the piston fully retracted in the cylinder, all play between the ends of the withdrawal lever has been taken up. Slacken the adjusting nut back 1.5 complete turns and secure with the locknut. At the pedal end, adjust the stop nut to the rear of the clevis on the pedal arm to give just

under $7\frac{1}{4}$ inches (183 mm) play measured between the top of the pedal pad and the floor (see FIG 5:8). Check that this gives full clutch withdrawal before the pedal touches the floor and, if necessary, adjust by setting back the clevis and locknut on the piston rod to the front of the pedal arm.

5:9 Propeller shaft and joints

The tubular propeller shaft terminates at both the gearbox and differential ends in universal joints with sealed needle bearings lubricated for life. At the forward end, a splined shaft and yoke receives the drive from the driven shaft of the gearbox while, at the rear end, the universal joint terminates in a flange coupling to the differential pinion.

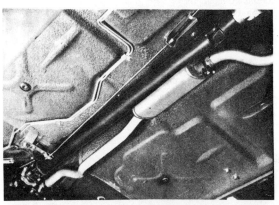

FIG 5:13 Underside of body showing exhaust displaced to facilitate removal of propeller shaft

FIG 5:14 Flange coupling between propeller shaft and differential pinion shaft

The shaft is of hollow steel construction welded to the forged yokes of the universal joints. The whole assembly is carefully balanced before installation and, when removing or servicing, great care must be taken to avoid upsetting either the balance or the straightness of the shaft or serious vibration will result in service.

To remove the propeller shaft for examination, first, ease the centre section of the exhaust system to one side (see **FIG 5:13**) and then unbolt the flange coupling at the rear axle (see **FIG 5:14**). Lower the shaft carefully to the ground, having marked both parts of the flange coupling for ultimate reassembly in the same positions, and ease the whole shaft to the rear to slide the forward end out of the gearbox. **Plug the exit to the gearbox temporarily to avoid spillage of the oil from within.**

The universal joints can be dismantled by, first, removing the circlips and tapping gently on one ear of the yoke with a wooden mallet. The needle bearings will emerge and can be extracted. Check that all are present and record the number for reassembly. Repeat for the opposite bearing. Turn the joint through 90 degrees and repeat for the other two sides. Extract both journals and spider. Wash all parts in petrol or paraffin and examine for wear. Replace parts worn or excessively marked by corrosion.

Reassemble, packing the bearings with Retinax A or equivalent lubricant, filling the race about one-third with the needle rollers in position. Install new gaskets and replace the circlips.

As the inner yokes are integral with the propeller shaft, any fault on the universal bearing yokes must be rectified by a complete new propeller shaft assembly, factory balanced.

The propeller shaft can now be reinstalled. This is straightforward but it is advisable to lubricate both splines and outside yoke with gear oil to facilitate installation and to ensure that the assembly goes back into service adequately lubricated.

5:10 Fault diagnosis

(a) Clutch will not disengage

1 Hydraulic fluid reservoir empty
2 Withdrawal lever nut worked loose
3 Faulty seal in master or slave cylinder
4 Leak in hydraulic line

(b) Clutch will not engage

1 Insufficient pedal free play
2 Weak or broken diaphragm or coil spring(s)
3 Control sleeve seized on splines
4 Worn facings on driven plate
5 Oil or grease on facings

(c) Clutch snatches

1 Damaged pressure plate
2 Unevenly worn facings
3 Pressure plate out of alignment
4 Withdrawal levers unbalanced (coil type clutch)

(d) Noisy clutch

1 Worn release bearing
2 Cracked diaphragm
3 Loose hub on coil spring clutch
4 Broken coil springs on cushion plate

(e) Heavy vibration

1 Propeller shaft out of balance
2 Damaged universal joint bearing
3 Loose flange plate coupling
4 One bolt missing from flange coupling
5 Propeller shaft bent

CHAPTER 6

THE MANUAL GEARBOX

6:1 Operation of the gearbox

The manual gearbox is of conventional pattern with three or four forward and one reverse gears according to which engine is installed. The forward gears are all synchromesh, the gears being of helical design permanetly meshed to give silent operation. The reverse gear is obtained by an intermediate gear inserted between the mainshaft and layshaft.

The gearbox is in two parts; a forward bellhousing and gearcase within which are contained the clutch and clutch lever, gear trains, selector forks and rods, and an extension housing for the speedometer drive and propeller shaft coupling and, in the four-speed box, the reverse gear train and gearshift control (see **FIGS 6:1** and **6:2**).

The main components comprise the main, or drive shaft, layshaft and gearshaft together with the selector rods and forks. The drive shaft, which transmits the drive from the gearbox to the propeller shaft, is supported at the forward end in a roller bearing housed in the gearshaft (transmitting the drive from the engine, through the clutch, to the gearbox), and in a ballbearing at the centre where it passes through the wall separating the gearcase from the extension housing. The hollow layshaft runs on needle bearings around a stationary spindle supported in the end walls of the gearcase.

The drive from the gearshaft 1 is transmitted to the layshaft 2 via the first pair of helical gears 3 at the forward end of the gearcase. Adjacent to the drive gear and integral with the gearshaft is the tooth wheel 4, which is engaged with the inner teeth of the sliding sleeve 5 to provide top, or direct drive.

In all other gears, the drive is via the layshaft and through one of two or three pairs of gears. The driven gear of each pair is a sliding fit on the drive shaft with each having a tooth wheel (sometimes referred to as a 'baulk ring') on the side adjacent to the sleeve as an integral part. Gear selection is by movement of one of the two sliding sleeves 5 or 6, which are splined to central hubs 7 or 8, keyed to the drive shaft. The internal splines of a sleeve, when moved left or right, mesh simultaneously with a tooth wheel of the adjacent driven gear and those of the hub to provide a positive drive to the drive shaft and beyond while leaving the remaining pairs of helical gears free to rotate without taking load.

The synchronizing feature is provided by a tooth wheel interposed on the shaft between the sleeve hub and the driven gear. The tooth wheel is friction driven on one side by the driven gear and locked by dogs on the other immediately prior to engagement with the tooth wheel by the sleeve. This ensures that both the sleeves and the

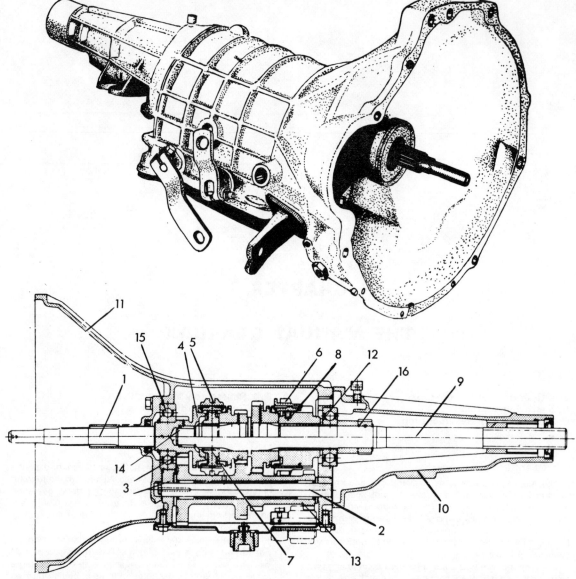

FIG 6:1 General view and section through three-speed gearbox

Key to Fig 6:1 1 Gearshaft 2 Layshaft 3 Gearshaft to layshaft drive gears 4 Tooth wheel 5 Sliding sleeve 6 Sliding sleeve 7, 8 Central hubs 9 Main or drive shaft 10 Rear extension casing 11 Bellhousing and gearcase 12 Ballbearing 13 Layshaft gear cluster 14 Needle roller bearing 15 Ballbearing 16 Speedometer drive shaft

driven gear are at the same speed of rotation before positive meshing.

The sleeves are moved by forked arms, embracing the circumferential groove of the sleeve, mounted on bearing rods passing through the walls of the gearcase and, in the four-speed box, terminating in a pair of adjacent slotted tabs either of which can be engaged by the tongue of the gearshift selector shaft while a third fork, when engaged, moves the reverse gear on the drive shaft in the extension housing into mesh with the intermediate gear. The latter

is driven within the gearbox, by the second-speed gear on the layshaft.

On a three-speed box, the bottom gear position is used to mesh the reverse gear train and the forks are moved by cross-shafts terminating in levers external to the case which are mechanically linked to the gear selector lever mounted on the steering column. Selection of the appropriate cross-shaft and lever is effected in the mechanism at the bottom of the steering column (see **Section 6:5**).

Mechanical interlocks are provided to ensure that the

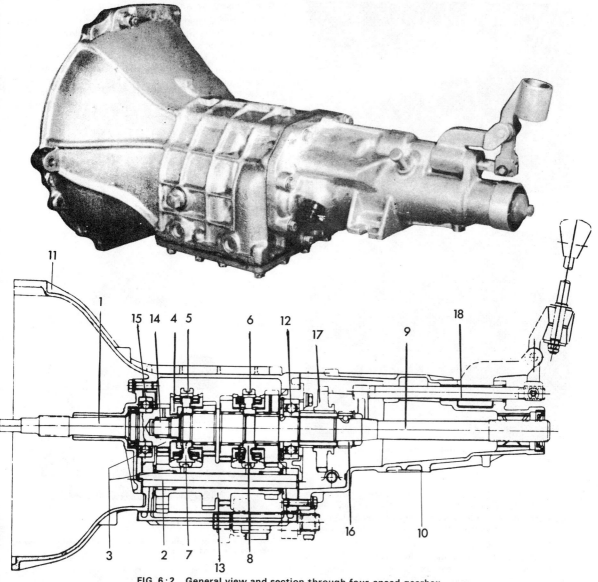

FIG 6:2 General view and section through four-speed gearbox

Key to Fig 6:2   1 to 16 see Fig 6:1   17 Reverse gear   18 Gear selection control rod

two gear selector forks cannot be moved simultaneously and that neither can be moved when the reverse gear is engaged.

The drive to the speedometer is provided by a helical gear, 9 on the drive shaft. The gear ratios vary according to the size of engine and details are listed in the Appendix.

6:2 Gearbox removal

The bottom position of the gearcase inspection cover enables examination of the gears to be carried out without removing the gearcase from the car. It is only necessary to raise the car on stands, or locate it over an inspection pit, drain the box through the drain plug and then remove the inspection cover. Movement of the selector mechanism and that of the sliding hubs on the shafts can be examined and the condition of the gear teeth can be determined. The presence of swarf, metal particles or broken teeth on the upper face of the cover when removed is an instant indication of causes of malfunction.

If the cursory examination discloses a need for overhaul, the gearbox must be removed to the bench for further dismantling. Before doing so, however, temporarily replace the cover.

Disconnect the battery positive lead, then the connections to the motor starter and unbolt and remove the starter. (It is presumed that the gearbox will now have

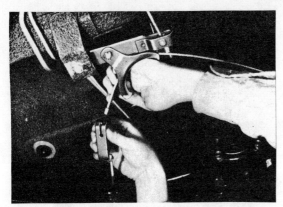

FIG 6:3 Removing the handbrake cable from the equalizer

FIG 6:4 Three-speed shift levers showing, arrowed, points of disconnection for gearbox removal

been drained.) Disconnect the handbrake cable at the equalizer (see **FIG 6:3**) and loosen the exhaust centre pipe clamps, easing the section with expansion chamber to one side of the propeller shaft. Remove the propeller shaft (see **Chapter 5**).

Disconnect the speedometer drive cable and, in the case of the three-speed gearbox, the remote control linkage at the points arrowed in **FIG 6:4**. Remove the clutch operating cylinder (see **FIG 1:7**). On the 1400 and 1600cc engines remove the gearlever from inside the car.

Support the engine with a jack placed under the sump but clear of the drain plug. Remove the two bolts securing gearbox to the rear engine crossmember and place a second jack under the gearbox. Unbolt and remove the crossmember.

Lower both jacks carefully to allow the complete engine/gearbox unit to slope downwards to the back on the forward engine mounting. Continue until it is clear that the gearbox can be removed without fouling the underside of the body. Extract the bolts securing the bellhousing to the crankcase and ease backwards until the gearshift is free of the clutch. Lower away and remove to the bench.

6:3 Inspection and dismantling

Thoroughly clean and dry the exterior of the gearcase and flush out the interior with paraffin and allow to drain. In the bellhousing, remove the clutch withdrawal mechanism including the bearing and sleeve. Remove the speedometer pinion assembly. **On the four-speed gearbox,** remove the clevis pin securing the control arm to the striker rod (see **FIG 6:5**). Unbolt and remove the rear extension housing. From this point there are differences between the procedure for the three-speed and four-speed gearbox.

FIG 6:5 Four-speed gearbox housing showing control rod, clevis and gearlever socket

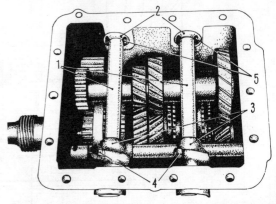

FIG 6:6 Interior view of three-speed gearbox showing arrangement of gears

FIG 6:7 Removing the intermediate gear from three-speed gearbox

Three-speed gearbox:

Turn the gearbox over with the underside upwards. The internal view will then appear as in **FIG 6:6**. Remove the circlip 3 on each cross-shaft, unscrew the nuts to the cotterpins 4 and extract the pins. Remove both cross-shaft 1. Extract the layshaft. Extract the shaft and remove the intermediate gear (see **FIG 6:7**) then remove the cotterpins securing the forks to the fork rods. Unscrew and remove the interlock plug and extract the interlock balls and springs, noting their order for reinstallation. If fitted, remove the reverse lamp switch (see **FIG 6:8**).

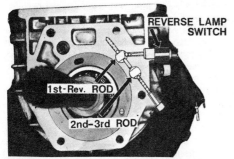

FIG 6:8 Interlocks in three-speed gearbox

FIG 6:9 Extracting the drive shaft from the three-speed gearbox

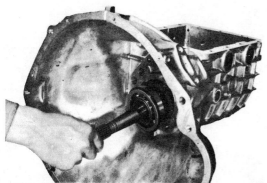

FIG 6:10 Extracting the gearshaft from the three-speed gearbox

FIG 6:11 Interior view of four-speed gearbox showing arrangement of gears

FIG 6:12 Removing the extension housing of the four-speed gearbox showing, arrowed, the control rod engagement feature

Extract the two striker rods and remove the forks from their positions. Ease the mainshaft assembly from the gearcase (see **FIG 6:9**) and, at the opposite end, extract the gearshaft (see **FIG 6:10**) taking particular care to check that the needle roller bearing is intact.

Four-speed gearbox:

Turn the engine over with the underside upwards. The internal view will then appear as in **FIG 6:11**.

When removing the rear extension housing, the gear selection control rod will come away with the housing from the gearcase. To permit this, care must be taken to ensure that the tab at the end is disengaged from the gates in the fork rods at the point arrowed in FIG 6:12.

Unscrew the plug and extract the interlock balls and springs noting their position for reassembly (see **FIG 6:13**). Extract the cotterpins securing the forks to the striker rods and remove both forks and rods. Slide the two coupling sleeves into mesh by hand at the same time to lock the gears. This is possible now that the striker forks have been extracted. Slacken the mainshaft nut seen to the extreme right in **FIG 6:11**.

Unbolt and remove the front cover and extension bearing in the bellhousing and, from this end, extract the shaft supporting the countershaft gear cluster and needle

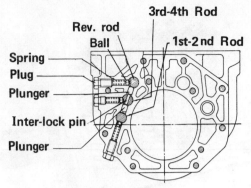

FIG 6:13 Interlocking arrangements in four-speed gearbox

FIG 6:14 Removing the intermediate gearing from the four-speed box

bearings. Remove the cluster. Remove the snap rings securing the intermediate gears to the splined shaft, and extract both gears and shaft (see FIG 6:14).

Remove the drive shaft bearing retainer from the rear of the gearcase (see FIG 6:15) and then withdraw the drive shaft assembly. At the opposite end, extract the gearshaft taking particular care to check that the internal needle roller bearing is intact.

Inspection:

Inspect all parts for signs of wear, damage of abnormalities and note before attempting to break the gear assemblies down further. Obtain replacement parts as necessary. Check the casings and covers for incipient cracks or indentations and determine whether they are of sufficient importance to warrant replacement.

Wash the bearings in a clean solvent, such as petrol or carbon tetrachloride, and examine for broken or deformed balls or races. Lubricate with light oil and check that they run smoothly without excessive noise. Check and reassemble the needle bearings and check that none are missing in the final assembly. When reinstalling the needles, coat the bearing with a little thick grease to hold the needle rollers in place during reassembly.

Examine all machined surfaces for burrs or deformations and check that the contact areas of mating gears are properly located and are not excessively deep. Check that all sliding parts on the shafts, splined and unsplined, move smoothly and that there is no excessive circumferential play in the splines.

Dismantling the gear cluster:

Should it be necessary to dismantle the gears on the drive shaft, carefully examine the assembly before dismantling and note the order and method of installing each component. The assemblies are mostly secured in position by snap rings encircling grooves around the splined areas of the shaft, or of the shaft itself as in the case of the speedometer gear. Always use proper pointed-nose pliers to remove and install the snap rings (see FIG 6:16).

Bearings are mostly a driving fit on the shafts and must be removed and reinstalled in a suitable press. **When fitting a bearing race by means of a press tool, always see that the inner race is properly supported and that the pressure for driving it into position on the shaft is directly applied. Severe damage can be done to a bearing if any of the fitting pressure is applied through the balls from the outer race.**

The synchronizing gear on the shafts is normally of the well established Borg-Warner pattern but in some gearboxes an alternative servo type of synchronizer may be fitted. This should present no real problems in overhauling providing that the dismantling and reassembly are carried out in an ordered manner.

 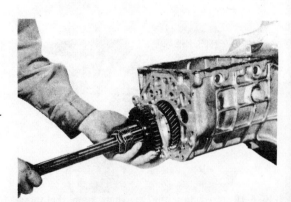

FIG 6:15 Left, removing the drive shaft bearing cover and, right, extracting the drive shaft from the four-speed gearbox

FIG 6:16 Removing a circlip from a gear cluster of the synchromesh pattern

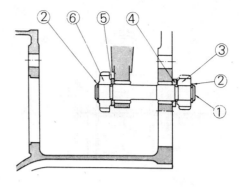

FIG 6:17 Diagrammatic view of four-speed intermediate gear arrangement showing the shaft 1, circlips 2, gears 3 and 6, and thrust washers 4 and 5

6:4 Reassembly and installation

Before commencing reassembly, have a small quantity of SAE.80.EP oil at hand and smear the surfaces of shafts and bearings with it before installation.

Assuming that the preassembly processes of installing the gears and bearings on the shafts has been carried out, main assembly commences with the installation of the gearshaft and drive shaft. The point to watch here is the insertion of the forward end of the drive shaft into the needle bearing in the end of the gearshaft. The same point applies to the fitting of the layshaft cluster on its bearings on the layshaft and, after this has been installed, the front cover in the bellhousing can be fitted, tightening the bolts to a torque of 12 lb ft.

Installation of the intermediate gear follows with the fitting of the speedometer gear, then the selector forks and rods, pinning the forks into place, and the interlock balls and springs. **When fitting the intermediate gear on the four-speed gearbox, check the end play and, if it is excessive, rectify by fitting a thicker circlip (see FIG 6:17). The end play should not exceed .012 inch and five thicknesses of circlip, in steps of .004 inch are available.**

Before inserting the interlock balls, lock the gears by sliding the two sleeves into mesh at the same time and tighten the drive shaft nut to a torque of 85 lb ft (four-speed box only).

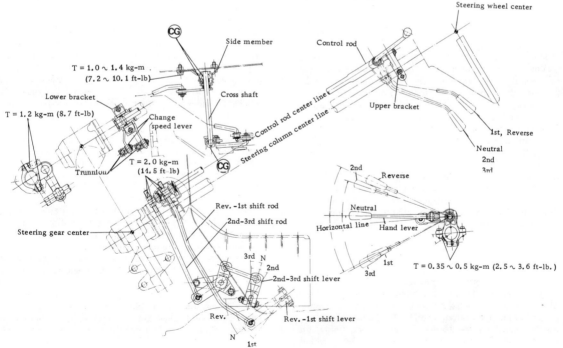

FIG 6:18 Column control of three-speed gearbox showing details of control linkage and adjustments

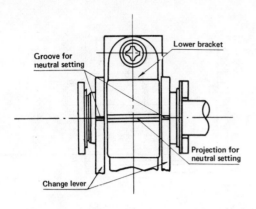
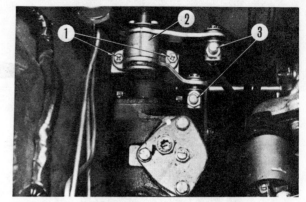

Groove for neutral setting

Lower bracket

Projection for neutral setting

Change lever

FIG 6:19 Location marks on bracket and levers for setting the neutral position of a column change mechanism

When the interlock balls have been inserted and the plugs tightened, check that it is impossible to move any fork and sliding sleeve with another in gear. Check that movement of any fork is possible from the neutral position without catching.

On the three-speed gearbox, install the cross-shafts and operating levers, inserting the cotterpins and securing with the locknut.

Install the rear extension housing, tightening the bolts to a torque of 21 lb ft, with, in the case of the four-speed gearbox, due care being taken to engage the striking rod tab with the selector rod gates. Finally, fit the bottom cover and gasket, tightening the bolts to a torque of 12 lb ft, insert the drain plug and reinstall the speedometer drive unit. Also, if it is fitted, reinstall the reversing light switch

Fill the gearcase through the side filler hole with about 3 pints of SAE.90 EP gear oil to the bottom level of the filler hole and replace the plug. (Alternative grades of oil are listed in the Appendix.) Reinstall the clutch withdrawal lever.

Transfer the gearbox to the underside of the car on a jack and raise to the level of the engine. Bolt the bellhousing to the crankcase, tightening the bolts to a torque of 22 lb ft, raise the complete assembly into position and reinstall the crossmember. Refix the two bolts between the crossmember and gearcase and reinstall the propeller shaft. Replace the central section of the exhaust and reconnect the handbrake cable.

On the three-speed gearbox, reconnect the gearshift linkage and adjust; on the four-speed gearbox, reinstall the gearlever in the car. On both gearboxes recouple the speedometer cable and the clutch slave cylinder. Reinstall the starter motor and remake the electrical connections. Reconnect the battery positive cable to the battery.

Remove the jacks and lower the car to the ground.

6:5 Gearlever adjustments

Of the two gearchange mechanisms, the three-speed column mounted is the most complex and likely to get out of adjustment. A central column, secured to the steering column at top and bottom by brackets, is capable of being rotated through some 20 degrees above and below the horizontal by the gearlever just below the steering wheel. In addition, the column is capable of movement along its axis through a short distance. Both movements are communicated to short lever arms at the foot of the column which, in turn, are linked, one directly and the other through a cross-shaft and second link, to the two shift levers at the underside of the gearbox communicating with the gearbox cross-shafts (see **FIG 6:18**).

Because of the differing lever arm lengths, the angular movement at the shift levers is less than that at the gearlever and the amount of play permissible throughout the mechanical linkage is strictly limited if clean gearchanges are to be effected. The interlocks in the gearbox prevent both shift levers being moved together and the selection of either is by the axial movement of the control rod. This is communicated to a pin in the lower bracket where it engages with either the upper or lower changespeed lever, movement from one to the other being possible only in the neutral position.

Adjustment of the complete linkage is effected at one position only, the trunnions at the extremes of the two changespeed levers. The two nuts, one above and one below, threaded on to the ends of the shift rods are adjusted to give perfect positioning of the shift levers in the neutral positions when the grooves cut on the change levers are in line with that cut on the bracket (see **FIG 6:19**). Providing that there is no excessive play in the remaining bearing linkages, this will give a clean and full change into the four gear positions. The adjustment cannot, however, compensate for wear at these points and if the play is excessive, the levers must be replaced or rebushed. Good lubrication and regular inspection at frequent intervals is, therefore, absolutely essential to consistent gearchanging.

Removal of the column change from the steering column is only rarely necessary. When the steering column itself is being overhauled, it is necessary only to disconnect the upper and lower brackets and to tie the control rod to the dashboard without further dismantling.

Looseness of the bolts securing the cross-shaft bracket to the body sidemember can also be responsible for play in the linkage.

The design of the gearchange lever on the four-speed gearbox is robust and simple and needs no adjustment. A spot of light oil applied to the clevis pin, in the oil hole on the control arm (see **FIG 6:5**) and to the shaft where it passes through both control arm and bracket is all the servicing needed.

6:6 Fault diagnosis

(a) Gear jumps out of mesh

1 Weak detent springs
2 Detent springs in wrong position
3 Broken or missing detent ball
4 Worn synchronizing rings
5 Worn shift forks
6 Worn sliding sleeve
7 Loose selector forks on rods
8 Linkage out of adjustment (three-speed column change)

(b) Noisy gearchange

1 Worn synchronizer rings
2 Broken dog springs
3 Clutch not disengaging
4 Wrong selection of gears

(c) Gearchange stiff

1 Bent selector rod
2 Rod tight in bearings
3 Sliding sleeves tight on shaft

CHAPTER 7

THE AUTOMATIC GEARBOX

7:1 Description of automatic gearbox

The Borg-Warner Model 35 automatic transmission comprises two main components, a fluid flywheel and a hydraulically operated gearbox embodying a set of epicyclic gears with controls providing three forward speeds and a reverse.

Both the fluid flywheel, or hydrokinetic converter, and the gearchange mechanism share a common oil supply and pump, the gearchanges being effected by the application of internal clutches and external brake bands to elements of the planetary gears in ordered sequence set by the selection of gear from a lever by the driver, engine speed as regulated by the throttle control and torque as determined by a governor.

Dealing first with the hydrokinetic converter, this comprises an impeller, bolted to the engine crankshaft through a special adaptor plate, the outer blades of which circulate the fluid through the peripheral vanes of a turbine rotor coupled to the gearshaft, the fluid returning through inner vanes of the rotor and a stationary set of vanes back to the impeller (see **FIG 7:1**).

The shape of the vanes is such that, when the impeller is turning at a rate faster than that of the turbine rotor, the drive is combined with a degree of torque multiplication.

This ranges from 2:1 at full throttle with the car stationary in gear, decreasing to 1:1 when impeller is running at about ten per cent above rotor speed. From this point the device acts as a simple fluid coupling, without torque multiplication. It is this feature that enables a three-speed gear train to be used to give better than the normal performance possible with a four-speed manual gearbox.

The transmission can be considered as two distinct mechanisms, a mechanical group, comprising planetary gears, clutches and brake bands, and a hydraulic group of pumps, valves, regulators and a governor.

The physical arrangement can be seen from the sectional view in **FIG 7:2**, the torque converter being on the left, the gear trains on the right and the hydraulic channels and valves in the section beneath. The hydraulic governor is in the extension housing with the speedometer drive beyond.

A schematic view of the transmission is given in **FIG 7:3**, with a more detailed cutaway view of the clutch and gear trains in **FIG 7:4**. The front clutch 6, links the input shaft 5, with the forward sun gears 13. The rear clutch links the input shaft 5, with the reverse sun gear 17, the latter being locked by the external brake band 8, in certain gear configurations. A unidirectional clutch 9, prevents the

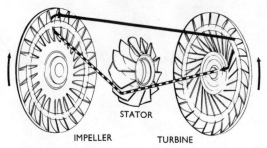

FIG 7:1 Diagrammatic impression of hydrokinetic converter operation

IMPELLER   STATOR   TURBINE

pinion carrier 11, from rotating in a direction opposite to that of the engine and permits the gearbox to freewheel in first gear. The rear brake band 10, when applied, locks the pinion carrier against rotation in either direction while the annulus 12, transmits the drive from the planetary pinions 15 and 16.

The planetary gear set comprises two sun gears, two sets of pinions, a pinion carrier and a ring gear or annulus. The teeth are helical involute throughout for quietness and efficient torque transmission. In all forward gears, the drive is through the forward sun gear 5 (see FIG 7:5), leaving by the ring gear 3, and, in reverse, the drive is through the reverse sun gear 8. Six pinions in all are mounted on the planet carrier, three being long pinions meshing between the reverse sun gear 8, and the internal teeth of the annulus at one end and between the forward sun gear 5, via the second set of three pinions 6, and the annulus teeth at the other.

Selection of gear is, primarily, by the gear selection lever on the steering column. This provides 5 positions, **Neutral, Drive, Reverse, Lock-up** and **Park,**indicated by the initial letters on a scale adjacent to the lever.

In the two drive positions, D and L, the bottom gear is mechanically selected on depression of the lever, changing up then being automatic according to throttle setting and torque. This is done by the hydraulic control mechanism. In P, the car is braked positively by a pawl mechanism providing a third brake apart from the hand and footbrake. **It must never be engaged while the car is in motion or serious damage to the transmission will result.**

The hydraulic control derives its supply of oil from a single pump, driven from the input shaft, to give pressures ranging from 57 lb/sq in to 160 lb/sq in according to speed. Part of the output is routed to the hydraulic converter and part is converted to lower pressures in regulator valves for other purposes within the transmission.

Apart from non-return valves, there are eight valves (two regulator, two shift, one manual, one throttle, one servo orifice and one modulator) a governor, two brake servos and two clutch servos interconnected by a complex network of channels. The manual valve is operated mechanically by the gear selector lever and the throttle valve by a cam linked with the throttle by a cable. All others are hydraulically operated and provide the automatic feature of the transmission.

The function of the manual valve, mechanically linked to the gear selector lever, is to direct the hydraulic fluid to, or exhaust it from, the clutch and servo pistons. In this manner the initial stages of power flow from the engine, through the gears, to the drive shaft is set up.

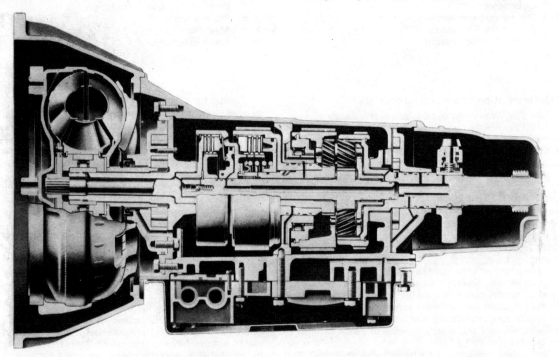

FIG 7:2 Section through complete gearbox and converter

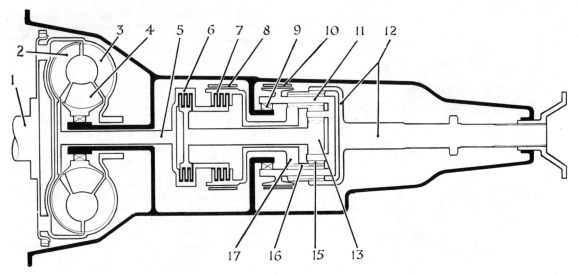

FIG 7:3   Schematic view of gearbox showing main elements

Key to Fig 7:3   1 Engine crankshaft   2 Turbine blading   3 Impeller blading   4 Stator blading   5 Gearshaft
6 Front clutch   7 Rear clutch   8 Front brake band   9 Unidirectional clutch   10 Rear brake band   11 Pinion carrier
12 Annulus and drive shaft   13 Forward sun gear   14 Parking pawl teeth   15 Short planetary pinion   16 Long planetary pinion
17 Reverse sun gear

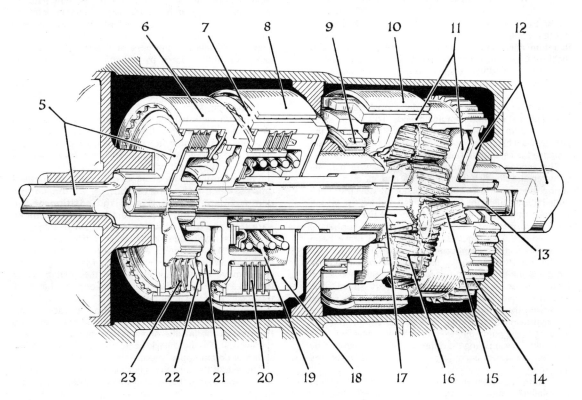

FIG 7:4   Cutaway section through clutches and planetary gears

Key to Fig 7:4   1 to 17 see Fig 7:3   18 Rear clutch piston   19 Rear clutch return spring   20 Rear clutch plates
21 Front clutch piston   22 Front clutch diaphragm spring   23 Front clutch plates

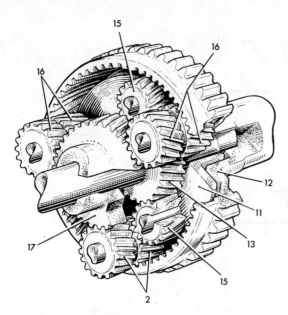

FIG 7:5 Cutaway section through planetary set

For key to numbers, see Figs 7:3 and 7:4

The throttle valve is set by a cam, cable-linked to the throttle control. Depression of the accelerator pedal, therefore, acts on both the carburetter butterfly valve and the throttle valve in a proportion set by the shape or contour of the cam. Actually, this is two valves in a common body each having a separate function and interlinked by a spring. The first is the downshift valve the function of which, at full accelerator depression, is to delay upshifts or effect downshifts at maximum engine speeds. This is the 'kick-down' feature which enables the driver to achieve the effect of a changedown with a manual gearbox to get increased acceleration if needed.

The second is the throttle valve proper which floats between the downshift valve spring and its own return spring, the return force being amplified by governor controlled throttle pressure, and transmits a hydraulic pressure, via the primary regulator valve, to control the clutch and servo units operating on the brake bands of the sun wheel and annulus. This regulates the clutch and brake band capacities to suit current operating conditions.

The governor valve is centrifugally operated and regulates the pressure to the modulator, shift and servo orifice valves according to output shaft speed. The regulator valves are, in effect, pressure reducing valves modifying the pump pressure to suit the requirements of the hydrokinetic converter, overall lubrication and the exhaust to the pump inlets. The modulator valve acts as a hydraulic relay applying the differing pressures required by the throttle valve according to the condition of the governor.

Though the underlying principles of the transmission are relatively simple, their translation into an effective and smooth running, reliable mechanism is the result of much development and experiment with valve dimensions, spring pressures and channel proportions all of which are permanently set in the dimensions of the component

parts. The only adjustments are the purely mechanical ones of taking up wear in the planetary brake bands, the linkage between the carburetter and the downshift cam and the link between the gear selector lever and the manual valve. The sole faults that are likely to occur in the valve and hydraulic system are those due either to the use of wrong hydraulic fluid, allowing the fluid level to fall too low or the admission of dirt or grit into the hydraulic system.

The adjustments to the linkages are made while the transmission is in the car. Adjustments to the planetary brake bands necessitate removal of the unit to a bench.

7:2 Gear selection

Manual gear selection is by a lever, mounted on the steering column below the steering wheel. Once this has been moved to any of the drive positions, subsequent gear selection is automatic as already described.

An exploded view of the gear selection mechanism, as fitted to a righthand drive car is shown in **FIG 7:6**. The lefthand drive arrangement is a mirror image of that shown. Movement of the lever 1, is communicated to the gear selector lever on the automatic gearbox via a control rod 2 pinned to a crank 3, linked by a rod 4, cross-shaft 5 and control arm 6, to the gear selector lever 7.

A gate 8 controls movement of the lever 1. Movement between Drive and Neutral can be effected without depression of the lever but passage through the gates to other positions necessitates depression of the lever for the stopper pin 9 to clear the gate detents. Return from these positions can however, be effected without further depression except in the case of Parking (P) which is locked-on until released by a second depression of the lever.

A pointer 12, secured to the shaft below the lever, shows the gear selected against an illuminated indicator in the housing 11.

A switch mounted on the gearbox inhibits operation of the starter motor when the engine is in any of the drive positions. This switch is in the solenoid circuit of the starter and, should the engine stall, the lever must be returned to N before it can be started again.

The engine can be started by handle or manual depression on the starter button in the engine compartment irrespective of the position of the lever. Before using these starting facilities, make sure that the gear selector lever is set in P.

To adjust the linkage, slacken back both locknuts on the control rod 4 at the crank 3, and set the lever 1 into position D (Drive). With rod 4 perfectly free in the eyebolt on the crank, move the selector lever 7 on the gearbox as far forward as it will go (the Parking position) and then back three 'clicks' of the lever detent.

Holding it in this position, take up the slack on the locknuts either side of the eyebolt, check that there is no free play in the linkage and tighten both equally about the eyebolt. Finally, check each position by the feel or sound of detent engagement.

The use of the L position is to keep the car running in the second gear, either as a means of controlling a coast downhill, or as an alternative to using the 'kick-down' to give increased acceleration while in top gear. At speeds below 5 mile/hr, the use of the L position automatically keeps the engine in first gear. **L should not be selected at speeds above 50 mile/hr, except in an emergency.**

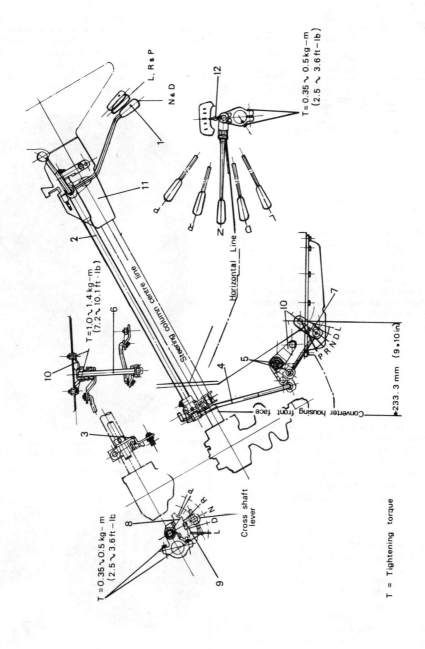

L, R & P

N & D

1

11

2

Steering column centre line

Horizontal Line

T=0.35∿0.5kg—m
(2.5 ∿ 3.6 ft—lb)

12

Z

N

D

L

T=1.0∿1.4 kg—m
(7.2∿10.1 ft—lb)

6

10

10

5

4

3

7

P R N D L

Converter housing front face

233.3 mm (9•10in)

T=0.35∿0.5 kg—m
(2.5 ∿ 3.6 ft—lb)

8

9

P
R
N
D
L

Cross shaft
lever

T = Tightening torque

FIG 7:6   Exploded views of column pattern gear selector unit

Key to Fig 7:6   1 Gearlever   2 Control rod   3 Crank   4 Rod   5 Cross-shaft   6 Control arm   7 Gear selector lever
8 Gate   9 Gearlever stop pin   10 Bracket   11 Housing   12 Pointer

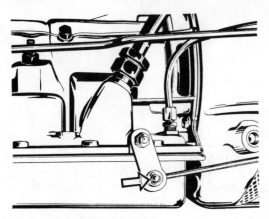

FIG 7:7 Terminal linkage of manual shaft control rod at the gearbox. Splitpin shown arrowed

The parking position P, is particularly useful for holding the car on steep gradients but it should always be applied in addition to, and not as a substitute for, the handbrake. If it is released with the hand or footbrake being applied, the car will immediately commence to roll and attempts to re-engage it can only result in damage.

When stopping on slight upward gradients, if the engine tick-over has been properly set, the car will remain stationary in Drive and not roll back. If the gradient is a little steeper, roll-back can be stopped by a small application of the accelerator ready for a quick move off. On level ground, the engine should be set to give a very slow crawl forward. The footbrake should always be applied before selecting gear and the foot transferred to the accelerator after the gear has been engaged. A very slight kick can be felt as the servo clutches operate.

7:3 The torque converter

The torque converter is a sealed unit with the impeller as an integral part of the housing, a stator mounted on a unidirectional clutch supported on the tube projecting from the gearbox and the turbine rotor splined to the gearshaft housed within the tube. Cooling blades and a drive ring are welded to the outer casing of the converter and the general view when extracted from the gearbox is shown in FIG 7:8. The sleeve seen projecting from the converter provides the drive to the front pump rotor, the projections fitting into the slots visible in FIG 7:9. Within this sleeve is the converter support tube, the splined end carrying the unidirectional clutch and stator. The gearshaft passes through the support tube to enter the splined boss of the turbine rotor.

The three units, impeller, stator and rotor, are self-supporting within the converter and the withdrawl of support tube or shaft does not affect their mechanical relationship. The hydraulic fluid from the pump enters the converter via an annular clearance between the sleeve and support tube, returning via a similar clearance between support tube and gearshaft.

The starter ring gear is shrunk on to the drive ring and the whole is mounted on an adaptor plate secured to the flywheel flange on the engine crankshaft by six bolts with hardened steel washers, four similar bolts and washers

being used to secure the drive ring to the adaptor plate (see FIG 7:10).

7:4 Power flow in gears

Torque transmission, or power flow, in the various gears is shown diagrammatically in FIG 7:11.

In the first of these, the gear selector is set in either N or P. The front and rear clutches are released and the rotor shaft turns without transmitting torque to either of the sun wheels. The only difference between the two positions is that, in P, the pawl brake is applied mechanically through linkage with the selector shaft and, purely for constructional reasons, the rear brake band is applied if the engine is running.

FIG 7:8 View of hydrokinetic converter removed from the engine and housing. The starter gear ring is not fitted in the picture

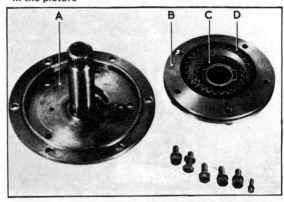

FIG 7:9 Front pump dismantled to show, A the converter support assembly, B the pump body, C the pump driven gear with drive sockets and D the pump driven gear

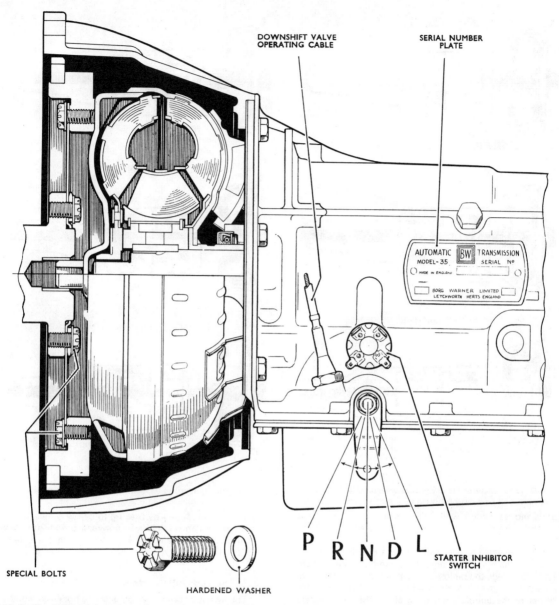

DOWNSHIFT VALVE OPERATING CABLE

SERIAL NUMBER PLATE

AUTOMATIC [BW] TRANSMISSION
MODEL-35   SERIAL Nº
○ MADE IN ENGLAND
BORG WARNER LIMITED
LETCHWORTH HERTS ENGLAND

P R N D L

STARTER INHIBITOR SWITCH

SPECIAL BOLTS

HARDENED WASHER

FIG 7:10 Part section through converter and housing showing the bolts securing the adaptor plates to crankshaft flange and converter and the positions of the operating cable connector, starter inhibitor switch, gear selector lever and serial number plate

When the Drive position is selected, the front clutch is applied connecting the converter to the forward sun gear. The unidirectional clutch prevents the pinion carrier from turning and the torque is transmitted through the pinions to the annulus providing a gear reduction of 2.393:1. On the overrun, the unidirectional clutch releases the forward drive and the car freewheels.

At a suitable point, set by the combination of governor pressure and throttle setting, the front brake band is applied holding the reverse sun gear, which has been freewheeling, stationary. This has the effect of reducing the gear ratio to 1.45:1.

With a further increase in engine speed for a given throttle setting, the front clutch is applied, connecting the converter to the forward sun gear. At the same time, the front brake band is released. With both sun gears now locked together, the gearing rotates as a whole to give a direct drive from converter to drive shaft.

Changing up and down from second to top gear is, therefore, effected by switching the locking between front

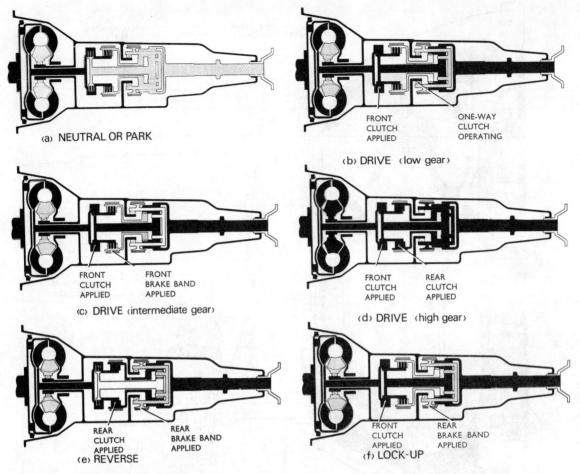

(a) NEUTRAL OR PARK

(b) DRIVE (low gear)
FRONT CLUTCH APPLIED   ONE-WAY CLUTCH OPERATING

(c) DRIVE (intermediate gear)
FRONT CLUTCH APPLIED   FRONT BRAKE BAND APPLIED

(d) DRIVE (high gear)
FRONT CLUTCH APPLIED   REAR CLUTCH APPLIED

(e) REVERSE
REAR CLUTCH APPLIED   REAR BRAKE BAND APPLIED

(f) LOCK-UP
FRONT CLUTCH APPLIED   REAR BRAKE BAND APPLIED

FIG 7:11   Power flow diaphragm for the main selector positions and hydraulically selected secondary positions

band and rear clutch, while changes between bottom and second are effected by applying or releasing the front brake band.

When Reverse is selected, the front clutch is released and both the rear clutch and rear brake band are applied. The latter holds the pinion carrier stationary and the drive is now through the rear sun wheel, via the gears on the carrier to the annulus and drive shaft, the intermediate gear in the pinion carrier reversing the direction of rotation of the annulus to that the converter. The reduction ratio is now 2.094:1.

If Lock-up (L) is selected instead of D, the rear brake band is applied instead of using the unidirectional feature of the in-built clutch. The gear ratio is the same as for Drive, namely 2.393:1, but the car can no longer freewheel and the engine can therefore be used for braking when descending hills. The other features of the L drive are inherent in the hydraulic system, but, in effect, the application of L when the car is stationary inhibits a change-up into second gear while a shift from Drive to L in second or top gear produces an immediate change-down into the gear below. Only one change is possible without further movement of the lever unless the speed

of the car is reduced by braking to below 5 mile/hr. The same effect can be achieved between 5 and 20 mile/hr by use of the accelerator kick-down with the selector lever in L.

7:5 The hydraulic system

The hydraulic system is complex and not easy to understand or dismantle. Even garage mechanics of long experience and skill have to undergo a course at the makers before they are able to dismantle, repair and re-adjust the hydraulics satisfactorily, so it is not advisable for the owner/mechanic to attempt to dismantle the assembly even under the most favourable home garage conditions. Fortunately, the makers supply a valve and body assembly as a complete unit and, should trouble be traced to this area the transmission, replacement of the unit is the recommended remedy. The procedure is dealt with in Section 7:6.

Operation of the system in the various settings of selector lever and throttle are outlined below with schematic diagrams to enable the owner/mechanic to appreciate something of what is going on during a journey.

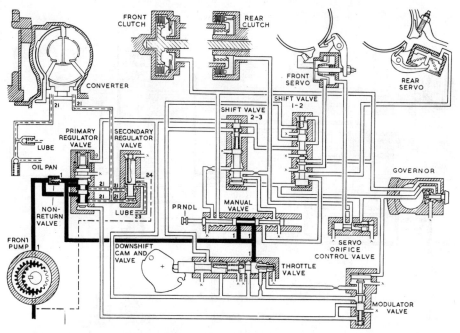

FIG 7:12 Operation of hydraulic circuit in N

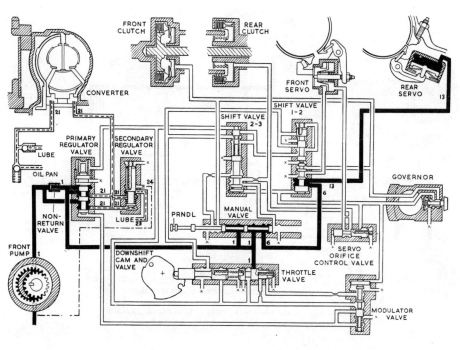

FIG 7:13 Operation of hydraulic circuit in P

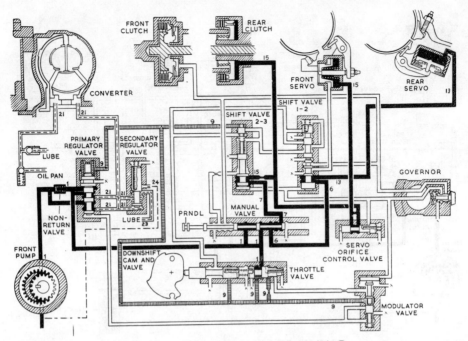

FIG 7:14   Operation of hydraulic circuit in R

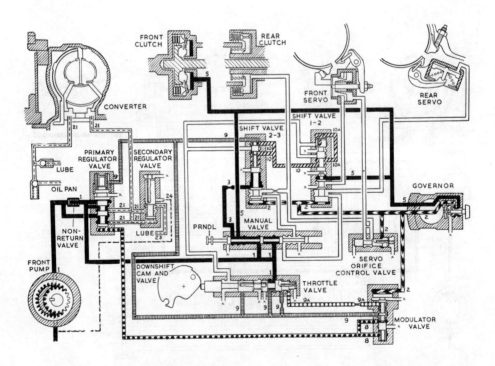

FIG 7:15   Operation of hydraulic circuit in D (low)

Lever in Neutral (N) (see Fig 7:12):

With the engine running, the front pump circulates the fluid to the primary regulator valve, manual valve and throttle valve, the former adjusting pressure to the hydro-kinetic converter and, via the secondary regulator valve, lubrication for the front gear trains. The latter serves as a pressure relief valve, exhausting to the pump inlet via 24, while ensuring that lubrication to the rear end of the gear train, via 23, is not maintained at the expense of that to the converter and front gear trains via 21. Both of the clutches are free and neither of the servo brake bands are applied. Fluid returned to the pump inlet passes either to the sump or to the pump inlet.

Lever in Park (P) (see Fig 7:13):

With the engine running, the hydraulic system is the same as for Neutral with the addition of a feed to the rear servo brake band. An extension to the selector rod lever setting the manual valve operates a toggle mechanism inserting a robust pawl into dog teeth integral with the driven shaft annulus or ring gear.

Strickly speaking, the application of the rear servo brake band has no useful purpose but the arrangement is the result of an extremely simple design of manual control valve.

Lever in Reverse (R) (see Fig 7:14):

With the engine running and the front pump circulating the hydraulic fluid, the manual valve opens the line to shift valves 1/2 and 2/3. The former redirects the pressure to apply the rear servo while the latter applies the rear clutch and, via the servo orifice valve (which serves no purpose at this stage) the front servo. The function of the throttle pressure line is to regulate the degree of pressure applied to the clutches and servos to suit the torque as a function of engine speed and throttle setting.

The application of the clutches and brakes is then as described in **Section 7:4** for Reverse.

Lever in Drive (D) (see Figs 7:15, 7:16 and 7:17):

The manual valve applies pressure to the front clutch at the same time opening the hydraulic lines to the shift valve 2/3, 1/2 and to the governor valve.

With the throttle in full open position as illustrated, the pressure 9, regulated by the modulator valve balancing governor pressure against feedback throttle pressure, opposes the throttle pressure in the primary regulator valve to adjust line pressure in the interests of smooth gearshifts. As the engine speed increases with fall-off in torque for a given throttle setting, the governor commences to regulate the flow and pressure of fluid to the shaft valves, servo orifice valve and modulator valve 2, balancing the throttle pressure 9, so adjusting the degree of application of the front clutch.

From this point onwards, the control of fluid flow through the primary regulator valve supplying the converter and lubrication, is set by the opposing forced and modulated throttle pressures 9 and 8. The former is controlled by the setting of the throttle valve and the latter by the modulator valve which, in turn, is regulated by governor pressure 2 (see **FIG 7:16**).

The shift takes place when the governor pressure 2 at one side of the 1/2 shift valve opposes the internal spring pressure and shift valve plunger pressure 10, to a point at which line pressure 5 is admitted to the front servo line 19, applying the front brake band. In the kick-down position as shown, the downshift cam has operated the throttle pressure line 9, to the modulated throttle pressure line 11, opposing the governor pressure in the two shift valves. The action of these is then inhibited and the changedown takes place or change-up is prevented, at least until the kick-down has been stopped or excessively high engine speed has caused the governor to resume control.

As the engine speed increases with reduced torque in intermediate gear, the governor pressure 2 also increases until a point is reached at which shift valve 2/3 also moves up to open the line 15, to both the rear clutch, applying it, and to the servo orifice control valve which is regulated by governor pressure 2. When this is sufficient to move the piston, fluid is admitted to the opposite side of the front servo and the brake band is released. With the two clutches engaged, the through drive is effected.

Any further retardation merely serves to reduce the throttle pressure and the transmission remains in top. Even when the car is coasting with the throttle closed, as in **FIG 7:17**, the existance of governor pressure is sufficient to prevent changedown. The only conditions which will induce a changedown is a serious fall in speed with load, resulting in a fall in governor pressure, or a sudden rise in throttle pressure as would result from a heavy depression of the accelerator either of which, or a combination of both, will result in shaft valve 2/3 closing to release the rear clutch and permit the 1/2 valve side of the front servo to overcome the rapidly falling counter pressure from the servo orifice control valve.

It must be appreciated that the operation of the valves and hydraulic pressures is not a step-by-step process but a constantly varying and interrelated condition which is functioning entirely in accordance with road and engine speed conditions, related to throttle opening, on a pre-arranged performance graph. The examples shown are merely typical conditions existing at selected points on this performance graph. Even the application of the clutches and servos is a graduated process giving smooth transitions from gear-to-gear, not just an on/off step. The exception to this is the front clutch which is directly applied by selection of any of the forward gears, the feed coming from the manual valve alone. The other three controls are dependent upon the position of the shaft valves.

Lock up:

The one position that has not been considered is the Lock-up (L) state (see **FIG 7:18**). Here the manual valve has sealed off the pressure to the shift valve 2/3 and provided a direct feed via 6 and 13 to the rear servo. Governor pressure acting on the two shift valves is unable to effect any changes and the bottom gear remains selected from a standing start.

If the transmission is already in D and running in top gear (see **FIG 7:17**), the effect of moving the manual valve to L is to open the line 3, from shift valve 2/3 to exhaust and the line 15 pressure drops releasing the rear clutch. A downshift to second gear results, governor pressure moving shift valve 1/2 up to seal off 6 and couple 13 to exhaust while opening 5 to 19 the front servo release. This is then the condition in **FIG 7:16**.

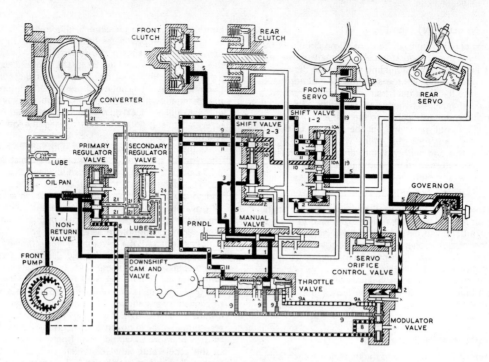

FIG 7:16   Operation of hydraulic circuit in D (intermediate)

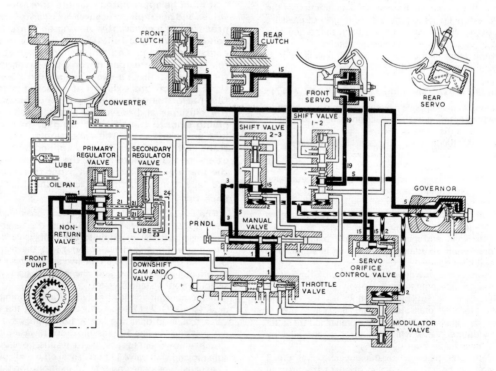

FIG 7:17   Operation of hydraulic circuit in D (high)

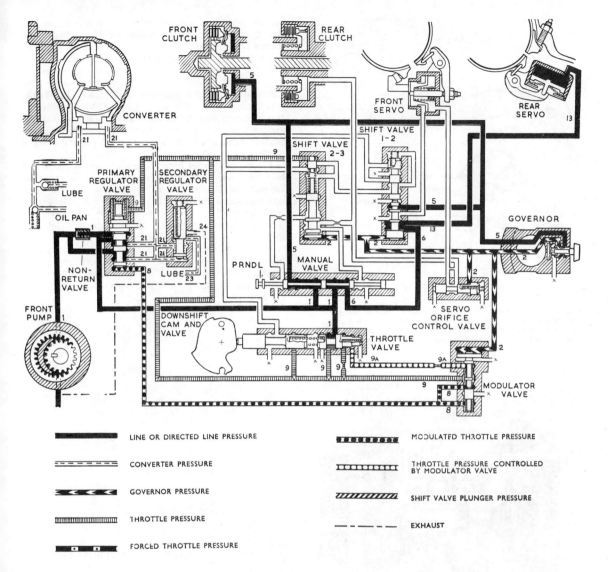

FIG 7:18 Operation of hydraulic circuit in L with key to flow lines

▬▬▬▬ LINE OR DIRECTED LINE PRESSURE	▨▨▨▨▨ MODULATED THROTTLE PRESSURE
═════ CONVERTER PRESSURE	▭▭▭▭▭ THROTTLE PRESSURE CONTROLLED BY MODULATOR VALVE
◄◄◄◄ GOVERNOR PRESSURE	▨▨▨▨▨ SHIFT VALVE PLUNGER PRESSURE
▥▥▥▥▥ THROTTLE PRESSURE	— ‧ — ‧ — ‧ EXHAUST
▬ ◼ ▬ ◼ FORCED THROTTLE PRESSURE	

D2 position:

On some cars the second drive position is provided, D2, which has the effect of inhibiting starting in bottom gear. When selected, the transmission then acts as a two-speed unit which, with large engines and a tendency to apply heavy accelerator on moving off, reduces the tendency of rear wheel spin.

The D2 position brings into service a second control valve interposed in the line between the governor and the shift valve 1/2. This valve seals the governor line 2 substituting line pressure to the shift valve 1/2 only. The front servo brake band is therefore held on so long as D2 is selected.

7:6 Dismantling and inspection

Raise the front of the car and mount on stands. Remove the drain plug and drain the fluid from the gearbox. **If the engine has been running recently before dismantling has been commenced, take care in draining as the temperature of the fluid can be above scalding point.** The drain plug has a hollow hexagon head and requires an Allen key $\frac{1}{4}$ inch AF to remove it. Draining the main gearcase will not allow the fluid to drain from the converter, so it is advisable to refit the plug before removing the converter/gearbox unit from the engine.

Disconnect the starter motor lead and remove the dipstick tube securing bolt. Loosen and remove the bell-

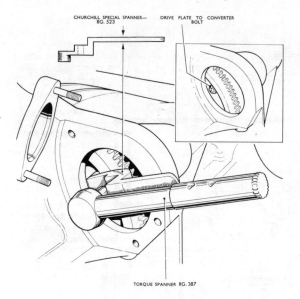

CHURCHILL SPECIAL SPANNER—
RG. 523

DRIVE PLATE TO CONVERTER
BOLT

TORQUE SPANNER RG. 387

FIG 7:19 Diagram showing access to bolts securing the converter to the adaptor plate throudh the starter aperture using the Churchill cranked spanner with torque spanner attached for tightening to a 28 lb ft setting

FIG 7:20 View of underside of transmission unit with oil pan removed showing, at A, the valve assembly securing bolts

housing bolts noting that one also secures the battery earth lead. Remove the upper mounting bolt and that securing the transmission filler tube to the support bracket. Disconnect the exhaust pipe from the manifold. Disconnect the downshift cable at the clevis pin and remove the connection to the inhibitor switch.

Mark the propeller shaft coupling flange for subsequent remarrying, loosen and remove the coupling bolts and lower the shaft at the rear to enable it to be withdrawn from the gearbox coupling splines. Free the handbrake

cables from their supports under the car and disconnect the equalizer from the gear selector rod by removing the rubber boot, extracting the clevis pin from the coupling block and moving the equalizer back on the pin to free it from the gearbox. Unbolt and remove the starter motor.

Through the starter motor hole, loosen and remove the converter-to-adaptor securing bolts (see **FIG 7:19**) rotating the crankshaft to bring each bolt opposite the hole. Loosen and remove the four bolts securing the engine rear plate to the converter and engine support bracket. Loosen and remove the speedometer cable and driven gear.

Place jacks under both the engine and gearbox and take their weight. Unbolt and remove the engine rear support from both engine and underframe, ease the gearbox rearwards to free it from the engine (the engine rear plate will be released by this and may fall away from the locating dowels), lower it on the jack and transfer to the bench or stand.

Place a tray under the joint between the converter housing and gearbox, remove the six bolts and spring washers securing the housing and carefully break the joint to enable the fluid within to drain away. Remove the housing.

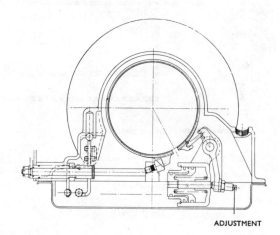

ADJUSTMENT

FIG 7:21 Adjustment of front brake band

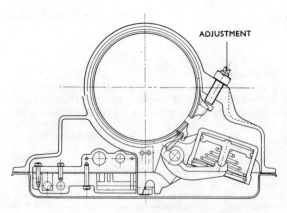

ADJUSTMENT

FIG 7:22 Adjustment of rear brake band

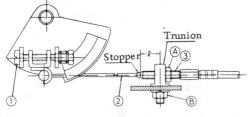

FIG 7:23 Carburetter end of downshift control cable showing throttle sector plate as fitted to a typical down-draught pattern carburetter. The carburetter termination may differ according to the type of carburetter installed but the control adjustments are similar. Adjustment is by the screw 1, operating on the cable 2 in the sleeve 3. B is the bracket locknut and A the sheath adjuster set to abut the stopper crimped on the cable in the idling position

The oil pan is of relatively light construction and, if the assembly is allowed to bear on it, some distortion will occur affecting the position of the oil tubes above. The weight must always be taken on the main casing and a special bench cradle, BT.4515 is available for this purpose.

FIG 7:24   Removing the pump

There may be some slight differences in the above procedure resulting from production changes in layout from time to time. However, these should become evident as the work proceeds and if a note is taken at the time, the reassembly will present no untoward difficulty.

Clean the exterior of the transmission and converter housings and drain the remnants of the hydraulic fluid from the transmission through the drain hole in the pan if this has not already been done.

Examine the converter body for signs of damage and check that the sleeve with the turbine rotor within rotates in the bearing without roughness or excessive friction. If any trouble has been experienced or there is any suspicion as to its efficient operation, fit a new converter returning the other to the makers for reconstruction. **The units being welded together, are not suitable for local repair.**

Turn the transmission over and mount on a suitable cradle with the hydraulics section uppermost. Unbolt and remove the oil pan. The pan supports four oil tubes each of which is a push fit into its socket. These can easily be damaged if the gearbox is allowed to rest its weight on the oil pan, so be careful. With the pan removed, carefully lever out the tubes, noting their positions for reinstatement. Unscrew the four studs securing the filter in place, clean the filter in petrol or carbon tetrachloride and allow to dry. **Do not use any fluffy material to wash or wipe down.**

Now remove the valve body assembly by extracting the three $\frac{7}{16}$ inch bolts indicated in **FIG 7:20**. (Two of these may have already been extracted when removing the filter.) Detach the cable from the downshift cam and carefully lift clear of the four oil tubes in the front of the gearbox. The two larger diameter tubes are the front pump inlet and outlet and the smaller are the feed and return for fluid to the converter. **Do not attempt to dismantle the valve body assembly.** The front pump is next to be removed giving access to the gear train from the front clutch end.

The two clutch assemblies may now be extracted, the front clutch by just pulling clear and the rear assembly,

FIG 7:25   Removing the front clutch and input shaft

FIG 7:26   Removing rear clutch and sun gears

FIG 7:27   Dismantling the rear clutch

FIG 7:28   Reinstalling the front clutch piston

FIG 7:29   Refitting the front clutch plates

FIG 7:30   Reinstalling the rear clutch piston

FIG 7:31   Refitting the rear clutch plates

FIG 7:32 Inserting the unidirectional clutch

FIG 7:33 Installing the front and rear clutch assembly

complete with forward sun gear, by easing through the open front clutch band. Separation is second procedure. The clutch band can then be squeezed together to free it from the servo and withdrawn through the front opening. The servo unit is secured by two $\frac{5}{16}$ inch bolts.

To remove the planet gears, the centre support must first be extracted. This is secured by two centre screws and the forward screw of the pair retaining the rear servo unit. Separation of the support and gears assembly is external to the casing after extraction. The rear brake band can be extracted through the front end, tilting it slightly on withdrawal.

The governor can be serviced on the drive shaft. To remove the rear cover, unscrew the five bolts and spring washers and withdraw.

Examine all bushes, thrust washers, friction surfaces of clutch plates and drums for signs of scoring and the brake bands for signs of burning. Replace all oil seals and any parts obviously damaged or worn.

The foregoing brief summary of dismantling assumes that minimum work is needed and, in the majority of cases, it is only to service one part which is suspect. Some of the operations are shown pictorially in FIGS 7:24 to FIG 7:38.

7:7 Reassembly and installation

Reassembly is a straightforward reverse process to dismantling, bearing in mind the following points. First, absolute cleanliness must be observed at all stages and the use of rags should be dispensed with or, at the minimum, only lint-free materials. Freshly washed nylon rag is quite suitable.

Always renew all gaskets and oil seals. Immediately before reassembly, all parts must have been cleaned in petrol or carbon tetrachloride and dipped in clean transmission fluid to facilitate installation.

All nuts and screws must be tightened to the appropriate torques as detailed in the Appendix as many of the threads are of light alloy and overtightening may damage them and render the fixing insecure. Be particularly careful not to cross threads when inserting. If possible, start the thread with the finger and take up slack with a tubular socket spanner without the use of a tommy bar or other lever device, using the torque wrench as the final stage.

From full dismantling, the assembly sequence is:

(a) insert shift rod, lever and parking pawls
(b) insert drive (output) shaft and annulus
(c) install rear adaptor plate
(d) fit governor and speedometer drive pinion
(e) install rear band and servo
(f) insert centre support and planet gear group
(g) install front servo and band
(h) install rear clutch
(i) install front clutch
(j) install front pump
(k) fit extension housing
(l) fit pump and converter oil tubes and install valve assembly

FIG 7:34 Fitting the rear adaptor plate

(m) fit four supply tubes and install oil pan

(n) install converter and housing in car

(o) reinstall transmission on housing in car

(p) reconnect propeller shaft and resupport gearbox on mounting

(q) remake all connections, electrical and mechanical, dissembled during the preparatory phase of dismantling.

Adjustments:

During the reassembly, certain adjustments have to be made. The first of these is for the front brake band (see **FIG 7:21**) and procedure is as follows. Slacken the adjustment locknut. With a torque screwdriver tighten the adjusting screw to a torque of 10 lb ft, then slacken off exactly four turns and secure with the locknut. **This is done with the oil pan removed.**

The rear brake band adjustment is external on the right-hand wall of the case (see **FIG 7:22**). Again, slacken the locknut, tighten the adjusting screw to a torque of 10 lb ft and slacken off one complete turn. Tighten the locknut.

To adjust the starter inhibitor switch, mounted above the gearshift lever on the transmission, place the selector lever in the D or L position. Couple the reverse connections (these tabs are set over at 45 deg.) to a battery and lamp and screw in the switch body to the unit until the lamp is extinguished. Make a mark on the body against a mark on the transmission casing and transfer the connections to the other two tags. Screw in further, counting the number of turns and parts of a turn, until the lamp lights. Turn back half this number to achieve a mid-point setting and secure with the locknut. Remake the proper connections.

To set the downshift valve cable, run the engine until warm and set the idling speed at 500 rev/min against a reliable tachometer, with the selector lever in N. Apply the handbrake and chock the wheels.

Check that the downshift cable and sleeve are secure at the transmission end, then adjust the nut at the throttle lever end (see **FIG 7:23**) until the end of the sleeve just abuts the adjustment stop crimped to the cable; that is, so that there is no free play in the sleeve. Secure by the locknut. Select D and note the fall in engine speed. This should be about 100 to 200 rev/min.

The only other adjustment is that for the selector lever which has already been detailed.

7:8 Maintenance

Maintenance is restricted to periodic checks of the hydraulic fluid using the dipstick in the breather tube to the rear of the engine. This should be done every 3000 miles and the check must be carried out on a level surface after the fluid has attained normal running temperature and while the engine is running. Bring the level up to the 'High' mark **but do not overfill.**

Routine fluid changes are unnecessary. At each service period, check the condition of the oil pan underside and the ventilating grilles beneath the converter housing. Clear away any caked road dirt or mud as the surfaces play an important part in cooling.

7:9 Modifications

Certain modifications have taken place since the Model 35 transmission was introduced. Generally speaking,

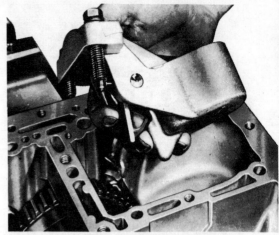

FIG 7:35   Installing the rear servo unit

FIG 7:36   Checking shaft end float

FIG 7:37   Mounting the governor on the shaft

FIG 7:38 Use of torque screwdriver to tighten valve body screws

these are only of significance when re-ordering new parts for replacement of their worn counterparts. Providing that the unit serial number, from the plate just above and to the right of the selector lever, is quoted, the correct part will be sent automatically.

All recent models now include a six position detent lever on the gear selector mechanism and this applies to units with or without the D2 position. If it is not present slight difficulty may be experienced in finding the N position when adjusting the selector linkage.

7:10 Fault diagnosis

Most faults in the transmission system can be located by a sequential process since an observed irregularity can be traced to more than one cause. The adjoining table shows how the most common symptoms can be checked to identify the cause in the quickest possible time. Clearly, those causes which do not need unit removal must be checked before the longer process is embarked upon. Intelligent use of the chart avoids this. Operation G to L do not need unit removal from the car but do need draining of the hydraulic fluid and lowering of the oil pan.

Key to Table

A	Check fluid level		M	Readjust starter inhibitor switch
B	Adjust manual linkage		N	Check pawl mechanism
C	Check carburetter full throttle		O	Check fit of rear clutch supply tube
D	Adjust engine idling speed		*	Remove transmission unit
E	Adjust downshift cable		p	Examine front pump and drive
F	Adjust rear brake band		q	Check front friction band
G	Examine rear servo		r1	Examine front clutch assembly and forward sun wheel seals
H	Adjust front brake band		r2	Examine plug in forward end of drive shaft
J	Examine front servo		s	Examine rear clutch assembly and seals
K1	Check valve block screws for tightness		t	Check unidirectional clutch
K2	Remove a clean valve block		u	Check rear friction band
L	Remove and clear governor		v	Examine planetary gear set
			w	Replace hydrokinetic converter

Fault	Operations that do not require unit removal															Operations requiring unit removal									
	A	B	C	D	E	F	G	H	J	K1	K2	L	M	N	O	*	p	q	r1	r2	s	t	u	v	w
No automatic upshifts																									
No 1 to 2 shift		1						3	4		5	2				6		7							
No 2 to 3 shift		1							4		5	2		3		6					7				
Incorrect shift speeds—quality of shift affected																									
Incorrect shift speeds			1		2				5		3	4				6									
Loss of kickdown			1		2							3													
Slip on 1 to 2 shift	1	3			2			4	5		6					7		8	9						
Slip on 2 to 3 shift	1	2			3				5		6				4	7		8			9				
Harsh 1 to 2 shift				1		2				3	4					5			7			6			
Harsh 2 to 3 shift				1		2				3						4						5			
Harsh 3 to 2 shift								1	3		2					4		5				6			
Harsh 2 to 1 shift				1	2											3			4			5			
Seizure 1 to 2						1				2						3					4	5			
Seizure 2 to 3								1	2	3															
Loss of drive—slip on takeoff																									
No forward drive	1	2			3						4	5				6			7	8			9	10a	10b
No drive in reverse	1	2				3	6				5				4	7					8		9		
Slip or squawk in L	1	2			3						4					5	8		6	7					
Slip or squawk in R	1	2			3	4	5				6					7	10				8		9		
Incorrect operation in L																									
Upshifts occur with L selected		1								3		2													
Excessive downshift delay—no engine braking. L selected from 30 mile/hr		1						2	3		4														
Miscellaneous																									
Incorrect starter or reverse lamp operation		1											2												
P position not holding vehicle		1												2											
Bumpy D, L or R engagement				1	2							3				4			5		6				
Delayed D, L or R engagement	1	2					5				4				3	6	10		7	8	9				
No neutral drive in neutral		1							2							3			4						
Drag in R								1								2			3						
Overheating	1					3		2								4									5

CHAPTER 8

REAR AXLE AND SUSPENSION

8 : 1 Description of rear axle

There are fundamental differences in design between the rear axles of the Datsun saloon and the estate car. On the saloon, a main crossmember mounted on, but insulated from, the body supports the two independently sprung suspension arms carrying the rear wheel bearings while the differential is comparatively rigidly mounted between the centre of the crossmember and a separate member at the rear. The drive to the rear wheels is then by telescopic shafts terminating in a universal coupling, of the Hardy-Spicer pattern, at each end (see **FIG 8 : 1**).

On the estate car, a more conventional arrangement of leaf springs and axle housing, with halfshafts communicating the drive from the differential to the wheel hubs and shock absorbers, is used (see **FIG 8 : 2**).

8 : 2 Dismantling and servicing the saloon suspension

To dismantle the rear suspension of the saloon, first raise the rear of the car and support it on stands. Remove the wheels and disconnect the brake linkage and the hydraulic hose connections, capping the latter against leakage of fluid.

Remove the exhaust tail pipe and silencer, mark the coupling flanges at the differential so that they will go together again in the same relationship when reassembling, then unbolt and withdraw the propeller shaft.

On each side, take the weight of the suspension arm on a jack and unbolt and remove the shock absorber from the arm, taking care to preserve the bushings. Remove the jack and the suspension arm will fall a short distance. Transfer the jack to under the central differential casing, remove the two nuts securing the differential mounting member 10 (see **FIG 8 : 1**) to the body and the two securing the crossmember 1. Lower the complete unit to the floor and ease clear of the car. Take care not to allow the assembly to fall sideways from the jack during the process (see **FIG 8 : 3**).

Thoroughly clean and examine all parts for signs of damage or excessive wear. In particular, check that the bushings in the arms, which are of the live rubber type (see **FIG 8 : 4**) are in first class condition as these are the main insulation against transmission of road vibration to the body. The dimension A, in the illustration should be not less than .2 inch, when installed with the car unladen. Replace, if necessary.

Remove and examine the coil springs and seatings. These must be in good condition and undistorted, with a

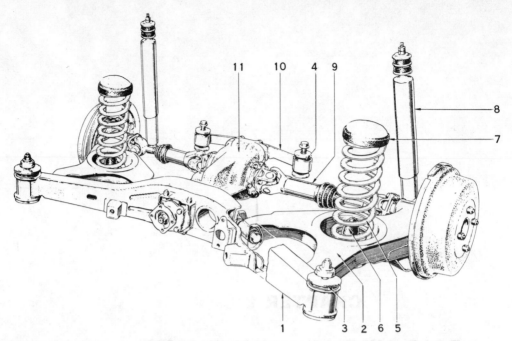

FIG 8:1   General view of rear suspension and differential drive assembly as fitted to the Datsun saloons

Key to Fig 8:1   1 Crossmember   2 Suspension arm   3 Suspension member mounting unit   4 Differential mounting unit
5 Coil spring   6 Bumper   7 Spring seating pad   8 Shock absorber   9 Drive shaft   10 Differential mounting member
11 Differential assembly

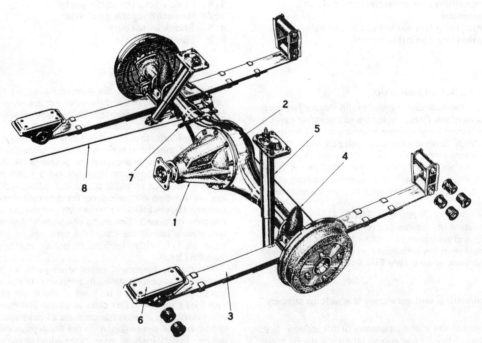

FIG 8:2   General view of rear suspension and axle arrangement as fitted to the Datsun estate cars

Key to Fig 8:2   1 Differential assembly   2 Rear axle casing   3 Leaf suspension spring   4 Bumper   5 Shock absorber
6 Forward mounting plate   7 Hydraulic brake line   8 Handbrake cable

free length of 12.2 inches on the standard 1300cc saloon, 12.0 inches on the 1600cc saloon and 11.8 inches on the deluxe models regardless of engine capacity. Replace if necessary. (This can, of course, be done without removing the complete suspension should circumstances warrant (see **FIG 8:5**).

Unbolt and remove the two telescopic shafts by un-coupling the flanges at each end, again marking the couplings for identical mating on reassembly. The shafts can be transferred to the bench for further examination and dismantling.

Wheel bearings:

The next step is to remove the wheel bearings. First remove the brake drum. This discloses the brake shoes and cylinder mechanism both of which are mounted on the backplate. Unless the brakes are being overhauled, in which case the procedure outlined in **Chapter 11** is followed, brush clear of dust and blow the loose matter away with an air jet. **It is not necessary to dismantle the brakes for removal of the axle and bearing.**

The exploded view of the hub components and a section through the assembly are shown in **FIGS 8:6** and **8:7**. To extract the bearing, first remove the hub nut from within the axle flange coupling, using a long-handled socket wrench while holding the flange against turning with the special tool ST49190000 (see **FIG 8:8**), or by other means, and pull off the coupling flange. The short stub axle and wheel mounting can then be extracted from the housing either by means of a hide mallet applied to the end of the shaft or by a sliding hammer tool bolted to the flange.

Remove the oil seal and inner bearing using the special drift ST49180000 designed for the purpose. Extract the distance piece and then withdraw the outer bearing. Thoroughly clean the interior of the housing and the bearings of all traces of old grease and the inspect all parts for signs of damage or deterioration. Replace as necessary.

On the exterior of the housing, a letter, A, B or C, will have been stamped. Check this against the letter marked on the distance piece and note that they are the same. If a new distance piece has to be installed, see that this too, bears the same letter as that on the housing. When assembled, the distance piece should be .002 inch less than the distance between the two inner races of the bearings so as to apply a small degree of preload when the assembly is tightened to the proper torque loading. This is ensured by the correct pairing of the markings.

When the inspection is complete and the necessary replacement parts have been obtained, the wheel bearings and stub axle can be reassembled. Reinstall the external bearing with the sealed side outermost, fit the bearing ring into place and insert the stub axle. From the other end, mount the distance piece on the axle and pack the space between the distance piece and housing with MP2 or MP3 bearing grease. Reinstall the inner bearing, again

FIG 8:3   Removing rear axle assembly from the Datsun saloon

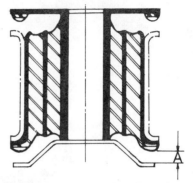

Suspension member mounting insulator

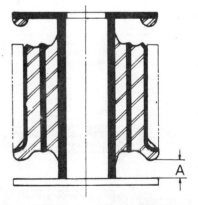

Differential mounting insulator

FIG 8:4   Details of the mounting insulators. In each case, A must not be less than .2 inch when unladen

with the sealed side outermost, and fit a new oil seal. Replace the coupling flange, washer and nut and tighten to a torque of 240 lb ft.

Check the end play, which should not exceed .006 inch, and the turning torque, which must be less than 4 lb inch. If either are out of limit, dismantle and fit a new distance piece.

FIG 8:5 Removing the coil suspension spring from the Datsun saloon

FIG 8:6 Exploded view of the rear hub assembly with, from left to right, the wheel mounting flange, brake backplate gaskets, seal, bearings and distance piece, oil seal, coupling flange, nut and washer

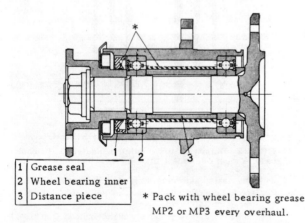

1	Grease seal
2	Wheel bearing inner
3	Distance piece

* Pack with wheel bearing grease MP2 or MP3 every overhaul.

FIG 8:7 Section through wheel hub assembly showing oil seal 1, bearing 2 and spacer 3. Greasing areas are marked with an asterisk

Suspension arm bushings

The two suspension arms are hinged in live rubber mounted bushings on the main suspension member. To remove, unscrew and remove the bolts passing through the bushings and lower the suspension arm. Examine the condition of the bushing and also that of the bolts. If it is necessary to replace the bushings, the old ones must first be extracted with a suitable tool (special tool ST49160000 has been designed for the purpose) and a new one installed with the same tool (see FIG 8:8).

When refitting the bearings, the nuts, being self-locking must be renewed. When tightening, set the torque spanner to 72 lb ft. Bushing renewal, can of course, also be carried out as a separate operation, should circumstances demand, without dismantling the rear axle assembly from the chassis.

Drive shafts:

The drive shafts can now be examined and serviced on the bench. An exploded view of the component parts is shown in FIG 8:9.

The purpose of dismantling the drive shaft assembly is, primarily to relubricate the ball splines, an operation required every 30,000 miles, or to replace a worn or faulty Hardy-Spicer bearing in the universal joint. As, however, the yoke of the universal joint is integral with each half of the shaft, a worn or damaged universal joint must be dealt with by complete replacement of the whole drive shaft assembly.

First, remove the universal joint spider at the differential end of the drive shaft (see Chapter 5, Section 5:9). Remove the circlip 7 and plug with washer 6. Compress the drive shaft assembly to bring the end of the drive shaft 1 to the inner end of the sleeve and yoke 8, and remove the circlip and stopper 4. Remove the boot band 6, on the sleeve yoke and ease the boot back over the shaft. Extract circlip and ring 7 and slide the shaft out of the yoke taking particular care not to loose any of the balls and spacers. Wash and clean all parts in paraffin and dry. Inspect for damage or wear and check the drive shaft for straightness. If any part is out of limit, replace the whole assembly.

Providing that the component parts are satisfactory and that there was no excessive radial play in the two parts

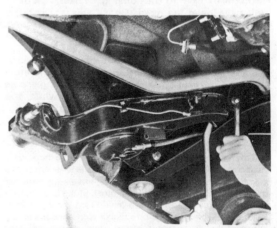

FIG 8:8 Removing a rear suspension arm

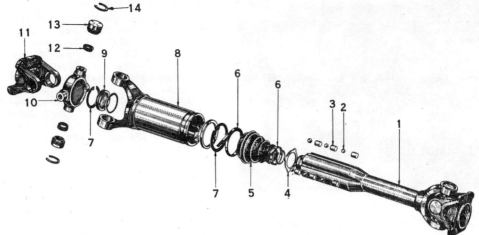

FIG 8:9   Exploded view of the rear wheel drive shaft assembly

Key to Fig 8:9   1 Drive shaft   2, 3 Spline balls and spacers   4 Stopper   5 Boot   6 Boot bands   7 Circlips
8 Sleeve and yoke   9 Yoke plug and washer   10 Spider   11 Flange coupling and yoke   12 Oil seal   13 Needle bearing
14 Circlip

before dismantling, reassemble in the reverse order, packing the areas around the balls, spacers and splines with
multi-purpose grease. Fit a new boot and boot bands and,
before reinstalling the sleeve yoke plug, insert 1.25 ozs of
of the same grease into the cavity beneath.

8:3 Dismantling the estate car suspension

To dismantle the rear suspension on the estate car,
raise the car on stands, disconnect the handbrake cables,
hydraulic brake hose at the three-way connector (see **FIG
8:10**), plugging the latter to prevent loss of fluid, and
remove the road wheels. Disconnect the shock absorbers
by removing the self-locking nuts and sliding the mounting
eyes from the pivot of the rear spring seat and then remove
the flange bolts connecting the propeller shaft to the
differential pinion coupling (see **FIG 8:11**).

Place a jack under the centre of the rear axle and then
remove the nuts from the U-bolts securing the axle casing
to the suspension spring (see **FIG 8:12**). Unbolt and
withdraw the rear end of the spring from the shackle (see
FIG 8:13), lower the spring and then withdraw the
U-bolts and ease the axle casing to the rear and away
from the car.

Overhauling the springs:

To remove the springs from the car, unbolt and remove
the front pin brackets (see **FIG 8:14**) and lower away. At
the bench, remove the centre bolt securing the spring to
the front bracket and commence to dismantle the four
leaves by extracting the centre bolt and clips. **Note that
the centre bolt is offset 2.36 inches to the front.**

Clean the leaves and examine for signs of wear, cracks,
fatigue or damage. If any leaf is faulty, replace the whole
pack. Providing that all are satisfactory, reassemble with
a good coating of grease on both surfaces and with the
liners in position at the leaf ends. Secure by the clips and
centre bolt. If necessary, rebush the eyes at each end of
the upper leaf. Check that the bushes are satisfactory too,
in the rear shackles.

FIG 8:10   Hydraulic brake 3-way hose connector

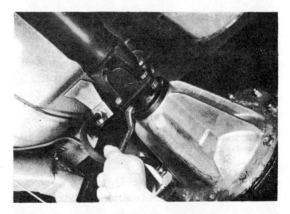

FIG 8:11   Disconnecting the coupling between propeller shaft and differential pinion

FIG 8:12 Detail of estate car rear mounting plate assembly with U-bolts and showing, arrowed, the self-locking nuts and shock absorber mounting pin and bush

FIG 8:13 Detail of rear leaf spring mounting shackle on the Datsun estate car

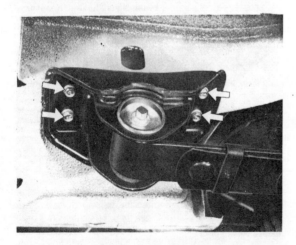

FIG 8:14 Detail of mounting bracket at forward end of leaf springs showing, arrowed, the mounting bolts

Removing halfshafts:

To remove the halfshafts, first remove the brake drums. Then, working through the two holes in the brake drum flange, unbolt and remove the four axle case end bolts. Remove the drain plug at the bottom of the banjo and drain the oil into a clean container. The oil may be re-used afterwards if in good condition and free from sludge or particles.

Using a sliding hammer, the plate of which is attached to the hub bolts, extract the halfshaft complete with bearing and bearing plate. **As the brake backplate is secured by the same four axle case end bolts, this will also be released but, unless it is desired to strip down the braking system at the same time, it can be replaced and held in position temporarily by the end bolts being reinserted in position.**

Thoroughly clean the halfshaft and bearings and examine the splined end for signs of wear or damage. If these are present, a new halfshaft will be required. The axle bearing and bearing end plate are secured in position by a bearing collar press-fitted to the shaft, the inner race of the bearing being gripped between the collar and a spacer resting on a step on the shaft immediately to the rear of the integral flange element (see **FIG 8:15**). **To replace a bearing, this collar must be cut or withdrawn in a press and discarded, a new collar being press-fitted on reassembly. The press load will have to be in the order of 4 to 5 tons.**

If the bearing is satisfactory, clean and repack with grease. Extract the old oil seal from the bearing housing and fit a new one, applying grease to the surfaces when fitting. Reinsert the halfshaft and secure in position, then check the end play in the shaft which should be between .012 and .02 inch and can be adjusted, if necessary, by changing the shims inserted between the brake backplate and the bearing housing. Tighten the axle case end bolts to a torque of 28 lb ft.

8:4 Dismantling the differential

The differential in the saloon differs from that in the estate car in several aspects, the former being mounted in its own casing while the latter is housed in the banjo section of the rear axle casing. The differences can be seen from a study of the two sectional diagrams, FIGS 8:16 and 8:17. The dismantling of the saloon differential will be dealt with in detail. That for the estate car will be left for the owner/driver to determine having regard to the differences shown in the diagrams and with general reference to the procedure for the saloon model.

Unbolt and remove the differential carrier from the suspension arm and unbolt and remove the rear mounting member from the carrier. Transfer to the bench and remove the drain plug, allowing the oil to drain into a suitable clean receptacle. It can be re-used again if in a good and clean condition.

Unbolt and remove the rear cover 10 (see **FIG 8:16**) and gasket. Unscrew and remove the two side bolts 19, and pull the side flanges 21 clear. Remove the side bearing retainer bolts 23 and, using a standard puller against a drift inserted in the central hole, pull out the side bearing retainers (see **FIG 8:18**). **Carefully mark the parts removed so that they can be returned to their**

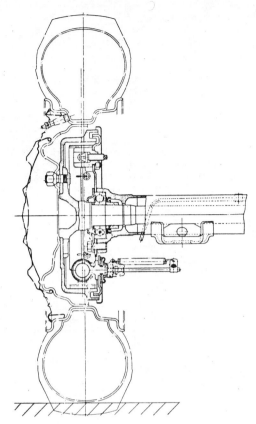

FIG 8:15 Section through rear wheel assembly as fitted to the estate car

original positions with the same shimming on reassembly. The differential gearcase 26, can then be extracted from the rear (see FIG 8:19).

Unbolt and remove the flange nut and washer 36, holding the flange from turning by suitable means, extract the dust cover 1 and oil seal 34, then press the pinion shaft out of the casing in a hydraulic or other press. The shaft 31 will come away with the rear bearing and race inner ring 27, leaving the centre and front bearings in position.

Unbolt and remove the front bearing cap 37, and extract the front spacer 31. Thoroughly clean the interior from old grease and repack the bearing 30 (the inner ring and race of which will have been released by removal of the spacer) with fresh grease. Unless the bearings, on examination, require renewal, it is not necessary to dismantle the outer rings of the taper roller bearings and the rear spacer 3 and washer 2, as these have been selected to give the right degree of preload on the bearings. If renewal is necessary, the next paragraph applies.

To renew the roller bearings 27 and/or 30, first extract the forward bearing outer ring by means of a drift or puller, then remove the rear bearing outer ring. The spacer 3 and washer 2, will have come out with the pinion shaft. Insert and press home the new outer rings. Reassemble the new bearings and spacers, with the original washer, on the

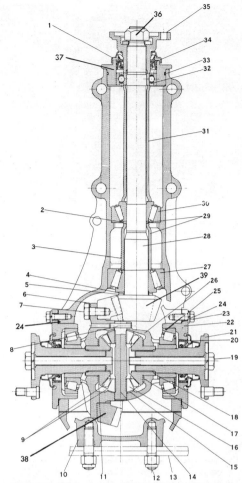

FIG 8:16 Section through the differential unit as fitted to the saloons

Key to Fig 8:16   1 Dust cap   2 Thrust washer
3 Spacer   4 Shim   5 Thrust washer   6 Locktab
7 Crownwheel stud   8 Pin   9 Free and side bevels
10 Rear cover   11 Thrust washer   12 Mounting bolt
13 Mounting member   14 Free bevel shaft   15 Washer
16 Free bevel   17 Washer   18 Side bevel
19 Flange coupling nut and washer   20 Oil seal
21 Side flange   22 Side bearing retainer
23 Side bearing retainer bolt   24 Preloading shim
25 Side bearing   26 Differential gearcase
27 Rear roller bearing   28 Bevel pinion shaft
29 Rear spacer and washer   30 Front roller bearing
31 Front spacer and washer   32 Ballbearing   33 O-ring
34 Oil seal 35 Coupling flange 36 Flange nut and washer
37 Front bearing cap   38 Crownwheel   39 Bevel gear

pinion shaft exactly as before dismantling and remount the coupling flange and nut. Tighten the nut to a torque of 145 lb ft and then determine the turning torque on the shaft. This should be not less than 97 oz inch nor more than 140 oz inch with new bearings. If the torque is outside these limits, dismantle and replace the washer 2, by a thinner one to decrease the turning torque or by a thicker one to increase it.

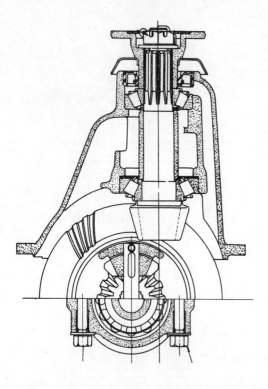 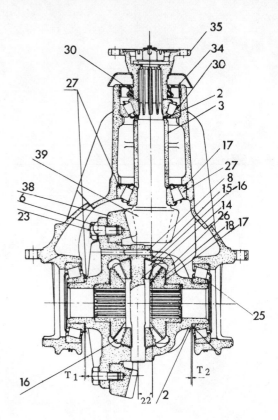

FIG 8:17 Section through the differential unit as fitted to the estate car. For key to the numbers, see Fig 8:16

After a period in service, the bearings wear in and the torque to be expected with old bearings should be not less than 40, nor more than 85 oz inch. If outside these limits, the washer thickness must be adjusted accordingly.

If it has been necessary to replace the pinion and shaft, the thrust washer shims 4 will also need adjusting. Check the figure, preceded by a + or − sign, on the head of the new pinion against that on the one it is replacing and measure the total thickness of the old shims. If the figure on the new pinion is **less** than that on the old (more negative or less positive) increase the shim pack thickness by the difference. If it is **greater** (less negative or more positive), decrease the shim pack thickness by the difference. For example, should the old head figure read −2 and the new +3 (that is 5 more) the shim pack thickness must be reduced by .05 mm. **The figures on the head relate to the variation in production from a design pinion datum in hundredths of a millimetre, so all measurements in this procedure must be made in millimetres.**

The above methods are a simplification of the setting up procedure in production, using dummy shafts and special gauges which are not easily accessible to the owner/ mechanic. It assumes that the original setting up procedure was properly carried out and that the shims or washers have not altered in thickness meanwhile. If however, on examination of the contact patterns on the teeth of the crownwheel and pinion are not central, the thickness of the shim packs will have to be adjusted once more. If the patterns are towards the heel (larger diameter) of the bevel pinion on the drive face of the tooth, the shim pack thickness must be increased; if they are towards the toe (smaller diameter) of the pinion, the shim pack thickness must be decreased. There is no method of establishing the correct amount of increase or decrease other than by trial and error. If the patterns are not sufficiently bright by themselves, lightly smear the tooth surfaces with red lead in oil and rotate the gears in mesh. The patterns will then instantly become visible.

To dismantle the differential gear cage, withdraw the races and inner bearing rings from the side bevels 18 (see **FIG 8:16**) using a suitable extraction tool, then flatten the lock straps, remove the bolts and detach the crownwheel from the casing. **Mark the position of the crownwheel before doing so and also identify each part removed so that it is returned to its original position on reassembly.**

Drive out the pin 8 from the free bevel shaft 14 and extract the shaft. This will release the free bevels 16 and thrust washers 15. Note how the pin 8 is secured, either by peening or caulking (both methods have been used) and either extract the caulking or ease the peening before driving out.

Extract the side bevels and thrust washers, carefully preserving the latter which determine the degree of back-

FIG 8:18 Extracting the side bearing retainer with puller

FIG 8:19 Removing the differential gearcase from the housing

FIG 8:20 Checking runout on crownwheel

FIG 8:21 Reinstalling differential gearcase and side bearing retainers

FIG 8:22 Reinstalling the differential assembly in the saloon showing rear mounting units being positioned for attachment

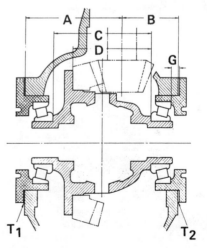

FIG 8:23 Determination of preload shim thickness on saloon type differentials

FIG 8:24 Positions of markings on differential case

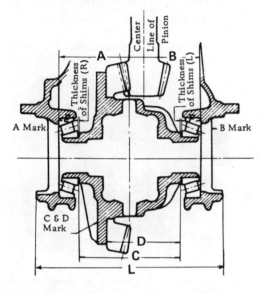

FIG 8:25 Determination of preload shim thickness on estate car differentials

FIG 8:26 Inserting estate car differential in the gear carrier with preload shims in position

lash in the assembly and are an important factor in quiet differential operation.

Examine all parts for damage or wear and obtain replacement oil seals, O-rings and other worn or damaged components.

8:5 Reassembling the differential

Reassemble the differential side bevels and free bevels in the reverse order to dismantling, applying gear oil generously to all surfaces. With the free bevel shaft in position but the locking pin 8 not fitted, check for backlash and, if necessary, adjust the thickness of the thrust washers. When properly set, there should be no backlash but the gears should rotate freely and without noise. Insert the locking pin.

Refit the crownwheel, using new lockstraps, tightening each bolt in steps, diagonally, and finally applying a torque of 58 lb ft to each. Press fit the side bearing cone and inner ring on to the differential casing and temporarily reassemble in the differential casing by means of the two retainer plates. Check the runout of the crownwheel with a dial gauge (see FIG 8:20) and if it exceeds .003 inch, readjust by slightly varying the torque on the bolts, lightly tapping the bolt heads at the same time. Secure by means of the lock straps.

Extract the differential cage assembly from the casing and reinstall the bevel pinion. Fit a new O-ring 33 and oil seal 34 (see FIG 8:16) and tighten the new self-locking nut 36 to a torque of 145 lb ft. Pack the area behind the oil seal 34 with bearing grease before inserting.

Reinsert the differential cage, carefully meshing the crownwheel with the bevel pinion, and reinstall the two side retainer plates, tightening the bolts to a torque of 9 lb ft (see FIG 8:21). Check the backlash on the crownwheel and pinion with a dial gauge and, if it exceeds .008 inch, readjust the thickness of the washer/shim pack behind the bevel pinion.

Fit the two oil seals in the retainer plates, greasing the upper lips and then fit the side flanges into place securing with the bolt and lockwasher tightened to a torque of 19 lb ft. Reinstall the rear cover and gasket, tightening these bolts also to a torque of 19 lb ft, and fill with 2 pints of Shell Spirax, heavy duty, Castrol Hypoid or equivalent gear oil. Refit the rear mounting member.

The differential gear assembly is then ready for remounting in the main suspension member on its vibration-proof mounts the bolts being tightened to a torque of 45 lb ft (see FIG 8:22).

8:6 Preloading the differential

In the foregoing procedure, it has been taken that the original shims inserted between the side retainer plates and the casing have been fitted and, as selected, are suitable for applying the correct preload on the taper roller bearings.

Should it be necessary to replace the differential casing, side bearing or retainer, a change in the shimming for correct preloading will possibly be necessary. In order to facilitate the determination of both shim thicknesses, each component is marked with a letter and figure which can be referred to in FIG 8:23. A and B are marked on the differential carrier, C and D on the differential cage (see FIG 8:24) and G and H on the side retainers and crownwheel respectively. E and F are the variations, in hundredths of a millimetre, from the standard 20 mm overall width of the side bearings as determined on a surface plate by dial gauge when under a load of 5½ lb.

The thickness of the left shim T_1, is then 76 plus the sum of A, C, G and H **less** D and E in hundredths of a millimetre. The thickness of the right shim T_2, is 76 plus the sum of B, D and G **less** F and H, also in hundredths of a millimetre.

On the estate car differential, the preloading is effected by shims inserted between the side bevels and inner ring of the taper roller bearings. The position of the marks, A, B, C and D, are shown in **FIG 8 : 25** while E and F are the same as in the saloon installations. The shim thicknesses are then on the crownwheel side derived from 7 plus the sum of A, D and C **less** E while that on the opposite side is derived from 6 plus the sum of B and F **less** D, both in hundredths of a millimetre.

The shims are mounted on the side bevel shaft before fitting the bearings and the assembly then has to be forced into position in the gear carrier by lightly hammering it home with a hide mallet before fitting the bearing caps into position (see **FIG 8 : 26**). After tightening the bearing caps (torque set to 35 lb ft), check the dimension across the outer rims of the caps with a gauge (see **FIG 8 : 27**). This should be between 7.811 and 7.817 inches for correct preloading.

8 : 7 Reinstalling the rear axles

Reinstallation is a simple reversal of the dismantling sequence both on the saloon and in the estate car. As far as possible, tighten the nuts and bolts to the recommended torque values. These are, on the saloon, flexible coupling nuts and bolts, 58 lb ft; suspension member mounting nuts, 73 lb ft; differential rear member mounting nuts, 62 lb ft; suspension arms to suspension members, 72 lb ft; and, on the estate car, shackle and front pin nuts, 33 lb ft; U-bolt nuts, 47 lb ft; front bracket fixing nuts, 17 lb ft; and propeller shaft flange nuts, 28 lb ft.

When fitting leaf springs on the estate car, remember that the centre holding bolt is not central between the two ends but is offset forward. It is easy to turn the springs round in assembling and if one should be the wrong way round, the axle will not lie properly across the car.

The use of soap solution applied to the rubber bushes will facilitate the assembling of the bushes in the eyes and sockets. One other point; always renew self-locking nuts. Although a self-locking nut may be used satisfactorily two or three times, there is no way of determining how many times it has already been fitted and removed.

8 : 8 Shock absorbers

On both the saloon and the estate car, the shock absorbers are of the double-acting, sealed hydraulic pattern and are not suitable for dismantling and servicing away from the makers. Always replace a faulty or suspect shock absorber by a new one.

On the saloon, the outer shaft is coupled to the body at the rear of the boot in a domed housing and is secured by two nuts with plain and domed washers, rubber composition bushings and packings (see **FIG 8 : 28**). At the lower end, the sliding member is secured to the axle housing mounting bracket by a bushing, washer and nut.

On the estate car, the upper end is bolted to a special domed plate which in turn, is secured by four bolts to the

FIG 8 : 27 Checking carrier spread as indicated of bearing preload

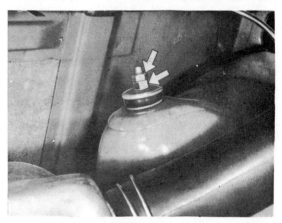

FIG 8 : 28 Top mounting of shock absorbers in rear of saloon car

FIG 8 : 28 Top mounting of shock absorbers in rear of estate car

body above (see **FIG 8 : 29**). At the lower end, the bushes eye is secured to a pin integral with U-bolt mounting plate (see **FIG 8 : 30**).

Replace the rubber bushings and washers if they become hardened or cracked and, when fitting the nuts and bolts, set the spanner to 18 to 20 lb ft torque.

FIG 8:30 Fitting bottom eye and bust of estate car rear shock absorber to mounting pin on rear suspension

8:9 Fault diagnosis

(a) Rear of car out of level

1 Uneven tyre pressures
2 Weak or broken spring
3 Faulty shock absorber

(b) Uneven tyre wear

1 Tyre treads not matched
2 Tyre pressures not matched
3 Weak or broken spring on one side
4 Faulty shock absorber on one side
5 Uneven vehicle loading

(c) Excessive rear tyre wear

1 Tyre pressures too low
2 Excessive use of acceleration

(d) Car pulls to one side

1 Rear axle out of alignment (estate car)
2 Tyre deflating (slow puncture)
3 Uneven tyre wear on rear wheels
4 One brake binding
5 Wheel nuts loose

(e) Excessive vibration

1 Wheel nuts loose
2 Propeller shaft joints loose
3 Worn shock absorber bushes
4 Faulty drive shafts and couplings (saloon)
5 Loose U-bolt nuts (estate car)
6 Wheels out of balance

(f) Noisy transmission

1 Excessive play in differential
2 Broken or damaged bearings in differential
3 Broken or damaged bearings in hubs
4 Worn shock absorber mounts
5 Broken or damaged teeth in differential
6 Damaged balls in shaft assembly (saloon)

CHAPTER 9

FRONT SUSPENSION AND HUBS

9:1 Description

The front suspension is of the single strut pattern, the shock absorber forming the spindle around which the steering turns. The front wheel hubs are welded to the foot of the strut outer casing with the top of the piston rod turning in a thrust ballbearing elastically mounted in a housing bolted to the car body frame. The substantial coil suspension spring is mounted at the upper end of the shock absorber being contained between two spring seats, one on the shock absorber outer casing and the other secured to the piston rod (see **FIG 9:1**).

The lower end of the assembly is bolted to a steering arm bracket turning in a sealed ball joint on a transverse link arm hinged to the front suspension crossmember. Lateral rigidity is provided by two tension rods secured to the ends of the link arms at one end and to the crossmember in live rubber mountings at the other. A stabilizer arm, secured to the underframe in rubber bushed brackets, and terminating at each link arm in a vertical rod, rubber bushed, ensures parallel vertical movement between the two arms and restricts forward movement of the body on the suspension. The combination of the three controls effectively removes excessive roll, buck or sway to provide a smooth ride regardless of adverse road surface conditions.

The ball joints at the foot of the struts are lubrication-sealed for life and the upper parts of the shock absorber are protected by a collapsible rubber boot within the coil spring. Excessive vertical movement is prevented by bump rubbers and rebound stoppers in each shock absorber.

The wheels are mounted on stub axles in substantial ball bearings of a design to take load at an angle to the vertical and are grease packed and sealed for a life of 30,000 miles.

The pressed steel wheels are secured to the brake hub flanges by four bolts and take 5.60 x 13 4PR tyres.

9:2 Dismantling wheel hub and bearing

Securely chock the rear wheels rear and front and raise the front of the car on stands. Remove the wheels, extract the cotterpin and unscrew the spindle nut. The hub assembly can then be drawn off the stub axle. To dismantle the hub assembly, extract the oil seal, remove the two inner bearing cages and examine the condition of the outer bearing cages press-fitted into the hub. A section through the hub assembly is shown in **FIG 9:2** with the exploded view showing the component parts in **FIG 9:3**.

Thoroughly wash all parts in paraffin and dry. If the bearing race or inner ring is damaged or worn, replace, removing the inner rings from the hub with a suitable diameter drift.

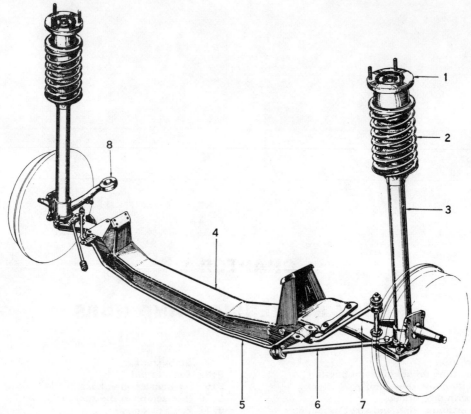

FIG 9:1   Diagrammatic view of front suspension arrangements

Key to Fig 9:1   1 Thrust bearing mount and housing   2 Suspension coil spring   3 Shock absorber   4 Crossmember
5 Stabilizer bar   6 Tension rod   7 Transverse link arm   8 Steering arm

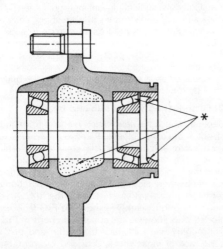

FIG 9:2   Section through wheel hub showing bearing and greasing points

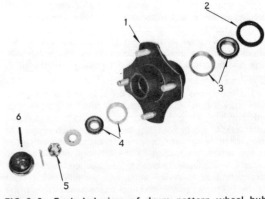

FIG 9:3   Exploded view of drum pattern wheel hub assembly

Key to Fig 9:3   1 Wheel hub   2 Oil seal
3 Inner bearing   4 Outer bearing   5 Castellated hub nut
6 Hub cap

FIG 9:4 Disconnecting hydraulic brake hose to front brake

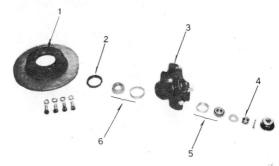

FIG 9:5 Exploded view of disc pattern wheel hub assembly

Key to Fig 9:5   1 Brake disc   2 Oil seal
3 Wheel hub   4 Castellated hub nut   5 Outer bearing
6 Inner bearing

9:3 Inspection and reassembly

Examine all parts for signs of damage or wear and replace as necessary. Discard the oil seal and obtain a new one. Check that the threads on the wheel supporting studs are in good condition and, if not, replace the hub. Examine the stub axle for signs of corrosion or out-of-truth. If either are present, the complete strut and shock absorber will have to be changed.

When all parts have passed inspection and spares obtained, reassemble in the reverse order, packing the bearings and hub cavities with MP2 or MP3 grease. Reinstall the oil seal, lightly grease the stub axle, partly to facilitate assembly and partly as protection against rusting in service, then fit the hub on to the axle and replace nut and washer.

Tighten the nut to a torque of 25 lb ft, oscillating the hub on the axle meanwhile, then turn the nut back about 90 degrees (a quarter of a turn) and fit the cotterpin. Replace the cap.

9:4 Hub with disc brakes

On the cars where disc brakes are fitted and the hub is integral with the brake disc, a slight modified dismantling procedure is necessitated.

First, disconnect the hydraulic brake hose at the position shown in **FIG 9:4** and then unbolt and remove the calipers. The hub nut can then be extracted and the hub dismantled as in the previous section. If necessary, the disc can be unbolted from the hub spider for resurfacing. The dismantled assembly then appears as in **FIG 9:5**.

When reassembling, tighten the disc-to-hub nuts to a torque of 38 lb ft and the caliper fixing bolts to 70 lb ft. Check that the bolts securing the brake backplate in position (and which do not need removing in this operation) are tightened to a torque of 27 lb ft. Adjust the hub nut as already described and check the brake disc, after assembly, for runout. Adjust as necessary.

9:5 Dismantling spring and strut assembly

With the car raised on stands, remove the wheels, hubs, brake drums or discs and backplate. Loosen and remove the two bolts securing the tension rod to the link arm, then

FIG 9:6 Unbolting the strut from the steering arm

FIG 9:7 Removing nuts securing the strut upper mount to the body structure

FIG 9:8 Removing the strut assembly from the front underside of the car

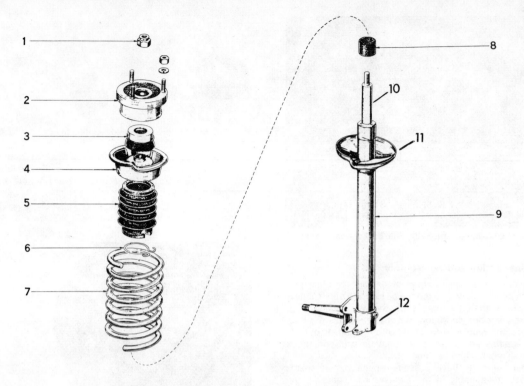

FIG 9:9   Exploded view of the suspension strut and shock absorber

Key to Fig 9:9   1 Self-locking nut   2 Elastic bearing mount   3 Thrust bearing   4 Upper spring seat   5 Rubber boot
6 Boot clip   7 Coil suspension spring   8 Bump rubber   9 Shock absorber   10 Piston   11 Lower spring seat
12 Stub axle and mount

unbolt and detach the steering knuckle from the foot of the strut (see **FIG 9:6**).

Raise the bonnet and from within the engine compartment sidemembers remove the three nuts securing the upper strut mount (see **FIG 9:7**) while taking the weight of the strut from underneath on a jack or other support. Lower the strut carefully, easing it clear of the link arm, and transfer to the bench (see **FIG 9:8**).

Compress the spring (a special tool ST49100000 has been designed for the purpose) and remove the self-

locking nut at the top of the assembly (1 in **FIG 9:9**). Remove the boot clip 6 from the lower end of the boot, release the spring pressure and extract the suspension mount 2, thrust bearing 3 and upper spring seat 4, with boot 5 attached. Remove the bumper rubber 8 from the piston rod 10. Remove the spring 7 from the lower spring seat 11.

Thoroughly clean all parts, making sure that all gritty particles have been removed, and dry. If it is required to renew the hydraulic fluid in the shock absorber, a special

FIG 9:10   Removing gland nut from the strut assembly

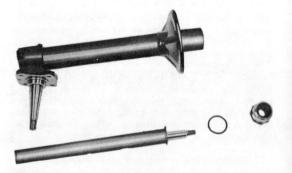

FIG 9:11   Exploded view of shock absorber showing outer casing with hub assembly, inner piston and cylinder, O-ring and gland nut

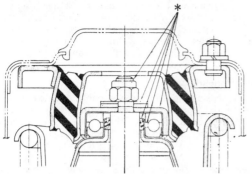

FIG 9:12 Section view through strut top mount showing live rubber support bush and thrust bearing with grease application points indicated by an asterisk

FIG 9:13 Removal of transverse link showing the mounting bush and nut assembly at 1

gland packing wrench will be required. This bears the tool number ST49130000 (see **FIG 9:10**).

Holding the strut upright, remove the packing gland at the top, first compressing the piston into the strut to enable the wrench to go over it on to the nut. Extract the O-ring from above the piston rod guide then extract the piston rod and cylinder assembly by pulling the piston rod upwards slowly (see **FIG 9:11**).

The shock absorber comprises a piston and cylinder housed within an outer casing with the annular space between cylinder and casing acting as the hydraulic reservoir. Both piston and cylinder incorporate special foot valves and it is not intended that the piston/cylinder assembly shall be dismantled further. Otherwise the two valves may be disturbed with adverse consequences to the efficient operation of the device. Do not therefore, attempt to break down the shock absorber, apart from removing the piston/cylinder assembly from the casing.

Drain the reservoir completely and dispose of the fluid. Wash all parts in petrol or carbon tetrachloride and dry off. Reinsert the piston/cylinder assembly carefully into the casing and fill the space between casing and cylinder with the correct amount of shock absorber oil obtained from the local Datsun agent. **It is important to use both the right grade and quantity of oil or performance will be affected.** For all saloon models other

that the 1300 cc standard saloon and the SSS, insert exactly 300 cc of oil. For estate cars, insert 325 cc and for the standard saloon and SSS, insert 290 cc.

Place a new O-ring on top if the piston rod guide and refit the oil seal and gland packing. Raise the piston by about 3½ inches and tighten the gland nut to a torque of 47 lb ft. To bleed the shock absorber, hold the strut upside down and pull the piston out steadily to its fullest extent. Reverse the strut and push the piston in. Repeat for about five times and check that the resistance to pull and push of the piston is about the same.

Clean and examine the thrust bearing and renew the self-locking nut and check the condition of the live rubber mount (see **FIG 9:12**). **If the rubber boot is perished, replace this too.**

The strut assembly may now be rebuilt in reverse order to dismantling and inserted in position in the car. Do not forget to fit the bump rubber on the piston rod before positioning the upper spring seat. Tighten the self-locking nut to a torque of 54 lb ft, applying MP2 or MP3 grease to the points indicated in **FIG 9:12**.

Tighten the three nuts securing the mount to the chassis to a torque of 37 lb ft and the two bolts securing the lower end to the steering arm to a torque of 58 lb ft. The nuts securing the tension rod to the link arm must be tightened to a torque of 45 lb ft.

FIG 9:14 Underside of transverse link showing, at 1, the bolts securing the ball joint assembly

FIG 9:15 Another view of the underside showing the tension rod 1, stabilizer arm and mounting bracket 2, link arm 3 and ball joint nuts 4

FIG 9:16 Installation of tension rod showing the elastic mount 1, on the chassis and two securing bolts 2, on the link arm

FIG 9:17 Position of the securing bolts and lockplate on the crossmember attaching it to the chassis

9:6 Transverse link

The transverse link is secured to the crossmember on a rubber bushed pin with a self-locking nut (see FIG 9:13). Before installing the strut, disconnect the link from the stabilizer bar at the upper end of the pillar and remove the link for closer examination both as regards its own condition and the condition of the ball joint. The latter is a sealed unit secured to the steering knuckle and to the transverse link, in the former by a tapered ball stud and nut and in the latter by two bolts (see FIG 9:14). Either of these can be disconnected to release the transverse link from the steering assembly.

Inspect the transverse link for distortion or cracks and the rubber bushes at the mounting pin and the stabilizer pillar. Examine the ball joint and replace if necessary. Reassemble in the reverse order tightening the self-locking nut (a new one) to a torque of 98 lb ft at the crossmember and to a torque of 12 lb ft at the stabilizer rod. When fitting the ball joint, tighten the nuts shown in FIG 9:14, to 18 lb ft.

9:7 Stabilizer bar

The stabilizer bar is connected to the front underside of the body in two rubber bushed brackets and terminates in rubber insulated eyebolt connections at the upper end of the two pillars on the transverse links. Should it be suspected that the bar has become twisted, dismantle it from the car and check on a level surface. When reassembling, tighten the bracket nuts to a torque of 18 lb ft (the bracket is clearly discernible in FIG 9:15) and to the vertical pillar to a torque of 12 lb ft.

9:8 Tension rod

The tension rod is threaded at one end for insertion in the bushed bracket on the chassis underframe (see FIG 9:16) and terminates at the other in a two-hole mounting end for attachment to the tension rod adjacent to the strut mounting. When dismantling the bracket end, note carefully the arrangement of washers and bushings and reassemble in similar order on completion. The tension rods must not be bent between the bracket and the mounting end and must be free from corrosion, rust or damage.

When reinstalling, the bracket end nut is torqued to 70 lb ft and the two smaller nuts at the link end to 45 lb ft.

9:9 Suspension member

The suspension crossmember should not need dismantling unless it has been dislodged or bent in an accident. Complete replacement is then necessary. Since the crossmember also supports the engine, it is necessary to suspend the engine on a chain within the front compartment while unbolting and removing the member. In addition, the transverse links must be disconnected from the end pins. The engine support mounting bolts can then be removed and, finally, the bolts securing the crossmember to the body (see FIG 9:17). When replacing, see that the holes go easily over the mounting studs, fit the locking plates and then tighten the nuts to a torque of 18 lb ft and the engine mounting bolts to a torque of 12 lb ft.

9:10 Reassembling the suspension

Reassembly is a straightforward procedure which needs no special instructions. Observe the torque loadings at the various points already mentioned and be careful to ensure that the parts go together without forcing. If they do not line up perfectly, check for faulty fitting on one component or other rather than attempt to deform or deflect the part or parts to secure attachment. Alignment of the front wheels after assembly is dealt with in Chapter 10.

9:1 Fault diagnosis

(a) Instability of steering

1 Tyre pressures too high
2 Faulty shock absorbers
3 Slack hub nut
4 Loose wheel nuts

(b) Car sways on cornering

1 Faulty shock absorber
2 Worn tension bar bushing

(c) Front of car not level

1 Faulty spring
2 Tyres unevenly inflated
3 Slow puncture on one side
4 Uneven loading of car

(d) Heavy on steering

1 Tyre pressures too low
   See also Fault Diagnosis section in Chapter 10.

CHAPTER 10

STEERING GEAR

10:1 Description

The steering gear is of the worm and nut pattern with recirculating balls as the link between the nut and the worm of the steering shaft within the steering column. The principle of recirculating balls is that the balls travel between grooves in the nut and in the worm as the worm rotates, the drive being taken as a shear across the balls between the drive and driven faces at a shallow angle dependent upon the difference between the radius of the balls and that of the grooves in which they are travelling. In the theoretically perfect mechanism in which the radii are identical and the clearance between the nut and the worm infinitely small, the shear would be across the balls parallel to the line of motion. In the practical application, the clearances are designed to give the best compromise between low friction drive and near-parallel shear.

The second feature of the recirculating ball mechanism is that, at the end of each complete turn, a ball will have moved one worm pitch away from its original position in the nut. Therefore, whether it be a single or multiple thread engagement, the balls must be disengaged from the thread and returned to the beginning of the groove in the nut by an external channel. In the present application, this transfer takes place in guide tubes clamped to one side of the nut and ball assembly which contains 58 balls in all. Of

these, the thrust is taken by 36 in and around the shaft, the remaining 22 being in transit through the guide tubes. Those in the guide tubes, of course, take no thrust during transition.

Lateral movement of the nut along the worm is transferred to a steering lever arm via a rocker shaft, the upper end of which embodies a toothed sector meshing with a rack on the side of the nut. The end of the lever arm is linked to the track rod, the opposing end of which is supported on a parallel relay arm. Adjustable link arms couple the ends of the track rod to the steering arms on the front hub assemblies (see **FIG 10:1**). Adjustable stops on the two hub steering arms limit the amount of turn as they are contacted by a stop plate welded to the side of each link arm.

The two-spoke steering wheel with horn bar and ring is secured to the top of the steering shaft by splines and a steering wheel nut. On the steering column is clamped a shell enclosing the direction and lighting control switch and, on the cars fitted with the three-speed gear or automatic transmission, the gear selector lever and control rod is also connected to and supported by the steering column.

The steering circle at full lock is 31 ft and the transition from lock to lock is effected by three full turns of the steering wheel.

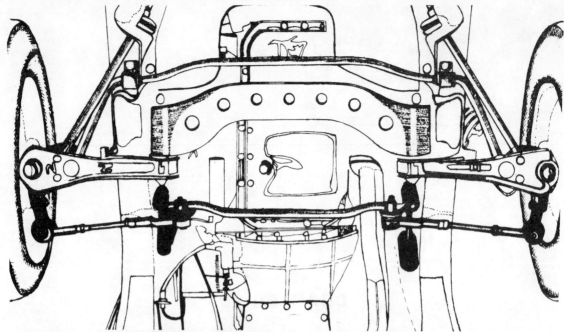

FIG 10:1　General view of steering linkage as seen from beneath the car

FIG 10:2　Removing the steering wheel nut

FIG 10:3　Removing the indicator and lighting switch from the steering column

10:2 Maintenance

Since all the ball joint assemblies are lubricated for life, routine maintenance is confined to a regular check of tightness of all nuts and bolts, checking the level of the oil in the steering box, the alignment of the steering and the condition of the rubber boots over the ball joints. Unless steering irregularities give rise to a suspicion that something is worn or loose, this maintenance check need only be done at the normal 6000 mile service.

10:3 Removing steering box and column

To remove the steering box and column, first disconnect the battery to enable the direction and lighting switch to be removed safely. Remove the horn bar and ring by depressing the centre and rotating the bar slightly anticlockwise to disengage it from the locking plate. The bar can then be lifted out.

Unloose and remove the steering wheel locknut. A special tool, ST46430000 is available for this purpose. Next, remove the steering column shell by removing the four clamping screws, remove the locating and fixing screws from the lighting switch unit and slip it clear over the head of the column (see **FIGS 10:2** and **10:3**).

If the car is fitted with column gearchange, either three-speed or automatic, unclamp and remove the top bracket (see **FIG 10:4**) and tie out of the way. Extract the two bolts securing the column support bracket to the instrument panel (see **FIG 10:5**).

At the foot of the column, remove the four bolts securing the bottom coverplate and remove the plate. Disconnect any gear linkages to the control column and remove the column (see **FIG 10:6**).

Disconnect the steering arm lever from the track rod using a proper extractor to pull the ball stud out of the lever

FIG 10:4 Removing the column change upper bracket from the steering column showing 1, the circlip, 2 and 3, the clamp nut and bolt

FIG 10:5 Position of the bolts securing the upper column bracket to the instrument panel

socket after removing the castellated nut and washer. **Do not hammer the lever or ball stud.**

From beneath the car, remove the three bolts securing the steering gearbox mounting plate to the body and ease the complete steering column out of the car from beneath.

10:4 Dismantling the steering box

Thoroughly clean the exterior of the steering box, remove the oil filler plug and drain the box of oil. Using a suitable puller, remove the steering nut and arm from the rocker shaft. Loosen the adjusting screw locknut and turn the screw a couple of turns in a counter-clockwise direction. Remove the cover fixing bolts and pull clear. The rocker shaft will come away with the cover until, when clear of the entry, the adjusting screw head can be slipped sideways out of the slot (see **FIG 10:7**). Extract the rocker shaft.

Remove the three bolts securing the steering column flange to the steering box and slide clear of the steering shaft. Carefully preserve the shims interposed between the flange and box. Extract the shaft with recirculating nut assembly in place (see **FIG 10:8**).

Note that the thread on the shaft, unlike many other similar types of steering mechanism, has a 'blind' end to

the worm (see **FIG 10:9**) and the nut cannot, therefore, be removed from the shaft simply by unscrewing. **To attempt to do so will damage the assembly.**

Remove the ball races from each end of steering column worm section and, from the steering box, extract the oil seal and, if necessary, the needle bearings for the rocker arm which are a press-fit in the housing. **Do not remove unless necessary.**

Holding the shaft and nut over a receptacle to catch the balls, remove the clamps holding the transfer tubes in place and extract the tubes. Empty the balls retained in the tube and check that there are eleven $\frac{1}{4}$ inch balls in each tube. Turning the nut rack face upwards, oscillate the shaft within the nut until all the balls have fallen out into the receptacle and check that 36 balls are present. Extract the shaft from the nut. The complete assembly should then include all the component parts shown in **FIG 10:10**.

Thoroughly clean all parts free from grease and examine for signs of wear. Clean out the interior of the housing with paraffin and repack the needle bearing with grease. If the bearing outer rings are in any way damaged in the steering column flange housing or in the opposing end of the box, extract and fit a new bearing, including the ball races. Should the worm track be worn or damaged, replace the steering shaft. Examine the nut, particularly at the points of entry and exit to and from the transfer tubes and replace nut and/or tubes as necessary.

FIG 10:6 Position of the bolts securing the steering column foot plate to the floor

FIG 10:7 Removing the steering box coverplate showing, arrowed, the slot in the rocker shaft end

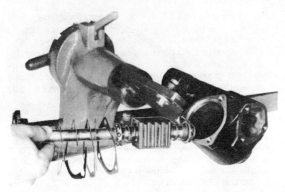

FIG 10:8 Dismantling the worm and nut from the steering box

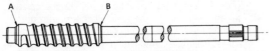

FIG 10:9 Detail of steering worm showing the blind end ball thread and bearing seatings at A and B

10:5 Reassembly and installation

Commence reassembly by reinstalling the nut on the steering shaft worm section. Positioning the nut centrally on the worm section with the holes upwards, insert the 36 balls in the holes, one at a time in each hole alternately, slightly oscillating the shaft meanwhile. This is facilitated if the balls are slightly oiled but as the column of balls within the nut extend, the balls may need slight pressure to force them in.

Grease the remaining balls in vaseline and insert them into the two transfer tubes until both are full. The presence of the vaseline should hold them in place while the tubes are fitted to the nut and clamped into position. There should be a clearance of about .02 inch between the underside of the transfer tubes and the nut when in position. Rotate the nut up and down the worm with a little oil on the threads but not too close to the ends of the worm. Check for end play on the shaft. This should be barely noticeable.

Reassemble the steering column in the steering box with the original shims, bearings and O-rings, tightening the studs to a torque of 18 lb ft. Check the turning torque on the shaft as a measure of the preload on the ballbearings. This should be not less than 60, nor more than 120 oz inch. A convenient means of determining this is to fit the steering wheel temporarily and measuring the torque with a spring balance hooked to the spoke, the torque to produce movement being the product of the radius from the centre of the wheel to the hooking point and the reading of the spring balance in ozs (see **FIG 10:11**). If the torque is outside these limits, adjust the shims between the column flange and the box. Four thicknesses of shim are inserted, .002, .005, .010 and .030 inch.

Next, reassemble the rocker shaft and sector in position, adjusting the worm and nut so that the nut is central and the sector teeth are at mid position (see **FIG 10:12**). Fit a new oil seal at the lower end. Remove the adjusting screw from the cover and check the play in the head groove of the rocker shaft when the original shim washer is inserted. This should be not greater than .001 inch, measured with a feeler gauge inserted below the head of the adjuster. If more, fit another shim washer. Insert the adjusting screw in position, lower the rocker shaft into the housing, properly centred, and replace the cover, screwing the adjusting nut in as the cover is lowered into place.

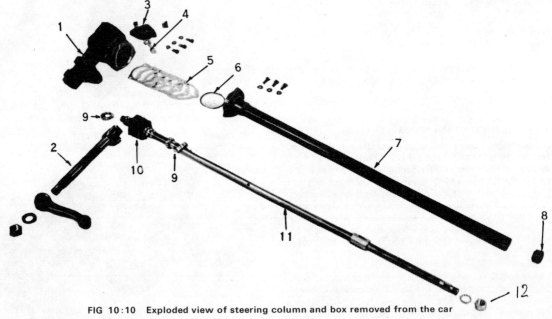

FIG 10:10 Exploded view of steering column and box removed from the car

Key to Fig 10:10   1 Steering box   2 Rocker shaft   3 Coverplate   4 Adjusting screw   5 Shims   6 O-ring
7 Steering column   8 Upper end bearing   9 Ballraces   10 Worm and nut   11 Steering shaft   12 Steering wheel nut

At the opposite end of the rocker shaft, reinstall the steering arm checking that it is positioned correctly by means of the alignment marks on arm and shaft. Check that the movement is smooth as the arm is moved from side to side by rotation of the shaft.

Using a dial gauge, measure the backlash on the end of the steering arm at the centre and each end of its travel and adjust by means of the adjusting screw in the cover. **From FIG 10 : 12, it will be seen that, as the teeth of the nut and those on the centre are inclined slightly to the axis of the rocker shaft, end-to-end movement by the adjusting screw brings the two parts into or out of close mesh, so adjusting rotational play on the shaft.**

When adjusted, fit the locknut, holding the adjusting screw against rotation meanwhile with a screwdriver, and then screw the adjuster in one-eighth of a turn and tighten the locknut to 15 lb ft.

Fill the gearbox with ½ pint of SAE.90 oil and install the filler plug.

Reinstall the steering gearbox and column in the car in the reverse order to dismantling, greasing the bearing at the top of the column before finally fitting the steering wheel.

10 : 6 Dismantling the steering linkage

First, jack up the front of the car on stands and chock the rear wheels securely. Remove the cotterpin and castellated nuts from the ball stud bearings at the two ends of each link arm and pull the studs out with a suitable puller. **Do not hammer.**

The link arms can then be detached but mark them so that they will go back on the same sides as they were originally. Free the track rod from the steering box arm and from the relay lever, then unbolt and remove the relay lever from the body underframe.

Examine all parts for rust or corrosion after cleaning, and check that the track rod is not bent and that the side rods are undistorted. Replace as necessary. A slightly bent track rod may be straightened in a press but if the distortion is at all severe, replace as a matter of safety.

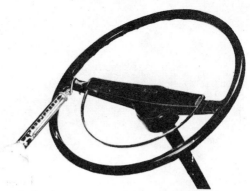

FIG 10 : 11   Checking wheel turning torque with spring balance

Examine the ball joints for smooth operation and freedom from play and, if necessary, replace the protective rubber boots. **Do not attempt to service a ball joint by trying to dismantle it. Fit a new balljoint if in doubt as to its condition.**

Examine the idler arm assembly (see **FIG 10 : 13**) and, if the torsion rubber bushing is hard or swollen, fit a new bushing using soapy water as a lubricant for facilitating entry into the housing.

Reassemble and reinstall in the car, checking that the two link arms are exactly the same length (12.185 inches) between centres initially. After assembly in the car, centre the steering before finally tightening the idler arm nut to a torque of 55 lb ft. The tightening torque for the steering arm to track rod bearing nut is 100 lb ft; that for the side arm bearing nuts is 55 lb ft.

10 : 7 Front wheel alignment

The full process of alignment comprises the setting of castor, camber, inclination and toe-in. The first three are not adjustable being inherent in the front suspension design. However, it is advisable to check them occasionally as any drift from the design setting can be attributable to

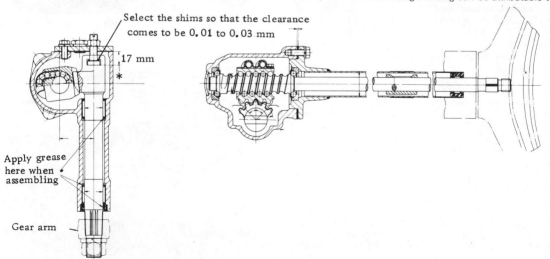

FIG 10 : 12   Sectional views of steering box showing position on nut and rocker shaft gear for straight-ahead position

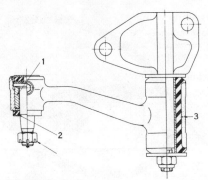

FIG 10:13 Detail section of relay lever showing, 1 nylon bushing, 2 dust cover and 3 rubber bush

FIG 10:14 Use of gauge for setting toe-in on front wheels

other factors. The tests need special equipment usually available only at a Datsun agents workshop. The tests have to be carried out on level ground, with the tyres correctly inflated and the car unladen.

Castor angle is that at which the pivoting axis of the front suspension is inclined from the vertical. Inclination rearwards is termed positive castor and inclination forwards is termed negative castor. The castor angle for the Datsun is 1 degree 40 minutes for the saloons and 2 degrees for the estate cars, both positive. If the garage check shows that the angle is outside these limits, check the stabilizer bar is not distorted and that the clamps are tight.

Camber angle is that at which the vertical centre line of the road wheel, viewed from the front, is inclined from the true vertical. Inclination outwards at the top is termed positive camber and inclination inwards is termed negative camber. On the 1300 cc saloon, the camber is 1 degree 30 minutes, on other saloons, 1 degree and on the estate cars 1 degree 10 minutes.

These two are, to some extent, interdependent. If the inclination is correct but the camber is outside limits, check the stub axles for distortion. If the camber angle is within limits but the inclination is out, examine the state of the link arms and the bearings at either end.

Toe-in, the angle made by the fore and aft centre lines of the wheels with the centre line of the car is adjustable and must be set to .2 inch on estate cars, .3 inch on saloons other than the 1300 cc and .4 inch on the 1300. That is to say, the distance between the tyre centres, with the steering set straight-ahead, must be .2 to .4 inch less than between the same two points with the wheel rotated through half a circle. This is determined by a gauge set between the two front wheels (see FIG 10:14). The adjustment is made by altering the length equally of the two link arms, the centre section of which is provided with left and righthand threads at opposite ends so that by turning it without disconnecting the ends, the effective length can be altered. Always tighten the locknuts after setting (see FIG 10:15).

The final adjustment is the lock limit, the function of which is to ensure that at extreme lock in either direction the tyre walls will not bear on the inner sides of the wheel housings. The stop is the head of a stud on the boss of the hub steering arms and it is set to bear on the stop plate welded to the suspension transverse link arms. Because of the design of the steering arms, the wheel on the outer side of the turning circle at full lock is not turned to as sharp an angle as that on the inner side and the stops are set to limit the angle of the outer wheel in either direction. On the Datsun, this is set to 23 degrees ± .5 degree from the fore and aft line. This automatically gives a limit of 39 degrees on the inner side.

To set the angle, use a scaled turntable under each wheel (see FIG 10:16).

FIG 10:15 Position of steering link arms and locknuts

FIG 10:16 Use of turntable to set wheel lock limit

10:8 Fault diagnosis

(a) Loose steering

1 Slack front wheel bearings
2 Faulty ballpin joints
3 Play in steering box mounting
4 Play in worm and nut adjustment

(b) Heavy steering

1 Seized shaft in relay or steering box
2 Low oil level in steering box

(c) Steering wander

1 Loose hub nuts
2 Excessive play in steering linkage
3 Loose ballpin joints

(d) Wander to one side

1 Toe-in out of setting
2 Uneven tyre pressures
3 Uneven tyre wear

(e) Excessive tread wear

1 Lock limit wrongly set (tyre wall rubbing)
2 Wrong toe-in
3 Tyre pressures too low

CHAPTER 11

THE BRAKING SYSTEM

11:1 Description

The braking system is hydraulic, operating on drum brakes at rear and front on early cars except the 1600 which has disc brakes on the front wheels. Later cars of both sizes are fitted with disc front brakes. The cable-operated handbrake applies the rear brakes only. The drum brakes on the front wheels incorporate two leading brake shoes while those on the rear wheels have one leading and one trailing brake shoe. The brake drums are 9 inches internal diameter all round but, where disc brakes are fitted to the front wheels, a larger diameter brake cylinder is incorporated in the rear brakes.

The pendant brake pedal operates directly on the master cylinder, which is equipped with its own reservoir, and also mechanically operates the brake light switch. The handbrake handle, mounted below the facia panel, is of the pull type, applying leverage to a Bowden cable which, in turn is linked to equalizing gear mounted centrally beneath the car body.

11:2 Servicing and maintenance

Servicing is confined to regular checks of brake fluid level in the reservoirs, topping-up with the correct fluid as necessary. The specified brake fluid is SAE.70.R3 and this includes a wide range of proprietary heavy duty brake fluids (Shell Donax B, Esso 400, Catraulic HD etc.). As a general rule, find out the fluid installed at the last brake overhaul and top up with the same make and grade. It is not advisable to change the grade unless the system has been completely emptied of the old fluid. While some of different name may be mixed without harm, the odd one may introduce some factor which will, in time, result in deterioration of the fluid or have adverse affect on the seals.

Routine maintenance covers, in addition, the checking of brake pads and shoes for wear, checking discs and drums for grooving, inspecting hydraulic lines and hoses, master and brake cylinder connections and checking for fluid leaks at the periods set down in the owners service handbook, renewing worn parts as necessary.

The hydraulic brakes are not self-adjusting for shoe lining or pad wear so, at regular intervals, adjustment of both rear and front wheels is necessary. As soon as it becomes evident that the depression of the foot pedal to achieve proper braking is excessive, or the handbrake has to be pulled far out to hold the car on a slight gradient, a check of brake adjustment is essential in the interests of road safety. The procedure is outlined in **Section 11:13**.

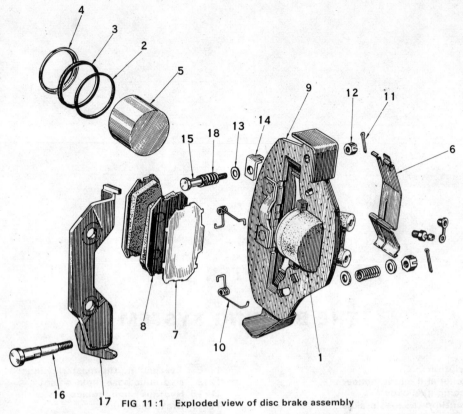

FIG 11:1 Exploded view of disc brake assembly

Key to Fig 11:1   1 Cylinder   2 Piston seal   3 Wiper seal   4 Retainer   5 Piston   6 Clip   7 Shim   8 Pad
9 Caliper plate   10 Torsion spring   11 Cotterpin   12 Nut   13 Washer   14 Bracket   15 Retainer pin   16 Pivot
pin   17 Mounting bracket   18 Spring

11:3 Replacing disc pads

To replace worn front disc brake pads, raise the front of the car on stands and remove the wheels. Study the exploded view of the brake assembly (see **FIG 11:1**) to familiarise yourself with the component parts and then proceed as follows.

First, remove the retaining pins and clips (see **FIG 11:2**) shown in the exploded view at 11 and 6. Slacken the bleed screw a turn then pull the caliper plate 9 away from the chassis to loosen the outer pad by depressing the outer piston 5 into the cylinder 1. With a pair of long-nosed pliers, grip the pad and withdraw sufficiently to extract with the fingers (see **FIG 11:3**). Repeat with the inner

FIG 11:2 Removing pad securing clip and pin

FIG 11:3 Extracting outer pad from disc brake

FIG 11:4 Disconnecting the hydraulic brake hose

FIG 11:5 Removing the caliper assembly from the front wheel

pad. Insert new brake pads into position, after cleaning the surfaces of the cylinders free from dirt or grease and checking that the old pads are not greasy or that there are any traces of grease on the discs, and secure with the original shims 7, clip and retaining pin.

Note carefully the way round that the pads are inserted. They are thicker at one end than the other and the assembly is mounted on the brake backplate at an angle to the disc faces. Always change all four pads at the same time and use only the correct grade, M78S, part No. 41060/70.16508 as supplied by the agent.

Tighten the bleed screws with the pedal depressed and then pump the pedal a couple of strokes to refresh the line.

Now depress the pedal to bring the pads into contact with the disc and check that the pads are free to move slightly and that the pins are not fouling the pads.

When both front wheels have been serviced, recheck the level of fluid in the reservoir and top up as necessary.

11:4 Dismantling the disc brakes

To dismantle the disc brakes for complete overhaul, raise the car on stands and remove the road wheels. Plug the reservoir outlet in the brake master cylinder, then unscrew and remove the front brake hose, capping it to prevent the ingress of dirt until reinstallation (see **FIG 11:4**).

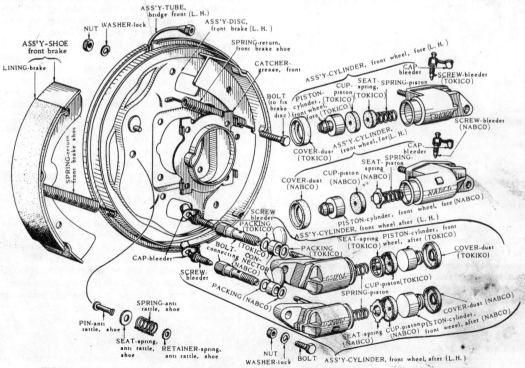

FIG 11:6 Exploded view of front wheel drum brake. Note the alternative cylinder assemblies

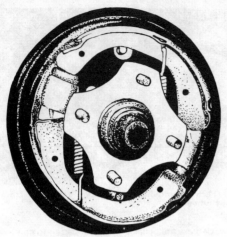

FIG 11:7 General view of assembled drum brake on front wheel

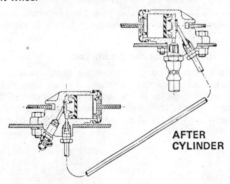

AFTER CYLINDER

FORE CYLINDER

FIG 11:8 Sectional view of fore and aft cylinders on drum brakes

Remove the two bolts securing the caliper assembly to the backplate and extract the caliper assembly (see **FIG 11:5**). Examine the faces of the disc for grooving or surface grease and check with a dial gauge for runout. Light grooving or scoring can be tolerated but heavy grooving will necessitate resurfacing or replacement. If any grease is present on the faces, locate the source and rectify.

On the bench, commence the dismantling of the caliper assembly after thoroughly cleaning the exterior. Remove the pin and clip and extract pads and shim. Remove cotter-pin 11 from the bracket retaining pin 17 and unscrew the nut 12. Extract pin, spring 18, washer 13 and retainer bracket 14. At the lower end of the bracket, remove cotter-pin, nut, spring and washers and extract the pivot pin 16. The mounting bracket 17 is then free from the assembly.

Ease the two torsion springs 10 from the seating on the cylinder 1 and extract from the holes in the caliper plate 9. The position of these when installed can be seen clearly in **FIG 11:3**. The cylinder can then be removed from the caliper plate. The piston 5 can be expelled from the cylinder by judiciously applying air pressure to the fluid inlet port. Extract the two seals and the retainer 2, 3 and 4.

The function of the piston seal 2, which is mounted in a groove in the inside wall of the cylinder is twofold. The first is that of rendering the piston and cylinder assembly proof against leakage of hydraulic fluid. The second is to act as a sprag on piston movement. Initial movement, of the order required to apply full braking pressure, is taken by distortion of the ring which returns to normal when the pressure is released the contact area between the ring and piston not being disturbed. As the pad wears, the movement to apply braking pressure exceeds the limits of distortion and the piston slides forward on the seal which takes up a new position. On release of the braking pressure, the ring, on recovery, with-draws the piston just clear of the pads, the wear on the pad faces now having been taken up by slightly increased fluid content in the cylinder. In this manner, the brakes are rendered self-adjusting as the pad thicknesses decrease.

11:5 Inspection and reassembling the disc brakes

Thoroughly clean all parts in brake fluid. **Do not use any other cleaning fluid or the seals may be impaired.** Examine all parts for signs of wear, distortion or damage. Check the condition of the cylinder assembly and replace if necessary. Should there be evidence of seal wear but the surfaces of both piston and cylinder walls are polished and free from abrasions, the three parts (two seals and retainer ring) can be renewed.

Rinse the cylinder bore with fluid and carefully insert the piston seal into the groove in the cylinder wall. Be careful not to damage it and then attach the wiper seal. Insert the piston without tilting it and refit the retainer. Next, push the piston home until the rim of the piston is almost flush with the retainer and reinstall it into the caliper plate securing it in position with the two torsion springs. Reinstall the bracket retaining pin, bracket, spring and nut, securing it with the cotterpin. Fit the mounting bracket into position by means of the pivot pin at the lower end and by lipping the upper end under the retaining bracket, which can be raised by means of a screwdriver against the spring pressure for the purpose. Check that the mounting bracket can slide, within limits, under the bracket around the pivot pin.

Install the caliper assembly in position on the backplate tightening the bolts to a torque of 27 lb ft. Attach a shim 7 to the rear face of the inner pad and, holding the two together and the caliper plate away from the disc, insert the pad, thick end down, into position between the piston and the disc.

Rock the assembly over on the pivot pin to provide the clearance between the rear of the disc and the caliper plate for insertion of the second pad and slip this into place. Reinstall the clip and pin.

Reconnect the hydraulic hose, slacken the bleed screw and pump the brake pedal until fluid begins to weep from the bleed screw. Carry out the bleeding procedure as described in **Section 11:11**.

Refit the road wheels and lower the car to the ground.

11:6 Dismantling drum brakes

Raise the vehicle on stands and remove the road wheels. Disconnect the hydraulic hose and plug the hydraulic line.

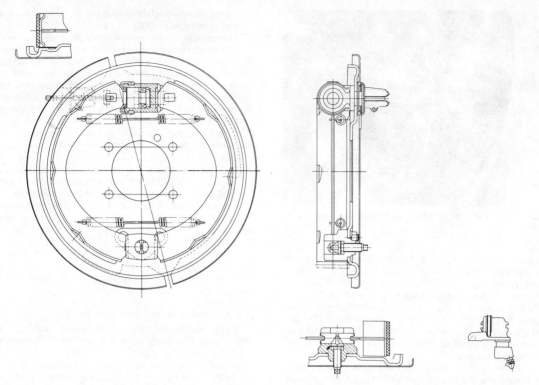

FIG 11:9   Diagrammatic presentation of rear drum brake assembly showing, bottom right, detail of brake adjuster unit

On the rear brakes, disconnect the handbrake cables by removing the clevis pins. **On the front wheels,** remove the hub assembly (see **Chapter 9, Section 9:2**). On all four, remove the brake drums.

Dealing first with the front brakes (an exploded view of which is shown in **FIG 11:6**) remove the short hydraulic connection between the two brake cylinders at the rear of the mounting plate, then unhook the two return springs from the brake shoes. The brake shoes can now be extracted from the assembly. **Note which is the upper and which is the lower shoe for replacement later (see FIG 11:7).** On some brakes, an anti-rattle pin and spring will be fitted which links each shoe to the mounting plate with a cushioning spring between. This is visible in the exploded view but is not fitted in **FIG 11:7**. Where fitted, this must be released before the shoes can be extracted and must be replaced on reassembly.

Unbolt and remove the two brake cylinders, again noting the positions for reassembly. **Alternative makes of brake cylinder are fitted to Datsun cars, both of which are shown in FIG 11:6. The cylinders are identified by the name, NABCO or TOKICO, on their exterior and the component parts differ slightly from each other. While the complete assemblies are interchangeable, the component parts are not. If, therefore, any difficulty is experienced in getting replacement components, replace the whole brake cylinder assembly.**

Brush the brake drums and the backplate free from dust and dirt and check that the adjusting cams are free to rotate in their bearings. If any grease or brake fluid is

FIG 11:10   Exploded view of rear drum brake with component parts

FIG 11:11 Position of brake adjusting cams on front brake

present, locate the source and rectify. Examine the return springs and replace if distorted, weak or rusted. Examine the shoe linings and check the thickness. If the thickness is less than .06 inch, replace the shoes. Though it is possible to reline existing brake shoes, it is more economic to obtain a replacement set from the agents and return the old shoes. Moreover, it ensures that the correct grade of brake lining is installed. The linings are bonded, and not riveted to the shoes.

If the lining thickness is satisfactory but the surfaces are greasy, clean with carbon tetrachloride and locate and rectify the cause.

Check the interior surfaces of the brake drum and, if heavily scored, or if the drums are not perfectly round, set up in a lathe and skim the interior surfaces. The skim should be as light as possible and if, after skimming, the internal diameter exceeds 9.04 inch, replace the drum.

At the bench, remove the dust covers from the ends of the brake cylinders and extract the pistons, cups and springs. Wash in brake fluid and examine for scoring or corrosion marks. The surfaces of the piston and cylinder interior should be almost mirror finish. Reassemble with new cups and covers. If there is any doubt as to the condition of the assembly, replace by a new assembly. A

sectional view through both fore and aft front wheel brake cylinders is shown in FIG 11:8.

Dismantling the rear wheel brake assemblies is similar apart from the fact that only one brake cylinder is involved. The lower ends of the brake shoes bear on the adjuster which comprises two slotted cam plates separated by a coned expander adjusted from the rear of the mounting plate (see FIG 1:9). This is secured to the mounting plate by two nuts while the brake cylinder is free to move in a slot at the upper end where it is retained by spring plates. This ensures that the braking force is applied equally between the two shoes irrespective of the wear on the linings.

To remove the brake cylinder, first extract the dust cover surrounding the handbrake lever and hydraulic fluid entry, then slide the slotted plates and shims away from their positions around the brake cylinder. The latter can be extracted through the hole in the cover, the handbrake lever and pin being released at the same time. The dismantled assembly appears as in FIG 11:10.

After cleaning, inspecting and making such replacements as are necessary (the procedure has already been outlined in previous paragraphs for the front brakes) reassemble and reinstall in the reverse order.

11:7 Reassembling the drum brakes

While reassembly of the drum brakes, both rear and front, should present little difficulty after dismantling, certain points require particular attention in order that the brakes should work effectively immediately on completion.

Dealing first with front brakes, note carefully which is the fore and which is the aft cylinder and check that they are inserted the right way round into the holes on the mounting plate. In the exploded view, the forward cylinder is shown uppermost (see FIG 11:6) whereas in the photograph (see FIG 11:7) it is shown to the left. A brief comparison with the latter illustration should remove any doubt as to whether the assembly is being made correctly. The hydraulic hose to the brake is connected to the forward cylinder and the bleeding is effected from the nipple in the rear cylinder. The short interconnecting tube, shown appearing over the top of the mounting plate in the exploded view, is connected between the remaining two unions as indicated in FIG 11:8.

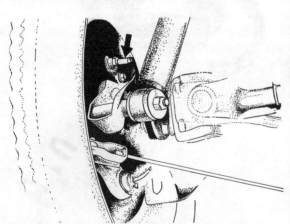

FIG 11:12 Position of brake adjuster on rear wheels for saloon left, and estate cars, right

After the assembly has been completed and the hub reinstalled and adjusted as set down in **Section 11 : 3**, the brake drum is next fitted and secured after which the free play in the shoes is taken up by the eccentric adjusters. There are two of these on each drum assembly and they are individually set. Spin the drum and slacken both back until the wheel hub runs free. Rotate the drum while the foremost adjuster is turned by means of a spanner applied to the adjuster head at the rear of the mounting plate, until a rubbing sound is heard. Turn the adjuster fractionally in the opposite direction until the sound ceases and carry out the same procedure on the other adjuster. The cams are shown in **FIG 11 : 11**.

On the rear brakes, the adjuster is on the upper end of the mounting plate and the end of the adjusting screw is a square shank. A notching device holds the adjuster and transition from notch to notch can easily be felt. The position of the adjuster and the method of turning the shank are both shown in **FIG 11 : 12**. The handbrake connection is, of course, located at the opposite end of the shoes.

Adjustment cannot take place until the system has been bled. This is because the brake shoes need to be centred, a simple enough operation which calls for the application of the footbrake after the brake drum has been fitted. Depression of the pedal two or three times causes the brake cylinder assembly to slide into a central position when the brakes are off and, at the same time, settles the return springs into their seatings.

During assembly, therefore, a thin film of grease is applied to the surfaces of the locking plates and shims before installing them into position in the slot at the rear of the cylinder assembly. The handbrake lever must, of course, be fitted at the same time after which the protective dust cover (or a new one if the old one is at all imperfect) is fitted into place. **Do not couple up the handbrake cable until after bleeding and setting the adjuster.**

With the shoes centred, turn the adjuster notch by notch until the shoes begin to bind on the drum. Do not be misled by the heavy binding which occurs between the clicks on some assemblies. Check only on the set positions. When binding begins, turn the adjuster back one notch and check that no binding re-occurs after application of the brake

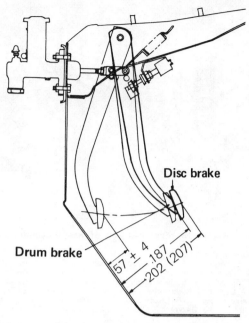

FIG 11 : 13   Diagrammatic view of pedal assembly showing settings for both disc and drum brakes

pedal. The clevis and pin connection can then be made to couple the handbrake cable or rod to the brake lever.

11 : 8 Overhauling the master cylinder

The master cylinder is mounted on the front bulkhead immediately ahead of the pedal assembly to which it is connected by a clevis fork and pin on the end of the operating rod passing through the bulkhead (see **FIG 11 : 13**). The pedal also operates the brake light switch mounted on a bracket below the dashboard.

A section through the master cylinder is shown in **FIG 11 : 14**, while the exploded view in **FIG 11 : 15** gives the breakdown of the component parts. The only difference

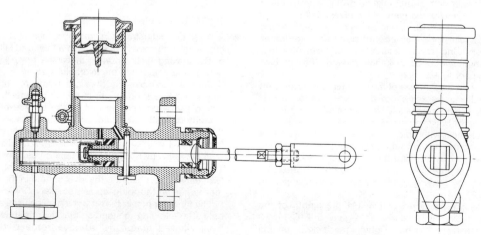

FIG 11 : 14   Diagrammatic section through the master cylinder

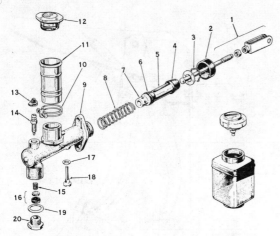

FIG 11:15   Exploded view of master cylinder

Key to Fig 11:15   1 Pushrod assembly   2 Dust cover
3 Spring clip   4 Secondary piston cup   5 Piston
6 Primary piston cup   7 Inlet valve assembly
8 Spring   9 Body and cylinder   10 Clip   11 Reservoir
12 Cap   13 Bleed screw cap   14 Bleed screw   15 Check
valve spring   16 Check valve   17 Packing   18 Stopper
pin   19 Gasket   20 Valve cap and union

between the master cylinder for cars with disc brakes at
the front is a larger reservoir of rectangular, instead or
circular, shape.

To dismantle, first remove the clevis pin from the fork
connecting the operating rod to the pedal and then disconnect the hydraulic line to the brake cylinders. Unbolt
and remove the master cylinder from the bulkhead and
transfer to the bench. Remove the reservoir cap and empty
the hydraulic fluid into a convenient container.

Remove the dust cover 2 and spring clip 3. The operating rod and washer can now be removed from the end of
the cylinder. Unscrew the stopper pin 18. Remove the
valve cap 20 and extract the check valve 16 and spring 15.
The extension of the spring 8 with the removal of the
stopper pin will cause the piston 5 with cups and valve to
emerge from the end. Extract carefully and transfer to a
clean container with clean brake fluid. Remove the bleed
valve 14 and unclip and remove the reservoir 11.

Examine all parts for signs of wear or damage and
replace as necessary. **Replace all cups and valves at
every servicing regardless of condition.** The two
cups, 4 and 6 should be soaked in brake fluid for at least
one hour prior to assembly.

Lightly coat the surfaces of the cylinder and piston with
brake fluid and reassemble in the reverse order to dismantling. When completely reassembled, remount in
position on the bulkhead and reconnect the hydraulic line.
Fill the reservoir with fluid. Temporarily insert the clevis
pin coupling the piston to the brake pedal and bleed the
master cylinder by opening the bleed valve and depressing the pedal until fluid commences to flow. Tighten the
valve while still flowing. Bleed the system as described in
Section 11:11.

Remove the clevis pin and adjust the length of the
operating rod to suit the dimensions given in **FIG 11:13**
and replace the clevis pin. Tighten the locknut on the
operating rod.

11:9 Hydraulic hose replacement

While little deterioration in the hydraulic pipelines
should be experienced over many years of service, the
hose connections between the brake cylinders and pipe
terminations are subject to deterioration by mud, dirt and
the oxidation effects of the engine exhaust-contaminated
atmosphere. It is, therefore, advisable to check these from
time to time and replace wherever necessary. The procedure is straightforward and replacement connections
are available, ready for installation, from the local Datsun
agent.

When installing hoses, always hold the end of the hose
connector in a grip or spanner while tightening the union
nut with another (see **FIG 11:4**). A twisted hose wears
rapidly and if it does not hang naturally between the pipe
and brake cylinder union, slacken the joint and readjust
until it does.

11:10 Hydraulic line replacement

In the unlikely event of the hydraulic lines being
damaged or punctured, new lines will have to be fabricated.
This is not a difficult task providing that the necessary
flaring tools are available and the proper stock is obtained.
This must be Bundy tubing with a wall thickness of .028
inch or equivalent. Pipe supplied for fuel lines is not
satisfactory.

However, most Datsun agents carry, or can obtain on
short notice, replacement pipes of double wall construction tubing ready bent and cut for installation in the
different runs. These are shown, with their identification
letters appended, for the saloon cars in **FIG 11:16**.
**Slightly different lines are available for the estate
cars, details of which can be obtained from the
Datsun agent.**

If it necessary to fabricate your own lines and the right
stock is available, take down the faulty line and feed a
length of copper wire from end to end, cutting the wire
about $\frac{3}{8}$ inch projecting from each end for flaring purposes.
Withdraw and straighten to give the developed length of
the line. Cut a length of stock to this and then shape to the
form of the damaged pipe using a proper tube bender to
give the right radius turns without flattening the tube.
Flare the ends to suit the adaptors and install in place.

11:11 Brake bleeding

After any adjustment of the hydraulic system, if the
fluid level in the reservoir has been allowed to fall too low
or the braking feels 'spongy' bleed the brake system to
get rid of air trapped in the hydraulic system.

To bleed, remove the dust cap from one front brake
nipple and fit a short length of rubber tube to the nipple,
letting the other end rest below the surface of a small
quantity of fresh brake fluid in a glass receptacle. Slacken
the bleed nipple back one turn, then proceed to pump the
brake pedal with long steady strokes and quick returns
until the fluid emerging from the pipe is free from bubbles.
Tighten the nipple and transfer to the other front, then the
two rear brakes, checking the level of fluid in the reservoir
meanwhile and topping-up as necessary.

The fluid trapped in the reservoir may be used again but
only after allowing to stand so that the entrapped air has
been allowed to escape. **Always replace the dust
caps on nipples after bleeding.**

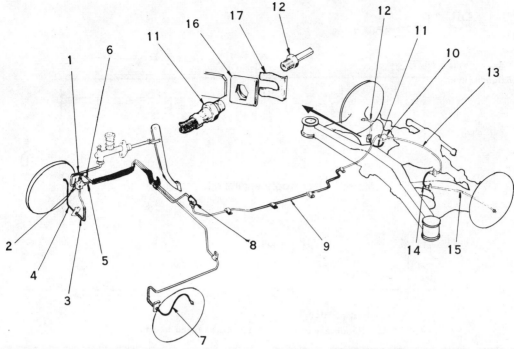

FIG 11:16   Hydraulic pipelines on the saloon car

Key to Fig 11:16
1 Brake tube A	**2** Front connector	**3** Brake tube B	**4** Hydraulic hose	**5** Brake tube C
6 Brake tube D	**7** Hydraulic hose	**8** Connector	**9** Brake tube E	**10** Rear connector	**11** Hydraulic hose
12 Brake tube F	**13** Brake tube G	**14** Hydraulic hose	**15** Brake tube H	**16** Lockplate	**17** Lockplate clip

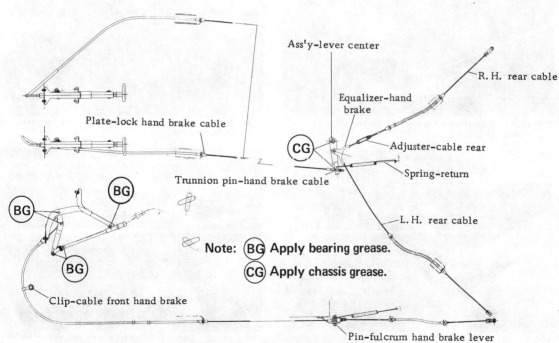

Ass'y-lever center

R. H. rear cable

Equalizer-hand brake

Plate-lock hand brake cable

Adjuster-cable rear

Spring-return

Trunnion pin-hand brake cable

L. H. rear cable

Note: **BG** Apply bearing grease.

CG Apply chassis grease.

Clip-cable front hand brake

Pin-fulcrum hand brake lever

FIG 11:17   Handbrake cable arrangements as fitted to saloon car

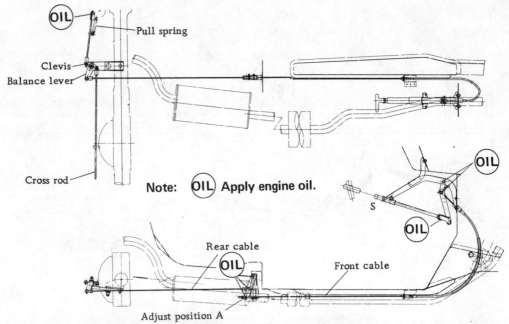

Note: **OIL** Apply engine oil.

FIG 11:18 Handbrake cable arrangements as fitted to estate car

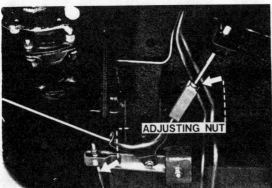

FIG 11:19 Adjustment for rear handbrake cable showing position of stirrup

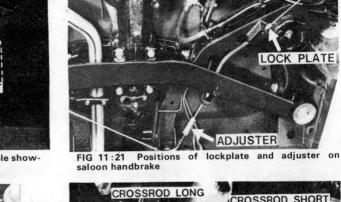

FIG 11:21 Positions of lockplate and adjuster on saloon handbrake

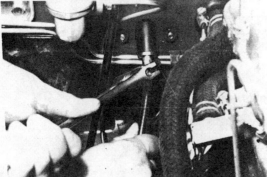

FIG 11:20 Front Bowden cable connection for handbrake cable

FIG 11:22 Details of estate car equalizer showing cable, crossrods and balance lever arm

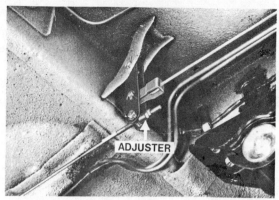
FIG 11:23 Adjustment for handbrake on estate car

11:12 Handbrakes

The handbrake cable runs and links are shown diagrammatically in **FIG 11:17** for the saloon and **FIG 11:18** for the estate car.

In each case the handbrake is operated by a pull handle the ratchet of which is released by rotating the handle and shaft through 90 degrees. Additional leverage is given by the cable coupling link at the foot of the shaft which communicates the pull, through a Bowden cable, to the underside of the chassis where the sheath terminates in a lockplate leaving the cable to continue to the equalizer.

In the saloon, the equalizer is in the form of a stirrup mounted on a second lever, the cables to the brake levers on the two rear wheels sliding over the curved inner race of the stirrup. The cables pass through protective sheaths for part of the way and adjustment is at two points. The first is at the end of the equalizer lever where the pull cable terminates in an adjusting screw and locknut; the second is at a tensioner in the equalizer cable close to the stirrup (see **FIG 11:19**).

In the estate car, different equalizing gear is installed. This is in the form of a balance lever pivoted to a point on the rear axle casing almost in direct line between the two brake levers and to which each of the idler arm ends is coupled by cross-rods (see **FIG 11:22**).

The pull off is assisted in each case by coil springs, on the saloon acting on the equalizer lever and on the estate car coupled to each of the cross-rods.

Replacement of springs and cables is a straightforward operation needing no detailed explanation. The points to watch are the entry of the Bowden cable beneath the footboard (see **FIG 11:20**) and the setting of the adjuster in relation to the stirrup and rear sheath in the saloon (see **FIG 11:21**).

Adjustment on the estate car is at a single point where the pull from the Bowden cable is transmitted to the equalizer cable via a lever (see **FIG 11:23**).

Handbrake adjustment is intended only to compensate for cable stretch and not to take up wear on brake shoe linings. All handbrake adjustments must therefore be preceded by a routine adjustment of the brake shoes as already described. Providing that this is observed, the replacement of brake shoes should not, in the normal course of events, necessitate a readjustment of the handbrake cables.

Routine maintenance of the handbrake is limited to periodic inspection of the cables and linkages, lubricating the Bowden cables where they enter the sheaths and greasing points of the balance and relay levers.

11:13 Fault diagnosis

(a) Brake locked on

1 Swollen brake pads on disc brakes through oil contamination
2 Blocked hydraulic lines
3 Master cylinder compensating hole blocked.
4 Hydraulic line connector blocked
5 Brake or pedal return springs weak or broken
6 Dirt in the hydraulic fluid

(b) Spongy brake action

1 Air in hydraulic lines
2 Master cylinder seals faulty
3 Low reservoir fluid level causing (1)

(c) Pedal yields under steady pressure

1 Faulty seals in master cylinder
2 Faulty seals in brake cylinders
3 Leak in hydraulic circuit.

(d) Unbalanced braking

1 Fluid leak in one cylinder
2 Unevenly worn tyres
3 Seized plunger in one brake cylinder
4 Blockage in hydraulic line connector

(e) Reservoir level falls rapidly

1 Leaks in pipeline
2 Deterioration in cylinder seals

CHAPTER 12

THE ELECTRICAL SYSTEM

12:1 Description

The electrical system is 12-volt, negative earth return, deriving its supply from a belt-driven alternator with integral rectifiers. That is to say, the alternator is, in reality, a d.c. generator in which the conventional practice of a rotating field with a stationary armature, or stator, common to a.c. generators has been adopted with silicon rectifiers taking the place of the commutator and brush rectification in the conventional d.c. generator.

The alternator floats across the terminals of the battery to produce a system voltage of 14-volts $\pm$ .3-volt when running, the voltage being regulated by a vibrating armature pattern regulator external to the alternator. No cut-out is necessary as the non-reversible current flow characteristics of the diodes provides this feature. The regulator is temperature compensated and incorporates a current operated coil in the circuit which extinguishes the pilot lamp on the instrument panel as soon as the charging current to the battery exceeds 5 amperes.

12:2 The battery

The battery is a six-cell, lead/acid type with a capacity of 40 amp/hr at the 20 hour discharge rate. The battery is mounted on a steel platform in the engine compartment and is retained in position by two stay bolts and a metal strap. In some cases the capacity of the battery installed is 50 amps/hr.

Maintenance is confined to a periodical check of electrolyte level and topping-up with distilled water as necessary. A battery in good condition should have all the cells with the same electrolyte specific gravity, as determined with a hydrometer (see **FIG 12:1**) ranging from 1.26 to 1.28 at full charge falling to 1.20 to 1.22 when discharged.

Inability of a battery to deliver heavy starting currents, though giving sufficient current for other purposes may be due to one faulty cell. The usual means of checking this is by measuring the voltage drop across each cell with a heavy discharge device. This practice is not always possible but a faulty cell will, in the majority of cases, reveal itself by having a lower specific gravity than the remainder.

12:3 The alternator

The alternator fitted is the Hitachi LT130.41 having a nominal output of 30 amps at 14 volts. This machine comprises a three-phase, star-connected stator with a wound rotating field, excitation of the field being from the battery at starting and from the alternator output while running.

FIG 12:1 Checking battery electrolyte specific gravity with hydrometer

The a.c. output at the stator winding terminals is rectified by a full-wave pack of silicon diodes, the neutral point being brought out to a separate terminal N, for connection to earth through the current coil of the regulator. It is belt-driven from the crankshaft pulley at 2.25 times engine speed. Belt tension must be checked periodically to ensure that the full output is available.

Silicon diodes are sensitive to high temperatures and are mounted on substantial heat sinks at the air intake end of the machine. It is imperative that a clear flow of cooling air be maintained, particularly at high ambient temperatures, and that no unnecessary obstruction to the air flow through the engine compartment shall be offered.

12:4 Removing and dismantling the alternator

Disconnect the negative terminal at the battery and remove the plug from the socket connector on the flying lead to the alternator. Slacken and remove the drive belt and unbolt the generator from its support on the engine. Transfer to the bench for overhaul.

Thoroughly clean the exterior of the alternator and then remove the cover at the rear end. Working through the aperture disclosed, remove the two caps covering the brush cavities and extract the caps. Carefully preserve and identify all screws and plates as they are removed to facilitate reassembly later.

Remove the three through-bolts and ease the pulley end with the shaft and rotor away from the rear portion. Remove the nut from the shaft and extract the pulley and fan. The rotor can then be withdrawn from the bearing by tapping the end of the shaft with a hide mallet while supporting the frame on blocks.

Turning to the rear portion, containing the stator, diode assemblies, brush holder and terminals, brush the interior clear of dust and blow through with a dry air jet. Carefully examine and identify the four leads, three-phase and one neutral, from the stator windings and unsolder them from the diode and terminal assembly. Remove the stator from the rear housing. The two diode assemblies with their interconnections and heat sinks will then be visible.

Again carefully examine the method of assembly and mounting and then remove the four nuts on the outside of the casing and extract the diode assemblies, with the securing bolts, from the housing. **Pay particular attention to the insulating bushes and washer and carefully preserve for reinstallation exactly as before dismantling when reassembling.** The brush holder will come away as a separate unit but the two diode heat sinks with the diodes in position will be coupled by the interconnecting wires. The component parts at this stage will appear as in **FIG 12:2.**

12:5 Overhauling and reassembling the alternator

First check the stator windings for continuity between the neutral lead and each of the three-phase terminations. Follow this up by a check of the individual diodes. Two types of diode are installed, a positive diode, in which the current will flow from the cap to the base but not in the reverse direction (the figures on the base are in **red**) and a negative diode in which the current will flow only from base to the cap. These are identified by **black** figures on the base (see **FIG 12:3**).

Using a battery, test lamp and two leads terminating in probes coloured red for the positive and black for the negative side of the battery, apply these between the plate and the cap electrode and check that, on the plate with the positive dioes, the lamp will light when the red probe is applied to the cap but not the black. On the plate with the negative diodes, the lamp must light when the black probe is applied to the cap but not the red (see **FIG 12:4**).

Should the lamp light in both directions, the diode junction has broken down and it is therefore useless. Similarly, if the lamp will not light in either direction, there is an open-circuit in the diode and this too is useless.

The diodes are a press-fit in the heat sink/terminal plate. To remove, unsolder the lead to the central electrode and press the diode out from below. Insert a new diode of the same type and number, obtainable from the agent, and press back into place, using a press tool which fits over the edge without bearing on the cap (see **FIG 12:5**). **The diodes must be removed and installed by steady pressure, not hammered in or out as shock can damage the delicate junction face within.**

Resolder the lead to the terminal with soft solder and using a small iron applied to the diode for the very minimum time. **All diodes are sensitive to heat and the application of soldering temperature to the junction, by conduction down the electrode can destroy it. A safe precaution is to hold the stem of the electrode in a pair of slim-nosed pliers while soldering, the function of the pliers being not so much a steady as a heat sink. Soldering diode connections is a task calling for some skill and the use of the right type of soldering iron. Do not attempt to do this unless you have had some experience.**

When all parts have been checked and the necessary repairs made, reassemble in the reverse order, noting carefully those points in the assembly which were observed when dismantling.

No mention has been made of the alternator bearings but, clearly, if these are faulty or worn, they must be replaced. Withdrawing the races and fitting new ones is just a normal procedure.

The foregoing dismantling routine has been described in case a replacement alternator should not readily be obtainable. It is of course, far better to exchange a faulty alternator for a new or

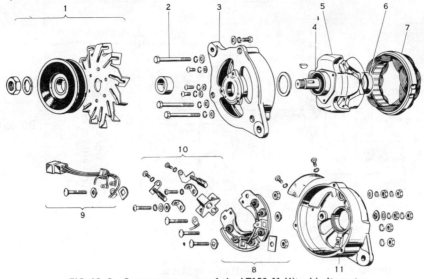

FIG 12:2   Component parts of the LT130.41 Hitachi alternator

Key to Fig 12:2   1 Fan and pulley assembly   2 Through-bolts   3 Forward casing shell   4 Rotor   5 Polepieces
6 Stator windings   7 Stator core   8 Diodes and heat sinks   9 Connector assembly   10 Brushgear   11 Rear casing
shell

reconditioned one at the agents, if in stock, which
will then carry the normal guarantee of satisfactory
performance.

12:6 The regulator

The regulator, Hitachi type TL1Z.17, comprise two relay
elements one of which is a vibrating pattern voltage
regulator and the other a contactor the primary purpose of
which is to light the generator/charging warning light on
the instrument panel. It also serves to bring the regulator
into circuit when the alternator has come on charge.

The regulator circuit is shown in **FIG 12:6** and a view
with the cover removed is illustrated in **FIG 12:7**.

Referring to the circuit diagram, the field coil of the
alternator is connected directly across the battery terminals
in series with the ignition switch and ballast resistor R_1.
On closing the ignition switch, the field is energized and,
as soon as the alternator rotor is turning, a.c. is induced in
the stator windings. This current, rectified in the full-wave
diode pack is applied through terminal A, to the positive
battery terminal and the return is via the system common
earth and coil VC_1 to the star point of the stator winding.
VC_1 is a current coil operating on contacts P_4, P_5 and P_6
and, until the current flowing through the coil exceeds
2A, P_4 and P_5 is closed, lighting the ignition warning lamp
through the ignition switch.

As the voltage rises, the charging current increases until,
at around 5A, P_4 and P_5 open, extinguishing the warning
lamp, and P_5 and P_6 close, energizing the voltage
regulator coil VC_2. This is also a current wound coil,
similar to VC_1, but the resistor R_2 in series converts it into
a voltage sensitive relay. The normally closed contacts of
this relay P_1 and P_2, shunt the ballast resistor R_1 to apply
full system voltage across the field and the generated
voltage rises steeply. At around 14 volts, the current flowing through VC_2 is sufficient to open P_1 and P_2, inserting

Red or Black figures

FIG 12:3   Position of identifying marks on diodes

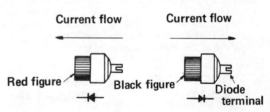

FIG 12:4   Current flow in diodes

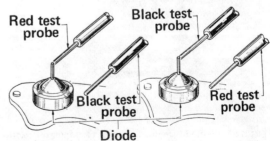

FIG 12:5   Testing diodes in situ with current probes

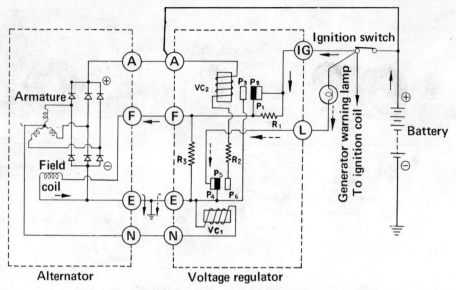

FIG 12:6 Alternator and regulator control circuit

the ballast resistor R_1 in circuit, and closing P_2 and P_3, quenching the field. The output voltage stops rising and commences to fall until VC_2 reverts to the normally open position applying full excitation.

That is to say, the contacts are continually opening and closing at a rate determined by the time constants of response of both field and stator windings to variations in load to give a mean excitation holding the output voltage constant regardless of load. The purpose of R_3 connected across the field is to provide suitable adjustment to the field response time constant and also to minimise the effects of sparking between P_2 and P_3.

The opening and closing currents are set by the biasing spring holding the armature over and by the contact gaps in each case. Variations in operating current with temperature (since the resistance of the coils themselves vary with temperature), are compensated by making the spring leaf of a bi-metal suitably chosen.

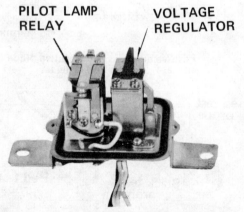

FIG 12:7 Hitachi regulator TL1Z.17 regulator with cover removed

While the regulator is capable of being readjusted should it fall out of setting, the procedure is a fairly critical one and, in normal circumstances, is best dealt with by exchange for a new factory set instrument.

12:7 Starter motor, description

The starter motor is of the pre-engaged type. That is to say, the pinion is mechanically engaged with the flywheel ring gear before current is switched on, a roller clutch drive in the pinion assembly enabling the pinion to freewheel on overdrive when the engine starts. The solenoid switch and

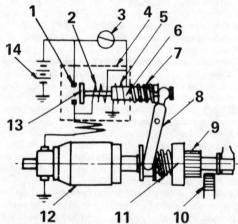

FIG 12:8 Pre-engaged starter circuit as fitted to Datsun cars

Key to Fig 12:8   1 Main contacts   2 Series winding
3 Starting contacts of ignition switch   4 Solenoid casing
5 Shunt winding   6 Solenoid armature   7 Return spring
8 Lever   9 Pinion   10 Ring gear   11 Roller clutch
12 Motor armature   13 Main moving contact

mechanical engagement are mounted on the motor yoke and cannot be engaged manually or energized apart from by the ignition switch.

The starter motor circuit will be understood from **FIG 12:8**. Energizing the series coil 2 from the ignition switch together with the shunt coil 5, pulls the plunger 7 over, taking with it the lever 8 which forces the drive pinion 9 into engagement with the flywheel ring gear 10. At the end of the stroke, with the gears engaged, the contacts 13 are closed to apply full battery voltage to the series wound starter motor 12. At the same time, the series winding 2 is disconnected.

As soon as the engine starts, the gears remain meshed but the roller clutch 11 enables the pinion to slip on over-drive until the starter switch, part of the ignition switch, is opened. The return spring 7 then disengages the pinion from the ring gear.

A view of the starter motor extracted from the engine is shown in **FIG 12:9** and an exploded view showing the component parts is in **FIG 12:10**. To remove the starter motor from the engine, first disconnect the battery negative and the solenoid and heavy duty cables from the motor, then remove the two bolts holding the motor to the clutch housing and withdraw the motor.

12:8 Dismantling the starter

Generally speaking, the starter motor is one of the more robust units on the car. Its life, in terms of hours used, is small compared with other electrical components and usually it should outlast the engine. Servicing is minimal and is confined to a clean up of the exterior and a brief examination of the brushes, solenoid contacts and pinion

FIG 12:9   View of pre-engaged starter removed from engine

teeth at the 12,000 mile routine servicing periods. If at any intermediate period, the starter motor fails to turn and/or there is a strong smell of burnt insulation, exchange the motor for a new one at the service station and reinstall.

Should it be necessary to dismantle the motor for other purposes, proceed as follows. First remove the three screws retaining the solenoid assembly (7 in **FIG 12:10**) in position and withdraw the assembly. Extract the through-bolts and remove the end cover 24.

Next, lift the four brushes in the holders allowing the springs to rest on the sides, instead of the top, so securing them clear of the commutator. Remove the end cover 10

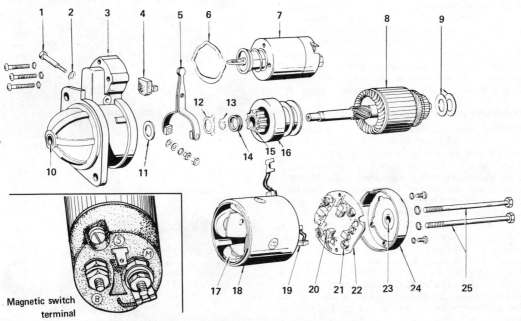

FIG 12:10   Exploded view of starter components

Key to Fig 12:10   1 Pivot pin   2 Washer   3 Forward casing   4 Dust cover   5 Lever   6 Grommet   7 Solenoid assembly   8 Armature   9 Washers   10 Forward bearing   11 Washer   12 Stop ring   13 Circlip   14 Pinion stop   15 Pinion   16 Roller clutch   17 Field coils   18 Yoke   19 Brush   20 Brush holder   21 Brush retaining spring   22 Backplate   23 Rear bearing   24 Rear casing   25 Through-bolts

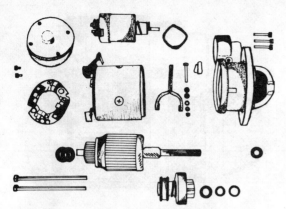

FIG 12:11 Component parts of the starter motor

from the yoke 18, complete with armature and engagement mechanism. Remove the pin 1 forming the pivot of the shift lever 5, and extract the armature, shift lever and pinion assembly from the end cover.

Ease the brush 19, connected to the field winding tail from the brush holder and separate the brush assembly from the yoke. On the armature shaft, push the stop ring 12 in against the pressure of the pinion sleeve ring and extract the snap ring 13. The roller clutch assembly can then be withdrawn.

Thoroughly clean all parts and examine for wear. **The roller clutch assembly is grease-packed for life so do not clean this with solvents.** Replace such parts as may be necessary and repack the bearings with grease (see **FIG 12:11**).

Reassemble in the reverse order and check for operation before installing in the engine. To do this, connect the battery negative to the terminal B on the starter and the positive to terminal S. Check that the pinion moves forward on the armature shaft into the meshing position for the ring gear. Then connect the battery positive to terminal M and again link the S terminal with the battery positive. The motor should run and the pinion move forward.

12:9 Direction indicators and control

The direction indicator switch is mounted on the steering column and is housed within a two-piece shell just below the steering wheel. It provides left and right direction flasher indication by movement forward or aft of the steering column, change from main to dip filaments by depressing towards the footboards, the operation controlling the headlamp relay, and headlight flashing by lifting towards the steering wheel. The latter operation is spring-returned on release. On the top of the unit, a spring contact provides the earth connection for the horn button.

A faulty unit should be replaced by a new one and no attempt be made to dismantle and repair. Before, however, determining that it is the unit that is faulty and not merely a broken lead or, more usually, a faulty earth, check the operation of each position by a link applied to the terminals revealed by removal of the shell. Check as follows.

Direction indicators:

Link the green cable termination to the green and black to check the 'turn right' indicator. Link the green cable to

the red and black to check the 'turn left' indicator. If neither operate, check the flasher unit by shorting the two terminals.

Horn button:

Earth the contact on top of the unit. If this fails to sound the horn, check the horn relay, first by earthing terminal 1 and then by linking terminals 2 and 3. (See wiring diagram in Appendix.) Check that fuse H on the fuseboard is not blown. **Note that although the horn button provides the earth connection to the relay coil, the relay contacts provide the live feed to the horns. Do not therefore, earth either terminal 2 or 3 at the relay or the fuse will be blown.**

Headlamp dipswitch:

Earth the black and red cable termination. Switch on the headlamps and check that the dip filament is glowing. If this fails, check by earthing terminal S of the headlamp relay. If neither filament glows on both headlamps, check the fuse L on the fuseboard.

Headlamp flasher:

Earth the brown and yellow cable termination. If this fails to light the headlamp main filament, check by earthing the brown and yellow cable termination at the passing light relay (see wiring diagram in Appendix). Also check

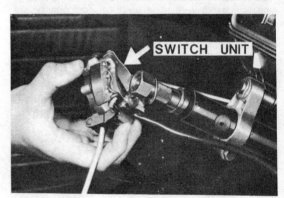

FIG 12:12 Removing the direction indicator switch unit

FIG 12:13 Adjusting horn for volume

by bridging terminals 2 and 3 on the relay. **The head-lamp flashing circuit is not fitted to the SSS model.**

To replace the direction indicator switch, first remove the steering wheel and column shells, then unscrew and remove the locating and fixing screws. The unit can then be slipped over the head of the column and the cable connections released (**FIG 12:12**). Reverse the procedure to reinstall.

12:10 Horns

The two horns are mounted at the front behind the grille, unscrew and remove the headlamp rim and extract need tampering with. However, if it is desired to increase the volume of sound, adjust the control by turning clock-wise the screw indicated in **FIG 12:13**. Secure in the new position by the locknut.

If the horn fails to sound and operation of the relay makes the terminal tag alive, a faulty earth connection is probably the cause. Dismount the horn and clean up the metal surfaces between the mounting bracket and chassis.

12:11 Lamps and lighting

Headlamps:

The outer headlamps are twin filament, sealed-beam units rated at 50 watt main beam and 37.5 watt dipped beam. The inner headlamps are single filament sealed-beam units rated at 37.5 watt. To replace, remove the front grille, unscrew and remove the headlamp rim and extract the faulty unit. Disconnect the plug connector at the rear. Reinstall a new unit in the reverse procedure (see **FIG 12:14**).

FIG 12:14   Replacing a sealed beam unit in the head-lamp

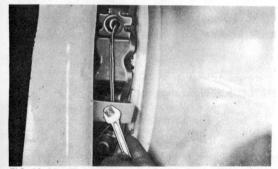

FIG 12:15   Removing the tail lighting assembly from the estate car

FIG 12:16   Removing the windscreen wiper motor and control linkage from the engine compartment

Front side and indicator lamps:

The front side lamps are rated at 8 watt and are housed behind the lens immediately beneath the headlamps. The lens is secured by a single central screw. The directional lamps, also in the same enclosure, are rated at 25 watt. **In some installations, a single twin filament lamp is used in place of the separate bulbs.**

Side directional lamps:

Side directional lamps, where fitted, are rated at 6 watt.

Rear directional lamps:

The rear directional lamps are a single filament bulb rated at 25 watt and is housed, with the stop, tail and reversing lamps, behind the composite lens at the rear of the car. In the saloon, all three lamps are accessible from behind by extracting the lampholder. In the estate car, the lamp unit has to be removed by loosening the nut from the inside (see **FIG 12:15**).

Tail and stop lamps:

The tail and stop lamps are rated at 8 watt and 25 watt respectively and are combined in a twin filament bulb behind coloured lens masks.

Reversing lamp:

The reversing lamp, operated by the switch on the gear-box when the gearlever is shifted to reverse, is rated at 25 watt and displays a white light to the rear.

License plate lamp:

The license plate lamp is housed behind the reflecting lens beneath the number plate at the rear and is rated at 8 watt.

Indicator and meter lamps:

Indicator and meter lamps are rated at 3 watt.

Interior light:

Interior lighting is provided by a 10 watt lamp.

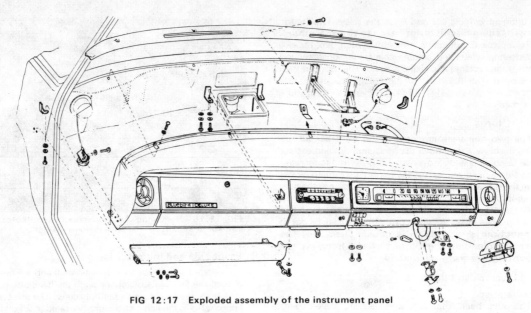

FIG 12:17   Exploded assembly of the instrument panel

12:12 Windscreen wiper

The windscreen wiper is electrically operated and controlled by a two-speed switch on the dashboard. The two wiper arms are oscillated by a link and pivot assembly attached to the motor and mounted on the outside of the air intake chamber under the grille (see **FIG 12:16**).

To remove, detach the wiper arms and blades from the shafts, unscrew the nuts around the shaft. From within the engine compartment, disconnect the motor wiring and remove the four screws holding the motor to the dashboard. The assembly can then be extracted.

While it is possible to dismantle and overhaul a faulty windscreen wiper motor, it is preferable to exchange it for a new, guaranteed one from the Datsun agent. Installation is a simple reversal of the dismantling procedure.

For efficient windscreen wiping, renew the wiper blades annually. Not only do the contact edges of the wiper strips deteriorate, but they tend to accumulate a film of silicon wax which makes the operation of wiping only partially efficient in light rain.

FIG 12:18   Removing the instrument cluster from the panel

12:13 Instruments

The instrument panel (see **FIG 12:17**) is secured to the body by five screws at the upper edge under the trim, and four beneath, two being at the outer edges and two at the centre in the glove box and behind the instrument cluster.

The instrument cluster comprises speedometer, fuel gauge and water temperature gauge, ignition and low oil pressure warning lights and pilot lights for main beam and directional indicator flashing.

The fuel and water temperature gauges are conventional ammeter movements operated from transmitters in the petrol tank and radiator head respectively. These are used in connection with a stabilized supply derived from a voltage stabilizer mounted at the rear of the panel and the car battery system.

The main beam and directional indicator pilot lamps are in parallel with the respective circuits while the ignition warning light is operated from the regulator relay and the low oil pressure warning light from a transducer inserted in the oil pump line.

In addition, the instrument illuminating lamps are installed and are replaceable, as are the other warning lamps, from the rear of the panel. To gain access, remove the two screws from the inner upper return of the instrument cluster (see **FIG 12:18**) and tilt the assembly forward. To completely remove, disconnect the speedometer cable, extract the temperature gauge and fuel meters and withdraw all lamps from their sockets.

12:14 Headlamp alignment

To align the headlamps, stand the car directly in front of a vertical wall or other surface and twenty-five feet distant. Check that the tyres are properly inflated, and that the car is unladen. On the wall, mark a horizontal line the exact distance above floor level as that of the headlamp centres. Then mark two vertical lines on each side of a vertical centre line, coincident with the at of the car, corresponding to the distances from the centre of each of the four headlamps.

Switch on the headlamps and select high beam. Remove the front grille and headlamp rims to gain access to the adjusting screws. Covering each lamp in turn, adjust the angle of tilt until each bright patch is centred on the horizontal line and the corresponding vertical line.

Select low beam and note the position of the beam patch on each of the lamps already adjusted. Covering one lamp at a time, adjust the remaining one of the inner headlamps so that the beam coincides with that of the outer for height but is centred on its own ahead line. When all four have been adjusted, the beam on the wall should be in the shape of an evenly lit oval the upper edge of which coincides with the horizontal line on the wall.

12:15 Fault diagnosis

(a) Battery discharged

1 Internal cell fault (replace battery)
2 External wiring fault (check wiring)
3 Alternator not charging
4 Ignition left on overnight

(b) Battery will not start engine

1 Faulty battery
2 Discharged battery
3 Open circuit on solenoid wiring
4 Starter main contacts not making

(c) Ignition light fails to extinguish

1 Loose or broken generator belt
2 Faulty regulator
3 Loose connection in charging circuit
4 Diode failure in alternator

(d) Lamps will not light

1 Fuse blown
2 Lamp burned out
3 Faulty earth connection
4 Loose connection in wiring

(e) Horns will not sound

1 Faulty wiring
2 Fault in horn relay
3 Bad earth connection at horn button
4 Bad connection at horns
5 Fuse blown

CHAPTER 13

THE BODYWORK

13:1 Body finish

The body structure is made up from a series of pressed steel sections joined together by welding. Damage to any section too great to permit of local rectification can be dealt with by replacing the section and welding it into position. As this is a process entailing, in many cases, realignment of the chassis or its assembly in a special jig, the work should not be attempted by the owner/mechanic but placed with a Datsun repair agent who is in possession of the necessary jigs and tools.

The stoved synthetic enamel finish is of a durable nature and will last many years if kept reasonably clean by regular washing and polishing. **Do not attempt to wipe road dust from the body with a dry cloth or its high finish will be impaired by fine scratches.** Always wash the dirt and dust away by copious flushing with water from a jet or hose. If very dirty, sponge over with a shampoo in warm, not hot, water until all is loose and rinse off with a hose before finally drying off with a chamois leather and polishing with a soft cloth.

The surfaces should be protected by a film of wax from time to time. There are two good indications of surface deterioration. The first is when water sprayed on to it tends to wet it evenly all over. Water should run off or, at least, stand in separate globules on the surface if the protective film is in good condition. The second is the 'feel' of the surface when polished after drying. If the clean duster slips easily over the surface with no effect, the film is present. If there is the slightest feel of drag, either the film has deteriorated and you are down to the base enamel of the film present is contaminated by ingrained dirt and must be removed.

Renovation is in two stages, the removal of the old film with its ingrained dirt and the replacement by a new wax surface. Many excellent proprietary cleaners and waxes are available and can be used with safety so long as the instructions are followed. The separate compounds are to be favoured but the polishing can be a long and arduous task which, however, pays good dividends. Combined cleaners and polishers are an acceptable second best.

Most products are now based on silicon waxes and should not be allowed to contaminate the windscreen. The water-repellant film a silicone leaves behind makes the use of the windscreen wiper inefficient in preserving clear vision when light rain is falling. The film is difficult to remove and, in any case, prevention is better than cure. To remove, use non-abrasive scouring powders with plenty of water or metal polish.

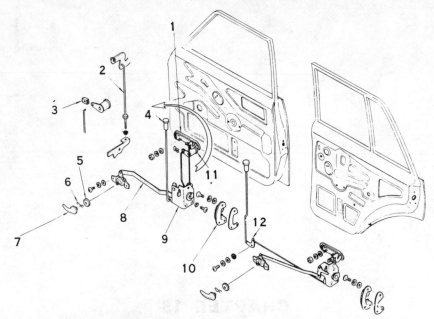

FIG 13:1   Exploded schematic view of front and rear door lock mechanisms

FIG 13:2   Removing lower sash and glass runner

FIG 13:3   Extracting door lock assembly

It is not generally known that chrome plating is porous and, despite its high finish, water can penetrate through it to the metal beneath causing pitting, bubbling and even stripping over large areas. The longer life of pre-war chrome plating was due to a heavy undercoat of non-porous copper plating and the more extensive use of brass in place of the present day die-casting alloys. The pores, however, can be closed by application of body wax and it is a good practice to go over all plated parts whenever body polishing is being done. On a new car, initial protection can be obtained by wiping over the surfaces with a solution of lanolin in white spirit, obtainable from any chemist. It must be applied warm and allowed to stand for a few hours. Then clean off the surface wax and what is left behind will give good protection for many years despite the use of chrome polishes.

Tar can be removed by the use of a little butter on a soft cloth, finishing off with an application of body wax. Bird droppings must be removed as soon as possible. Wipe off with a rotary motion using a very wet cloth and minimum pressure until all is clear. Rinse, dry and renew the wax. Most bird droppings have constituents which eat through the wax and affect the colour of the enamel beneath, leaving a lighter colour area.

Scratches and abrasions of the paintwork can be rectified by rubbing down and spraying over with a cellulose base paint. Tins of spray paint in pressurized containers are quite suitable for small areas but care must be taken in matching the colour. When spraying, use many coats of thinly applied paint rather than a single application heavily applied. For large areas, it is better to put the work in hand with a professional paint sprayer who will be able to match the existing colour rather more efficiently. All paint

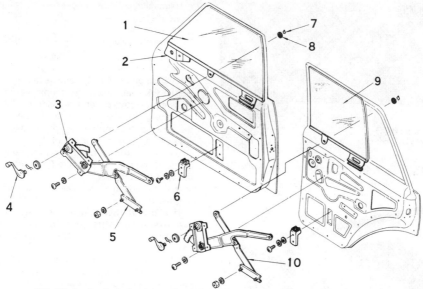

FIG 13:4   Exploded schematic view of front and rear window raising gear

Key to Fig 13:4   1 Front window glass   2 Bottom channel   3 Winding gear assembly plate   4 Winding handle
5 Cross-arm roller guide   6 Window stop   7, 8 Clip and washer   9 Rear window glass   10 Cross-arm

surfaces change in colour over the years and repainted areas, though they may match at the moment of application, tend to become more noticeable with time.

13:2 Upholstery and trim

Clean the plastic covered panels, seats and roof lining with a wet cloth and soap or soap liquid. Proprietary detergents (Handy Andy, Flash, etc.) can also be used but not those which contain ammonia in any form. **Do not use spirit cleaners or soda.**

Brush out the interior and the upholstery at frequent intervals, using a vacuum cleaner, if possible, to extract the dirt from crevices otherwise out of reach. The upholstery is waterproof and can be sat in immediately after cleaning.

13:3 Locks and hinges

Locks and hinges must be kept in good condition and oiled regularly. Be sparing with the oil, however, as any excess will work its way into positions where it can dirty the hands or clothes of the occupants.

The doors are secured by locks which are operated by a handle from the outside and a lever from the inside. A safety lock is provided with the internal handle and the driving door is fitted with a cylinder pattern lock on the outside.

Should it become necessary to replace the lock, first remove the door panel. The window raising and lock handles are retained in position on the panel by spring clips and come away with it. The panel can then be eased from the place around the edges where it is retained by spring clips. Remove the glass run channel (see **FIG 13:2**) and disconnect and remove the inside lock knob (4 in **FIG 13:1**). From the front edge of the door, extract the three fixing screws securing the lock 9 in place and the two

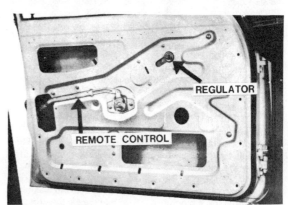

FIG 13:5   Location of regulator and locking mechanisms in door

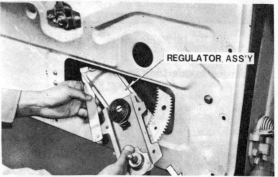

FIG 13:6   Removing window raising gear from door panel

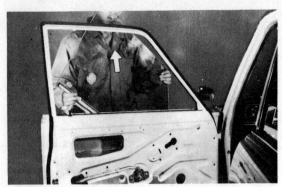

FIG 13:7 Removing glass from front window

FIG 13:8 Disconnecting tailgate from torsion bars

screws holding the remote control link plate in position. The lock and remote control assembly can then be extracted as shown in **FIG 13:3**.

13:4 Window raising gear

The window raising gear is of the rack and cross-link pattern the details of which are shown in **FIG 13:4**. To remove first take out the panel as for the door locks and, in addition, extract the plastic water deflection screen without tearing.

Lower the window glass and extract the clip and washer 7 and 8 from the pin on the cross-arm and ease the cross-arm away from the window bottom channel 2, to disengage the pin from the channel. (The pin can be seen at the bottom righthand corner of the upper left aperture in **FIG 13:5**.)

Remove the two roller guide securing nuts from the bracket at the opposite end of the cross-arm (these are located above the remote control lever in the recess) and ease the roller guide 5 out of position in the door recess. Extract the four screws holding the assembly plate 3 to the inner panel and ease the complete assembly out through the rectangular aperture at the foot of the door (see **FIG 13:6**). As the upper roller on the opposing arm will still be in the guide on the window bottom channel, it will be necessary to raise the window glass manually in order to manoeuvre the roller out from the guide before the assembly is free for extraction.

The window glass, complete with bottom channel, can then be eased out through the window aperture (see **FIG 13:7**).

Reinstallation is a simple reversal of the dismantling sequence.

13:5 Windscreen and backlight glazing

Both the windscreen and backlight glazing are secured in position by weatherstrip providing a watertight seal around the outer edge. To remove the windscreen, first dismantle the windscreen wiper arms, visors and rear mirror. Place a protective cover over the front of the car to prevent scratching the enamel. On the inside, loosen the lip of the weatherstrip around the edge of the glass with a suitable tool and, with an assistant to take the weight of the glass on the outside, push firmly on the window from the inside, using a suitable tool to assist the weatherstrip over the spot welded flange.

If the windscreen has been broken, carefully clear all fragments of glass from the weatherstrip and surrounds. **If a metal insert has been incorporated in the weatherstrip, this should be removed before attempting to extract the glass as it serves as a form of lock.**

Clean off traces of old sealant from the weatherstrip and around the window aperture and check that the aperture edge is clean, smooth and free from indentations. Check that the new glazing is suitable for the aperture and that the curvature of glass and aperture is identical. A windscreen inserted in a frame with only the slightest variation in curvature goes into service with an unrelieved tension that soon leads to another breakage.

Apply a suitable window sealant to the inner groove of the weatherstrip and fit it carefully around the windscreen. Insert a strong cord around the outer groove with a crossover at the bottom centre and enough to spare for a good grip. With an assistant holding the glass in place at the front of the car and the operator inside, pull the cord firmly to lip the inner flange of the weatherstrip over the inner edge of the window aperture. Seal the outer edge of the weatherstrip to the glass by sealant at any point at which that already in the groove has not exuded through to the surface and clean off any excess from the glass.

To replace the rear windscreen, follow a similar pattern of operations.

13:6 Tailgate and torsion bar

On the estate car, the tailgate is partially supported by substantial torsion bars to facilitate opening and to keep it in the raised position unassisted when open.

The two bars run alongside each other across the roof above the tailgate trim cover and are secured at one end to the tailgate hinge plate. At the opposite end a double crank, inserted in a crutch of a link hinged to curved tailgate hinge and restrained by a hook in the hinge plate at that end, applies a force which, at one extreme, holds the tailgate closed and, as the link passes over centre on opening, assists to overcome the weight of the tailgate on the hinge and prevents it closing under gravity.

To remove the tailgate, the links must first be disengaged from the cranked ends of the torsion bars using a lever to force the bar out of crutch link (see **FIG 13:8**). **While doing this, the tailgate must, of course, be supported.**

The hinge fixing screws can then be removed and the tailgate dismantled from the body. **Do not attempt to remove the tailgate with the torsion bars tensioned.**

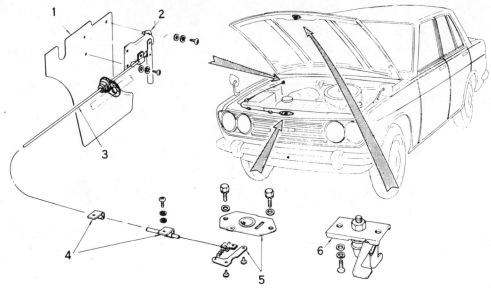

FIG 13:9   View of bonnet locking mechanism

Key to Fig 13:9   1 Side trim panel   2 Bonnet lock release lever   3 Cable   4 Bracket clips   5 Bonnet lock   6 Spring-loaded plunger and safety lock assembly

13:7 Air extractor

In addition to the air intake at the front of the car, an air extractor is fitted at the rear. This comprises a duct across the back of the car to which are coupled the outlets from the interior, mounted in the corners. Air is exhausted from the duct by a grille located in an area of the rear where a degree of atmospheric depression is induced by the forward motion of the car. Extraction therefore becomes automatic and a flap valve behind the louvre prevents a reverse flow through a strong tail wind at low speeds or while the car is stationary. The extractor needs no attention during the life of the car.

FIG 13:10   Adjusting spring-loaded plunger mechanism

13:8 Bonnet and boot

The bonnet of the car over the engine compartment is hinged at the rear and can be supported, when open, by a spring-erected support rod mounted on a bracket at the rear of the compartment.

To remove the bonnet, scribe around the hinge straps on the underside of the bonnet with a pencil and then remove the bolts. With the aid of an assistant, lift the bonnet clear.

The bonnet is locked by a cable-operated mechanism from the interior of the car. The general arrangement is shown in **FIG 13:9**. The spring-loaded lock plunger can be adjusted for centre in the lock by releasing the nut at the upper end and sliding it over (see **FIG 13:10**). The safety catch, which is unlocked by raising the front arm after the main lock has been released, is also clearly shown in the figure.

The boot lid is supported by torsion bars, similar to those on the tailgate of the estate car.

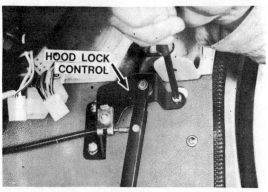

FIG 13:11   Adjusting hood lock mechanism

APPENDIX

TECHNICAL DATA

WIRING DIAGRAMS

HINTS ON MAINTENANCE

GLOSSARY OF TERMS

INDEX

TECHNICAL DATA

ENGINE
(Dimensions are in inches unless otherwise stated)

Number of cylinders	4
Firing order	1—3—4—2
Position of No. 1	Front of vehicle
Bore and stroke	
1296 cc	83 x 59.9
1428 cc	83 x 66
1595 cc	83 x 73.7
Compression ratio	
1300	8.5:1 (L13)
1400	9.0:1 (L14S)
1600 (single carburetter)	8.5:1 (L16S)
(twin carburetter)	9.5:1 (L16T)
Bore diameter	
Standard	82.99 mm to 83.04 mm
25 oversize, for rebore	83.22 mm to 83.27 mm + .035
50 oversize, for rebore	83.47 mm to 83.52 mm + .035
75 oversize, for rebore	83.72 mm to 83.77 mm + .035
100 oversize, for rebore	83.97 mm to 84.02 mm + .035
150 oversize, for rebore	84.47 mm to 84.52 mm + .035
Cylinder liners	
Inside diameter	82.45 mm to 82.55 mm
Outside diameter:	
400 undersize	87.00 mm to 87.05 mm
450 undersize	87.50 mm to 87.55 mm
500 undersize	88.00 mm to 88.05 mm
Pistons	
Material	Cast aluminium
Type	Slipper skirt, invar strut
Rings	2 compression, 1 scraper
Gudgeon pin	Floating, steel, hollow
Located by	Press-fit in conrod
Bore clearance	.025 mm to .045 mm
Diameter:	
Standard	82.99 mm to 83.04 mm
Oversize 1	83.22 mm to 83.27 mm
Oversize 2	83.47 mm to 83.52 mm
Oversize 3	83.72 mm to 83.77 mm
Oversize 4	83.97 mm to 84.02 mm
Oversize 5	84.47 mm to 84.52 mm
Ring groove:	
Compression	2.00 mm wide
Scraper	4.00 mm wide
Connecting rod	
Type	H-section steel forging
Length between centres:	
1300	5.235 to 5.237
1600	5.507 to 5.509

Crankshaft

Number of bearings	5
Type	Steel shell, whitemetal lined
Throw:	
1300	30 mm
1600	36.85 mm
Journal diameter	2.1631 to 2.1636
Crankpin diameter	1.9670 to 1.9675
Main bearing thickness:	
1300	.0719 to .0722
1600	.0717 to .0722

Camshaft

Number of bearings	4
Type	Steel-backed whitemetal bush
Inner diameter:	
1st	1.8898 to 1.8904
2nd	1.8898 to 1.8904
3rd	1.8898 to 1.8904
4th	1.8898 to 1.8904
Journal diameter:	
1st	1.8877 to 1.8883
2nd	1.8877 to 1.8883
3rd	1.8877 to 1.8883
4th	1.8877 to 1.8883
End play	.0031 to .0150

Cylinder block

Type	Block and integral crankcase
Material	Cast iron
Water jackets	Full length

Cylinder head

Type	Aluminium alloy, vertical valves
Valve guides	Steel, press-fit

Valves

Head diameter:	
Inlet, single carburetter	1.5000
Inlet, twin carburetters	1.6500
Exhaust	1.3000
Valve stem diameter	.3100
Valve length:	
Inlet	4.5600
Exhaust	4.5700
Spring free length:	
1300	1.89
1600 inner	1.77
1600 outer	2.05
Clearance hot:	
Inlet	.010
Exhaust	.012
Clearance cold:	
Inlet	.008
Exhaust	.010
Seat angle	45 deg.

FUEL SYSTEM

Carburetters

1300:

		Primary	Secondary
Bore	... ...	26 mm	30 mm
Venturi	... ...	21 x 8 mm	27 x 12 mm
Main jet	... ...	96	150
Main air bleed	... ...	80	90
Idle jet	... ...	43	180
Idle air bleed	... ...	220	100
Power jet	... ...	40	

1400:

Bore	... ...	28 mm	32 mm
Venturi	... ...	21 x 7 mm	28 x 10 mm
Main jet	... ...	96	165
Main air bleed	... ...	60	60
Idle air bleed (1)	... ...	1.0 mm	—
Idle air bleed (2)	... ...	220	100
Slow economizer	... ...	1.6 mm	—
Power jet	... ...	50	

1600:

Bore	... ...	28 mm	32 mm
Venturi	... ...	22 x 7 mm	29 x 10 mm
Main jet	... ...	102	165
Main air bleed	... ...	60	60
Idle air bleed (1)	... ...	1.0 mm	—
Idle air bleed (2)	... ...	180	100
Slow economizer	... ...	1.6 mm	—
Power jet	... ...	45	

1600:

Type	... ...	Twin HJL 38 W6 (SU Type)
Bore	... ...	38 mm
Needle	... ...	M76
Jet diameter	... ...	2.34 mm
Spring	... ...	No. 23

COOLING SYSTEM

Capacity	... ...	11.2 pints
Type	... ...	Pressurized, forced circulation
Thermostat		
Opening temperature	... ...	82°C
Fully open at	... ...	95°C
Type	... ...	Wax pellet
Location	... ...	Cylinder head
Maximum valve lift	... ...	.315 to 95°C
Cap relief valve pressure	... ...	12.8 lb/sq in
Radiator		
Type	... ...	Corrugated fin
Cooling capacity	... ...	360 Kcal/hr/°C
Water pump		
Type	... ...	Rotary impeller
Drive	... ...	V-belt from crankshaft
Fan clutch		
Operating temperature:		
On	... ...	65°C
Off	... ...	54°C
Installed with	... ...	Car heating systems only

CLUTCH

Type	Single dry plate, diaphragm spring
Operation	Hydraulic
Master cylinder bore	.675

GEARBOX

Manual

1300:

Type	Synchromesh, three-speed and reverse
Gear ratios:	
Top	1:1
Second	1.645:1
Bottom	3.263
Reverse	3.355
Model No.	R3W56L
Gearshift	Column-mounted lever

1600:

Type	Synchromesh, four-speed and reverse
Gear ratios:	
Top	1:1
Third	1.312:1
Second	2.013:1
Bottom	3.382:1
Reverse	3.364:1
Model No.	F4W36L
Gearshift	Floor-mounted lever

Automatic

1600:

Type	Borg-Warner, model 35
Gear ratios:	
Top	1:1
Second	1.450:1
Bottom	2.393:1
Reverse	2.094:1

FRONT SUSPENSION

Type	Independent, coil spring and strut, stabilizer bar
Springs	
Type	Coil
Inside diameter	5.12
Number of coils	8
Effective turns	6.5
Free length	14.55
Strut	
Outside diameter	2.00
Piston rod diameter	.787
Cylinder inner diameter	1.181
Shock absorber type	Double-acting, telescopic

REAR SUSPENSION

Type
Saloons	...	...	...	...	Coil, semi-trailing arm
Estate cars	...	...	...	...	Semi-floating, leaf spring

Differential

Saloons:
Type	...	...	...	...	Self-contained
Final drive ratio:					
1300	...	...	...	...	4.375:1
1600	...	...	...	...	3.700:1
Automatic	...	...	...	...	3.900:1
Rear wheel drive	...	...	...	...	Telescopic drive shafts
Shock absorber	...	...	...	...	Double-acting telescopic

Estate cars:
Type	...	...	...	...	Enclosed in axle casing banjo
Final drive ratio	...	...	...	...	3.700:1
Rear wheel drive	...	...	...	...	Halfshafts
Shock absorber	...	...	...	...	Double-acting, telescopic

STEERING

Type	...	...	...	...	Recirculating ball and nut
Ratio	...	...	...	...	15.00:1
Turns, lock to lock	...	...	...	...	3
Turning circle	...	...	...	...	31 ft
Steering angle					
Inner	...	...	...	...	38 deg.
Outer	...	...	...	...	32.5 deg.

BRAKING SYSTEM

Type
Early cars except 1600	...	...	Hydraulic, drum front and rear
1600 and later 1400	...	...	Hydraulic, disc front, drum rear

Brake drum diameter	...	...	...	9.00
Brake disc diameter	...	...	...	9.13
Master cylinder diameter	...	...	...	.75

Brake cylinder
Front drum	...	...	...	...	.875
Front disc	...	...	...	...	2.000
Rear drum	...	...	...	...	.875 (.815 with front discs)

ELECTRICAL EQUIPMENT

Battery
Type	...	...	...	...	Lead/acid
Capacity	...	...	...	...	40 amp/hr
Voltage	...	...	...	...	12

Ignition coil	...	...	...	...	Compound filled, 12-volt
Generator	...	...	...	...	Hitachi, LT130.41
Regulator	...	...	...	...	Hitachi, TL1Z.17

Starter motor
Type	...	...	...	...	Pre-engaged
Controlled from	...	...	...	...	Ignition switch
Number of teeth on pinion	...	...	...	9
Number of teeth on ringwheel	...	...	...	120
Engagement shift	...	...	...	...	Magnetic

Sparking plugs

Size		14 mm
Make		NKG
Type		See **Section 3:6**
Reach		19 mm
Gap		.030 to .035

BODY

Dimensions

Overall length, standard	160.2
delux	162.2
estate	163.2
Overall width	61.4
Height, saloons	55.1
estate	56.5
Wheelbase	95.3
Minimum road clearance	7.4

Tyres

Front, saloon	5.60 x 13 4PR
SSS	5.60 x S13 4PR
estate	5.60 x 13 4PR
Rear, saloon	5.60 x 13 4PR
SSS	5.60 x S13 4PR
estate	5.60 x 13 4PR

Inflation

Normal front and rear	24 lb/sq inch
High speeds front and rear	28 lb/sq inch

AUTOMATIC TRANSMISSION—TORQUE CHART

Crankshaft to drive disc bolts	40 lb ft
Drive disc to converter bolts	32 lb ft
Transmission case to converter housing	9 lb ft
Extension housing to transmission case	9 lb ft
Oil pan to transmission case	9 lb ft
Front servo to transmission case	9 lb ft
Rear servo to transmission case	12 lb ft
Pump adaptor to front pump body —$\frac{5}{8}$ bolt (24 UNC)	2 lb ft
—$\frac{5}{16}$ bolt (18 UNC)	20 lb ft
Pump adaptor to transmission case	12 lb ft
Centre support to transmission case	12 lb ft
Lever to manual valve shift	6 lb ft
Oil pan drain plug	12 lb ft
Oil tube collector to lower body	2 lb ft
Governor line plate to lower body	2 lb ft
Lower body end plate	2 lb ft
Upper body end plate	2 lb ft
Upper body to lower body	2 lb ft
Body assembly to transmission case	5 lb ft
Downshift cam bracket to valve body	5 lb ft
Front pump strainer to lower body	2 lb ft
Governor body to sleeve	2 lb ft
Cover plate to governor body	2 lb ft
Front servo lever adjustment nut	17 lb ft
Rear servo adjustment locking nut	27 lb ft
Starter inhibitor switch locknut	5 lb ft
Filler tube to connector sleeve nut	17 lb ft
Downshift cable adaptor to transmission case	25 lb ft
Stone guard bolts	1.5 lb ft

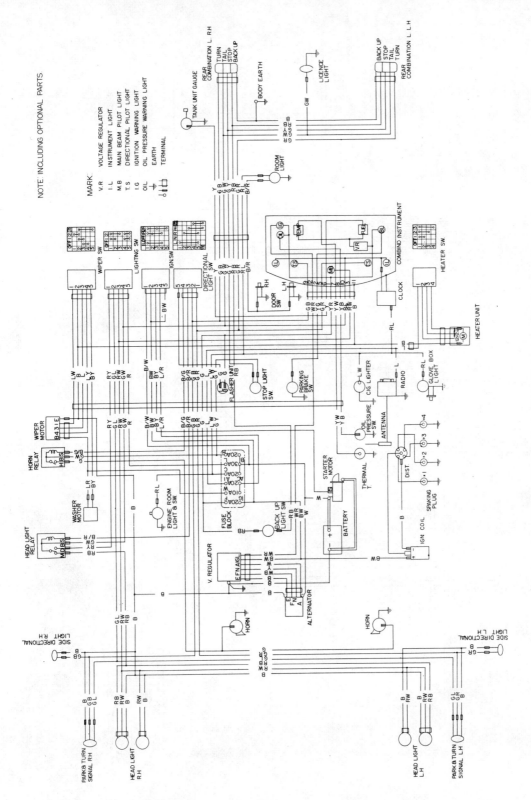

FIG 14:1   Standard wiring without passing light

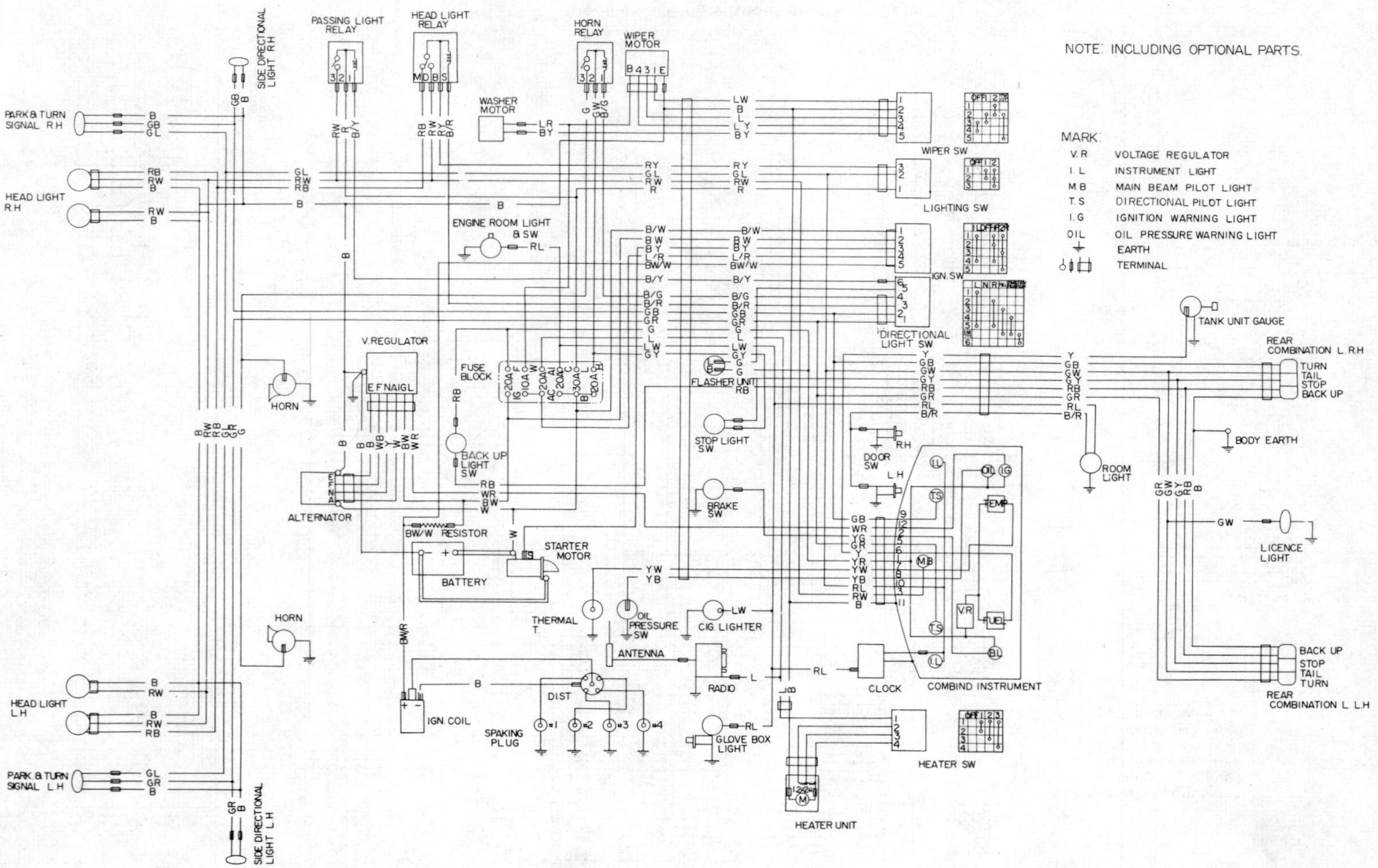

FIG 14:2 Standard wiring with passing light

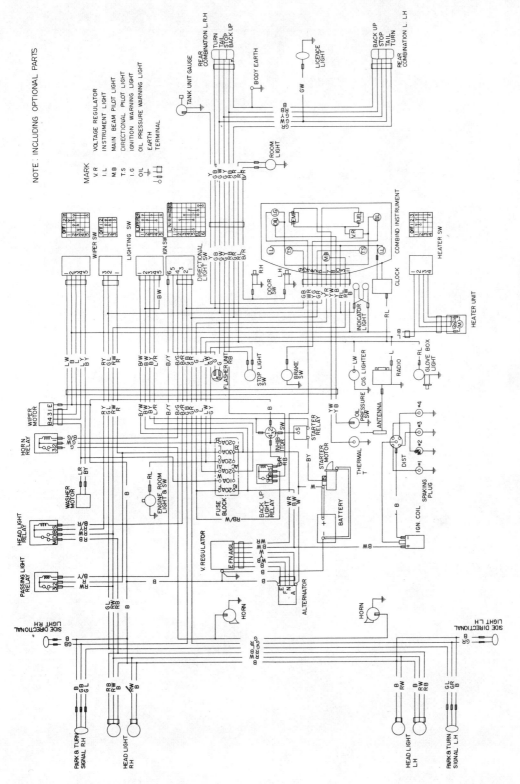

FIG 14:3 Wiring for automatic gearbox and passing light

HINTS ON MAINTENANCE AND OVERHAUL

There are few things more rewarding than the restoration of a vehicle's original peak of efficiency and smooth performance.

The following notes are intended to help the owner to reach that state of perfection. Providing that he possesses the basic manual skills he should have no difficulty in performing most of the operations detailed in this manual. It must be stressed, however, that where recommended in the manual, highly-skilled operations ought to be entrusted to experts, who have the necessary equipment, to carry out the work satisfactorily.

Quality of workmanship:

The hazardous driving conditions on the roads to-day demand that vehicles should be as nearly perfect, mechanically, as possible. It is therefore most important that amateur work be carried out with care, bearing in mind the often inadequate working conditions, and also the inferior tools which may have to be used. It is easy to counsel perfection in all things, and we recognize that it may be setting an impossibly high standard. We do, however, suggest that every care should be taken to ensure that a vehicle is as safe to take on the road as it is humanly possible to make it.

Safe working conditions:

Even though a vehicle may be stationary, it is still potentially dangerous if certain sensible precautions are not taken when working on it while it is supported on jacks or blocks. It is indeed preferable not to use jacks alone, but to supplement them with carefully placed blocks, so that there will be plenty of support if the car rolls off the jacks during a strenuous manoeuvre. Axle stands are an excellent way of providing a rigid base which is not readily disturbed. Piles of bricks are a dangerous substitute. Be careful not to get under heavy loads on lifting tackle, the load could fall. It is preferable not to work alone when lifting an engine, or when working underneath a vehicle which is supported well off the ground. To be trapped, particularly under the vehicle, may have unpleasant results if help is not quickly forthcoming. Make some provision, however humble, to deal with fires. Always disconnect a battery if there is a likelihood of electrical shorts. These may start a fire if there is leaking fuel about. This applies particularly to leads which can carry a heavy current, like those in the starter circuit. While on the subject of electricity, we must also stress the danger of using equipment which is run off the mains and which has no earth or has faulty wiring or connections. So many workshops have damp floors, and electrical shocks are of such a nature that it is sometimes impossible to let go of a live lead or piece of equipment due to the muscular spasms which take place.

Work demanding special care:

This involves the servicing of braking, steering and suspension systems. On the road, failure of the braking system may be disastrous. Make quite sure that there can be no possibility of failure through the bursting of rusty brake pipes or rotten hoses, nor to a sudden loss of pressure due to defective seals or valves.

Problems:

The chief problems which may face an operator are:
1 External dirt.
2 Difficulty in undoing tight fixings.
3 Dismantling unfamiliar mechanisms.
4 Deciding in what respect parts are defective.
5 Confusion about the correct order for reassembly.
6 Adjusting running clearance.
7 Road testing.
8 Final tuning.

Practical suggestions to solve the problems:

1 Preliminary cleaning of large parts—engines, transmissions, steering, suspensions, etc.,—should be carried out before removal from the car. Where road dirt and mud alone are present, wash clean with a high-pressure water jet, brushing to remove stubborn adhesions, and allow to drain and dry. Where oil or grease is also present, wash down with a proprietary compound (Gunk, Tepol etc.,) applying with a stiff brush—an old paint brush is suitable—into all crevices. Cover the distributor and ignition coils with a polythene bag and then apply a strong water jet to clear the loosened deposits. Allow to drain and dry. The assemblies will then be sufficiently clean to remove and transfer to the bench for the next stage.

On the bench, further cleaning can be carried out, first wiping the parts as free as possible from grease with old newspaper. Avoid using rag or cotton waste which can leave clogging fibres behind. Any remaining grease can be removed with a brush dipped in paraffin. If necessary, traces of paraffin can be removed by carbon tetrachloride. Avoid using paraffin or petrol in large quantities for cleaning in enclosed areas, such as garages, on account of the high fire risk.

When all exteriors have been cleaned, and not before, dismantling can be commenced. This ensures that dirt will not enter into interiors and orifices revealed by dismantling. In the next phases, where components have to be cleaned, use carbon tetrachloride in preference to petrol and keep the containers covered except when in use. After the components have been cleaned, plug small holes with tapered hard wood plugs cut to size and blank off larger orifices with grease-proof paper and masking tape. Do not use soft wood plugs or matchsticks as they may break.

2 It is not advisable to hammer on the end of a screw thread, but if it must be done, first screw on a nut to protect the thread, and use a lead hammer. This applies particularly to the removal of tapered cotters. Nuts and bolts seem to 'grow' together, especially in exhaust systems. If penetrating oil does not work, try the judicious application of heat, but be careful of starting a fire. Asbestos sheet or cloth is useful to isolate heat.

Tight bushes or pieces of tail-pipe rusted into a silencer can be removed by splitting them with an open-ended hacksaw. Tight screws can sometimes be started by a tap from a hammer on the end of a suitable screwdriver. Many tight fittings will yield to the judicious use of a hammer, but it must be a soft-faced hammer if damage is to be avoided, use a heavy block on the opposite side to absorb shock. Any parts of the steering system which have been damaged should be renewed, as attempts to repair them may lead to cracking and subsequent failure, and steering ball joints should be disconnected using a recommended tool to prevent damage.

3 It often happens that an owner is baffled when trying to dismantle an unfamiliar piece of equipment. So many modern devices are pressed together or assembled by spinning-over flanges, that they must be sawn apart. The intention is that the whole assembly must be renewed. However, parts which appear to be in one piece to the naked eye, may reveal close-fitting joint lines when inspected with a magnifying glass, and, this may provide the necessary clue to dismantling. Left-handed screw threads are used where rotational forces would tend to unscrew a right-handed screw thread.

Be very careful when dismantling mechanisms which may come apart suddenly. Work in an enclosed space where the parts will be contained, and drape a piece of cloth over the device if springs are likely to fly in all directions. Mark everything which might be reassembled in the wrong position, scratched symbols may be used on unstressed parts, or a sequence of tiny dots from a centre punch can be useful. Stressed parts should never be scratched or centre-popped as this may lead to cracking under working conditions. Store parts which look alike in the correct order for reassembly. Never rely upon memory to assist in the assembly of complicated mechanisms, especially when they will be dismantled for a long time, but make notes, and drawings to supplement the diagrams in the manual, and put labels on detached wires. Rust stains may indicate unlubricated wear. This can sometimes be seen round the outside edge of a bearing cup in a universal joint. Look for bright rubbing marks on parts which normally should not make heavy contact. These might prove that something is bent or running out of truth. For example, there might be bright marks on one side of a piston, at the top near the ring grooves, and others at the bottom of the skirt on the other side. This could well be the clue to a bent connecting rod. Suspected cracks can be proved by heating the component in a light oil to approximately 100°C, removing, drying off, and dusting with french chalk, if a crack is present the oil retained in the crack will stain the french chalk.

4 In determining wear, and the degree, against the permissible limits set in the manual, accurate measurement can only be achieved by the use of a micrometer. In many cases, the wear is given to the fourth place of decimals; that is in ten-thousandths of an inch. This can be read by the vernier scale on the barrel of a good micrometer. Bore diameters are more difficult to determine. If, however, the matching shaft is accurately measured, the degree of play in the bore can be felt as a guide to its suitability. In other cases, the shank of a twist drill of known diameter is a handy check.

Many methods have been devised for determining the clearance between bearing surfaces. To-day the best and simplest is by the use of Plastigage, obtainable from most garages. A thin plastic thread is laid between the two surfaces and the bearing is tightened, flattening the thread. On removal, the width of the thread is compared with a scale supplied with the thread and the clearance is read off directly. Sometimes joint faces leak persistently, even after gasket renewal. The fault will then be traceable to distortion, dirt or burrs. Studs which are screwed into soft metal frequently raise burrs at the point of entry. A quick cure for this is to chamfer the edge of the hole in the part which fits over the stud.

5 **Always check a replacement part with the original one before it is fitted.**

If parts are not marked, and the order for reassembly is not known, a little detective work will help. Look for marks which are due to wear to see if they can be mated. Joint faces may not be identical due to manufacturing errors, and parts which overlap may be stained, giving a clue to the correct position. Most fixings leave identifying marks especially if they were painted over on assembly. It is then easier to decide whether a nut, for instance, has a plain, a spring, or a shakeproof washer under it. All running surfaces become 'bedded' together after long spells of work and tiny imperfections on one part will be found to have left corresponding marks on the other. This is particularly true of shafts and bearings and even a score on a cylinder wall will show on the piston.

6 Checking end float or rocker clearances by feeler gauge may not always give accurate results because of wear. For instance, the rocker tip which bears on a valve stem may be deeply pitted, in which case the feeler will simply be bridging a depression. Thrust washers may also wear depressions in opposing faces to make accurate measurement difficult. End float is then easier to check by using a dial gauge. It is common practice to adjust end play in bearing assemblies, like front hubs with taper rollers, by doing up the axle nut until the hub becomes stiff to turn and then backing it off a little. Do not use this method with ballbearing hubs as the assembly is often preloaded by tightening the axle nut to its fullest extent. If the splitpin hole will not line up, file the base of the nut a little.

Steering assemblies often wear in the straight-ahead position. If any part is adjusted, make sure that it remains free when moved from lock to lock. Do not be surprised if an assembly like a steering gearbox, which is known to be carefully adjusted outside the car, becomes stiff when it is bolted in place. This will be due to distortion of the case by the pull of the mounting bolts, particularly if the mounting points are not all touching together. This problem may be met in other equipment and is cured by careful attention to the alignment of mounting points.

When a spanner is stamped with a size and A/F it means that the dimension is the width between the jaws and has no connection with ANF, which is the designation for the American National Fine thread. Coarse threads like Whitworth are rarely used on cars to-day except for studs which screw into soft aluminium or cast iron. For this reason it might be found that the top end of a cylinder head stud has a fine thread and the lower end a coarse thread to screw into the cylinder block. If the car has mainly UNF threads then it is likely that any coarse threads will be UNC, which are not the same as Whitworth. Small sizes have the same number of threads in Whitworth and UNC, but in the $\frac{1}{2}$ inch size for example, there are twelve threads to the inch in the former and thirteen in the latter.

7 After a major overhaul, particularly if a great deal of work has been done on the braking, steering and suspension systems, it is advisable to approach the problem of testing with care. If the braking system has been overhauled, apply heavy pressure to the brake pedal and get a second operator to check every possible source of leakage. The brakes may work extremely well, but a leak could cause complete failure after a few miles.

Do not fit the hub caps until every wheel nut has been checked for tightness, and make sure the tyre pressures are correct. Check the levels of coolant, lubricants and hydraulic fluids. Being satisfied that all is well, take the car on the road and test the brakes at once. Check the steering and the action of the handbrake. Do all this at moderate speeds on quiet roads, and make sure there is no other vehicle behind you when you try a rapid stop.

Finally, remember that many parts settle down after a time, so check for tightness of all fixings after the car has been on the road for a hundred miles or so.

8 It is useless to tune an engine which has not reached its normal running temperature. In the same way, the tune of an engine which is stiff after a rebore will be different when the engine is again running free. Remember too, that rocker clearances on pushrod operated valve gear will change when the cylinder head nuts are tightened after an initial period of running with a new head gasket.

Trouble may not always be due to what seems the obvious cause. Ignition, carburation and mechanical condition are interdependent and spitting back through the carburetter, which might be attributed to a weak mixture, can be caused by a sticking inlet valve.

For one final hint on tuning, never adjust more than one thing at a time or it will be impossible to tell which adjustment produced the desired result.

GLOSSARY OF TERMS

Allen key — Cranked wrench of hexagonal section for use with socket head screws.

Alternator — Electrical generator producing alternating current. Rectified to direct current for battery charging.

Ambient temperature — Surrounding atmospheric temperature.

Annulus — Used in engineering to indicate the outer ring gear of an epicyclic gear train.

Armature — The shaft carrying the windings, which rotates in the magnetic field of a generator or starter motor. That part of a solenoid or relay which is activated by the magnetic field.

Axial — In line with, or pertaining to, an axis.

Backlash — Play in meshing gears.

Balance lever — A bar where force applied at the centre is equally divided between connections at the ends.

Banjo axle — Axle casing with large diameter housing for the crownwheel and differential.

Bendix pinion — A self-engaging and self-disengaging drive on a starter motor shaft.

Bevel pinion — A conical shaped gearwheel, designed to mesh with a similar gear with an axis usually at 90 deg. to its own.

bhp — Brake horse power, measured on a dynamometer.

bmep — Brake mean effective pressure. Average pressure on a piston during the working stroke.

Brake cylinder — Cylinder with hydraulically operated piston(s) acting on brake shoes or pad(s).

Brake regulator — Control valve fitted in hydraulic braking system which limits brake pressure to rear brakes during heavy braking to prevent rear wheel locking.

Camber — Angle at which a wheel is tilted from the vertical.

Capacitor — Modern term for an electrical condenser. Part of distributor assembly, connected across contact breaker points, acts as an interference suppressor.

Castellated — Top face of a nut, slotted across the flats, to take a locking splitpin.

Castor — Angle at which the kingpin or swivel pin is tilted when viewed from the side.

cc — Cubic centimetres. Engine capacity is arrived at by multiplying the area of the bore in sq cm by the stroke in cm by the number of cylinders.

Clevis — U-shaped forked connector used with a clevis pin, usually at handbrake connections.

Collet — A type of collar, usually split and located in a groove in a shaft, and held in place by a retainer. The arrangement used to retain the spring(s) on a valve stem in most cases.

Commutator — Rotating segmented current distributor between armature windings and brushes in generator or motor.

Compression — The ratio, or quantitative relation, of the total volume (piston at bottom of stroke) to the unswept volume (piston at top of stroke) in an engine cylinder.

Condenser — See capacitor.

Core plug — Plug for blanking off a manufacturing hole in a casting.

Crownwheel — Large bevel gear in rear axle, driven by a bevel pinion attached to the propeller shaft. Sometimes called a 'ring wheel'.

'C'-spanner — Like a 'C' with a handle. For use on screwed collars without flats, but with slots or holes.

Damper — Modern term for shock-absorber, used in vehicle suspension systems to damp out spring oscillations.

Depression — The lowering of atmospheric pressure as in the inlet manifold and carburetter.

Dowel — Close tolerance pin, peg, tube, or bolt, which accurately locates mating parts.

Drag link — Rod connecting steering box drop arm (pitman arm) to nearest front wheel steering arm in certain types of steering systems.

Dry liner — Thinwall tube pressed into cylinder bore

Dry sump — Lubrication system where all oil is scavenged from the sump, and returned to a separate tank.

Dynamo — See Generator.

Electrode — Terminal, part of an electrical component, such as the points or 'Electrodes' of a sparking plug.

Electrolyte — In lead-acid car batteries a solution of sulphuric acid and distilled water.

End float — The axial movement between associated parts, end play.

EP — Extreme pressure. In lubricants, special grades for heavily loaded bearing surfaces, such as gear teeth in a gearbox, or crownwheel and pinion in a rear axle.

Fade	Of brakes. Reduced efficiency due to overheating.	**Journals**	Those parts of a shaft that are in contact with the bearings.
Field coils	Windings on the polepieces of motors and generators.	**Kingpin**	The main vertical pin which carries the front wheel spindle, and permits steering movement. May be called 'steering pin' or 'swivel pin'.
Fillets	Narrow finishing strips usually applied to interior bodywork.		
First motion shaft	Input shaft from clutch to gearbox.	**Layshaft**	The shaft which carries the laygear in the gearbox. The laygear is driven by the first motion shaft and drives the third motion shaft according to the gear selected. Sometimes called the 'countershaft' or 'second motion shaft.'
Fullflow filter	Filters in which all the oil is pumped to the engine. If the element becomes clogged, a bypass valve operates to pass unfiltered oil to the engine.		
FWD	Front wheel drive.	**lb ft**	A measure of twist or torque. A pull of 10 lb at a radius of 1 ft is a torque of 10 lb ft.
Gear pump	Two meshing gears in a close fitting casing. Oil is carried from the inlet round the outside of both gears in the spaces between the gear teeth and casing to the outlet, the meshing gear teeth prevent oil passing back to the inlet, and the oil is forced through the outlet port.		
		lb/sq in	Pounds per square inch.
		Little-end	The small, or piston end of a connecting rod. Sometimes called the 'small-end'.
		LT	Low Tension. The current output from the battery.
		Mandrel	Accurately manufactured bar or rod used for test or centring purposes.
Generator	Modern term for 'Dynamo'. When rotated produces electrical current.	**Manifold**	A pipe, duct, or chamber, with several branches.
Grommet	A ring of protective or sealing material. Can be used to protect pipes or leads passing through bulkheads.	**Needle rollers**	Bearing rollers with a length many times their diameter.
Grubscrew	Fully threaded headless screw with screwdriver slot. Used for locking, or alignment purposes.	**Oil bath**	Reservoir which lubricates parts by immersion. In air filters, a separate oil supply for wetting a wire mesh element to hold the dust.
Gudgeon pin	Shaft which connects a piston to its connecting rod. Sometimes called 'wrist pin', or 'piston pin'.		
		Oil wetted	In air filters, a wire mesh element lightly oiled to trap and hold airborne dust.
Halfshaft	One of a pair transmitting drive from the differential.		
Helical	In spiral form. The teeth of helical gears are cut at a spiral angle to the side faces of the gearwheel.	**Overlap**	Period during which inlet and exhaust valves are open together.
		Panhard rod	Bar connected between fixed point on chassis and another on axle to control sideways movement.
Hot spot	Hot area that assists vapourisation of fuel on its way to cylinders. Often provided by close contact between inlet and exhaust manifolds.		
		Pawl	Pivoted catch which engages in the teeth of a ratchet to permit movement in one direction only.
HT	High Tension. Applied to electrical current produced by the ignition coil for the sparking plugs.	**Peg spanner**	Tool with pegs, or pins, to engage in holes or slots in the part to be turned.
Hydrometer	A device for checking specific gravity of liquids. Used to check specific gravity of electrolyte.	**Pendant pedals**	Pedals with levers that are pivoted at the top end.
Hypoid bevel gears	A form of bevel gear used in the rear axle drive gears. The bevel pinion meshes below the centre line of the crownwheel, giving a lower propeller shaft line.	**Phillips screwdriver**	A cross-point screwdriver for use with the cross-slotted heads of Phillips screws.
		Pinion	A small gear, usually in relation to another gear.
Idler	A device for passing on movement. A free running gear between driving and driven gears. A lever transmitting track rod movement to a side rod in steering gear.	**Piston-type damper**	Shock absorber in which damping is controlled by a piston working in a closed oil-filled cylinder.
		Preloading	Preset static pressure on ball or roller bearings not due to working loads.
Impeller	A centrifugal pumping element. Used in water pumps to stimulate flow.	**Radial**	Radiating from a centre, like the spokes of a wheel.

Radius rod	Pivoted arm confining movement of a part to an arc of fixed radius.	**TDC**	Top Dead Centre. The highest point reached by a piston in a cylinder, with the crank and connecting rod in line.
Ratchet	Toothed wheel or rack which can move in one direction only, movement in the other being prevented by a pawl.	**Thermostat**	Automatic device for regulating temperature. Used in vehicle coolant systems to open a valve which restricts circulation at low temperature.
Ring gear	A gear tooth ring attached to outer periphery of flywheel. Starter pinion engages with it during starting.	**Third motion shaft**	Output shaft of gearbox.
Runout	Amount by which rotating part is out of true.	**Threequarter floating axle**	Outer end of rear axle halfshaft flanged and bolted to wheel hub, which runs on bearing mounted on outside of axle casing. Vehicle weight is not carried by the axle shaft.
Semi-floating axle	Outer end of rear axle halfshaft is carried on bearing inside axle casing. Wheel hub is secured to end of shaft.		
Servo	A hydraulic or pneumatic system for assisting, or, augmenting a physical effort. See 'Vacuum Servo'.	**Thrust bearing or washer**	Used to reduce friction in rotating parts subject to axial loads.
Setscrew	One which is threaded for the full length of the shank.	**Torque**	Turning or twisting effort. See 'lb ft'.
Shackle	A coupling link, used in the form of two parallel pins connected by side plates to secure the end of the master suspension spring and absorb the effects of deflection.	**Track rod**	The bar(s) across the vehicle which connect the steering arms and maintain the front wheels in their correct alignment.
		UJ	Universal joint. A coupling between shafts which permits angular movement.
Shell bearing	Thinwalled steel shell lined with anti-friction metal. Usually semi-circular and used in pairs for main and big-end bearings.	**UNF**	Unified National Fine screw thread.
Shock absorber	See 'Damper'.	**Vacuum servo**	Device used in brake system, using difference between atmospheric pressure and inlet manifold depression to operate a piston which acts to augment brake pressure as required. See 'Servo'.
Silentbloc	Rubber bush bonded to inner and outer metal sleeves.		
Socket-head screw	Screw with hexagonal socket for an Allen key.	**Venturi**	A restriction or 'choke' in a tube, as in a carburetter, used to increase velocity to obtain a reduction in pressure.
Solenoid	A coil of wire creating a magnetic field when electric current passes through it. Used with a soft iron core to operate contacts or a mechanical device.	**Vernier**	A sliding scale for obtaining fractional readings of the graduations of an adjacent scale.
Spur gear	A gear with teeth cut axially across the periphery.	**Welch plug**	A domed thin metal disc which is partially flattened to lock in a recess. Used to plug core holes in castings.
Stub axle	Short axle fixed at one end only.	**Wet liner**	Removable cylinder barrel, sealed against coolant leakage, where the coolant is in direct contact with the outer surface.
Tachometer	An instrument for accurate measurement of rotating speed. Usually indicates in revolutions per minute.		
		Wet sump	A reservoir attached to the crankcase to hold the lubricating oil.

INDEX

Alfa Romeo Giulia
1962 on
Aston Martin 1921-58
Audi 100 1969 on
(Austin, Morris etc.)
1100 Mk. 1 1962-67
(Austin, Morris etc.) 1100
Mk. 2, 1300 Mk. 1, 2,
America 1968 on
Austin A30, A35, A40
Farina
Austin A55 Mk. 2, A60
1958-69
Austin A99, A110 1959-68
Austin J4 1960 on
Austin Maxi 1969 on
Austin, Morris 1800
1964 on
BMC 3 (Austin A50,
A55 Mk. 1, Morris
Oxford 2, 3 1954-59)
Austin Healey 100/6, 3000
1956-68
(Austin Healey, MG)
Sprite, Midget 1958 on
BMW 1600 1964 on
BMW 1800 1964-68
BMW 2000, 2002 1966 on
Chevrolet Corvair 1960-69
Chevrolet Corvette V8
1957-65
Chevrolet Vega 2300
1970-71
Chevrolet Corvette V8
1965-71
Chrysler Valiant V8
1965 on
Chrysler Valiant Straight
Six 1966-70
Citroen DS 19, ID 19
1955-66
Citroen ID 19, DS 19, 20,
21 1966-70
Datsun 1200 1970 on
Datsun 1300, 1600
1968 on
Datsun 240Z Sport
1970 on
De Dion Bouton
1899-1907
Fiat 124 1966 on
Fiat 124 Sport 1966 on
Fiat 125 1967 on
Fiat 500 1957 on
Fiat 600, 600D 1955-69
Fiat 850 1964 on
Fiat 1100 1957-69
Fiat 1300, 1500 1961-67
Ford Anglia Prefect 100E
1953-62
Ford Anglia 105E,
Prefect 107E 1959-67
Ford Capri 1300, 1600
1968 on
Ford Capri 2000 GT,
3000 GT 1969 on
Ford Classic, Capri
1961-64
Ford Consul, Zephyr,
Zodiac, 1, 2 1950-62
Ford Corsair Straight
Four 1963-65

Ford Corsair V4 1965-68
Ford Corsair V4 1969 on
Ford Cortina 1962-66
Ford Cortina 1967-68
Ford Cortina 1969-70
Ford Cortina Mk. 3
1970 on
Ford Escort 1967 on
Ford Falcon V8 1964-69
Ford Thames 10, 12,
15 cwt 1957-65
Ford Transit 1965 on
Ford Zephyr Zodiac
Mk. 3 1962-66
Ford Zephyr V4, V6,
Zodiac 1966 on
Hillman Avenger 1970 on
Hillman Hunter 1966 on
Hillman Imp 1963-68
Hillman Imp 1969 on
Hillman Minx 1 to 5
1956-65
Hillman Minx 1965-67
Hillman Minx 1966-70
Hillman Super Minx
1961-65
Holden Straight Six
1948-66
Holden Straight Six
1966 on
Jaguar XK120, 140, 150,
Mk. 7, 8, 9 1948-61
Jaguar 2.4, 3.4, 3.8
Mk. 1, 2 1955-69
Jaguar 'E' Type 1961 on
Jaguar 'S' Type 420
1963-68
Jaguar XJ6 1968 on
Jowett Javelin Jupiter
1947-53
Landrover 1, 2 1948-61
Landrover 2, 2a, 3 1959 on
Mercedes-Benz 190b,
190c 200 1959-68
Mercedes-Benz 220
1959-65
Mercedes-Benz 220/8
1968 on
Mercedes-Benz 230
1963-68
Mercedes-Benz 250
1965-67
Mercedes-Benz 250
1968 on
Mercedes-Benz 280
1968 on
MG TA to TF 1936-55
MGA MGB 1955-68
MG MGB 1969 on
Mini 1959 on
Mini Cooper 1961 on
Morgan 1936-69
Morris Marina 1971 on
Morris Minor 2, 1000
1952-71
Morris Oxford 5, 6 1959-71
NSU 1000 1963 on
NSU Prinz 1 to 4
1957 on
Opel Ascona, Manta
1970 on
Opel G.T. 1900 1968 on

Opel Kadett, Olympia
993 cc, 1078 cc
1962 on
Opel Kadett, Olympia
1492, 1698, 1897 cc
1967 on
Opel Rekord C 1966 on
Peugeot 204 1965 on
Peugeot 404 1960 on
Peugeot 504 1968-70
Porsche 356a, 356b, 356c
1957-65
Porsche 911 1964-69
Porsche 912 1965-69
Reliant Regal 1962 on
Renault R4, R4L, 4
1961 on
Renault 6 1968 on
Renault 8, 10, 1100
1962 on
Renault 12 1969 on
Renault R16 1965 on
Renault Dauphine
Floride 1957-67
Renault Caravelle 1962-68
Rover 60 to 110 1953-64
Rover 2000 1963 on
Rover 3 Litre 1958-67
Rover 3500, 3500S
1968 on
Saab 95, 96, Sport
1960-68
Saab 99 1969 on
Saab V4 1966 on
Simca 1000 1961 on
Simca 1100 1967 on
Simca 1300, 1301, 1500,
1501 1963 on
Skoda One (440, 445, 450)
1957-69
Sunbeam Rapier Alpine
1955-65
Toyota Corolla 1100
1967 on
Toyota Corona 1500
Mk. 1 1965-70
Toyota Corona 1900 Mk. 2
1969 on
Triumph TR2, TR3,
TR3A 1952-62
Triumph TR4, TR4A
1961-67
Triumph TR5, TR250,
TR6 1967 on
Triumph 1300, 1500
1965 on
Triumph 2000 Mk. 1, 2.5 PI
Mk. 1 1963-69
Triumph 2000 Mk. 2, 2.5
PI Mk. 2 1969 on
Triumph Herald 1959-68
Triumph Herald 1969-71
Triumph Spitfire Vitesse
1962-68
Triumph Spitfire Mk. 3
1969 on
Triumph GT6, Vitesse 2
Litre 1969 on
Triumph Toledo 1970 on
Vauxhall Velox, Cresta
1957 on

Vauxhall Victor 1, 2, FB
1957-64
Vauxhall Victor 101
1964-67
Vauxhall Victor FD 1600,
2000 1967 on
Vauxhall Viva HA 1963-66
Vauxhall Viva HB 1966-70
Vauxhall Viva, HC Firenza
1971 on
Vauxhall Victor 3300,
Ventura 1968 on
Volkswagen Beetle
1954-67
Volkswagen Beetle
1968 on
Volkswagen 1500 1961-66
Volkswagen 1600
Fastback 1965 on
Volkswagen Transporter
1954-67
Volkswagen Transporter
1968 on
Volvo P120 1961-70
Volvo P140 1966 on
Volvo 160 series 1968 on
Volvo 1800 1961 on

NOTES